2023 NINJA SmartLid Recipe Book

600 Frugal, Healthy & Delicious Recipes for Beginners with Ninja Foodi SmartLid Multi-Cooker

Claire W. Harris

Copyright © 2021 by Claire W. Harris- All rights reserved.

The content contained within this book may not be reproduced, duplicated, or transmitted without direct written permission from the author or the publisher. Under no circumstances will any blame or legal responsibility be held against the publisher, or author, for any damages, reparation, or monetary loss due to the information contained within this book, either directly or indirectly.

Legal Notice: This book is copyright protected. It is only for personal use. You cannot amend, distribute, sell, use, quote or paraphrase any part, or the content within this book, without the consent of the author or publisher.

Disclaimer Notice: Please note the information contained within this document is for educational and entertainment purposes only. All effort has been executed to present accurate, up to date, reliable, complete information. No warranties of any kind are declared or implied. Readers acknowledge that the author is not engaged in the rendering of legal, financial, medical, or professional advice. The content within this book has been derived from various sources. Please consult a licensed professional before attempting any techniques outlined in this book. By reading this document, the reader agrees that under no circumstances is the author responsible for any losses, direct or indirect, that are incurred as a result of the use of the information contained within this document, including, but not limited to, errors, omissions, or inaccuracies.

CONTENTS

NINJA FOODI SMARTLID 101 11

WHY THE SMARTLID? 11
How Does the Foodi SmartLid Works? 11
Benefits of the Foodi SmartLid 12

SNACKS, APPETIZERS & SIDES RECIPES 13

Shallots With Mushrooms 13
Fried Pin Wheels 13
Herb Roasted Mixed Nuts 13
Mini Shrimp Tacos 13
Sweet Pickled Cucumbers 14
Spinach Hummus 14
Mushrooms Stuffed With Veggies 14
Mini Crab Cakes 15
Cauliflower Gratin 15
Shallot Pepper Pancakes 16
Cheesy Bacon Brussel Sprouts 16
Hand-cut French Fries 16
Pistachio Stuffed Mushrooms 17
Turkey Scotch Eggs 17
Cumin Baby Carrots 17
Beef Chicken Meatloaf 17
Hot Crab Dip 18
Cheesy Onion Dip 18
Glazed Walnuts 18
Spicy Honey Wings 18
Cheesy Fried Risotto Balls 19
Herbed Cauliflower Fritters 19
Garlicky Tomato 20
Honey Bourbon Wings 20
Fried Beef Dumplings 21
Asian Chicken Nuggets 21
Zucchini Chips 21
Brie Spread With Cherries & Pistachios 22
Herby Fish Skewers 22
Gingered Butternut Squash 22
Italian Pita Crisps 22
Cauliflower Nuggets 23
Spicy Glazed Pecans 23
Bacon-wrapped Halloumi Cheese 23
Japanese Eggs 23
Apple Pecan Cookie Bars 24
South Of The Border Corn Dip 24
Bacon Wrapped Scallops 24
Chicken And Vegetable Egg Rolls 25
Sweet Potato Fries 25
Crispy Delicata Squash 26
Horseradish Roasted Carrots 26

White Bean Hummus	26
Jalapeno Salsa	26
Tangy Jicama Chips	27
Parmesan Butternut Crisps	27
Scalloped Potatoes	27
Steak And Minty Cheese	28
Chili Chicken Dip	28
Artichoke Bites	28
Chicken Pork Nuggets	29
Almond Lover's Bars	29
Chicken Bites	29
Caponata	30
Crispy Spiced Cauliflower Bites	30
Tiny Tostadas	30
Cheesy Tomato Bruschetta	31
Cheesy Jalapeno Boats	31
Buttery Chicken Meatballs	31
Wrapped Asparagus In Bacon	32

BREAKFAST RECIPES 32

Maple Dipped Asparagus	32
Strawberry Oat Breakfast Bars	32
Pumpkin Pecan Oatmeal	33
Stuffed Baked Potatoes	33
Pumpkin Coconut Breakfast Bake	33
Deviled Eggs(2)	33
Soft-boiled Eggs	34
Baked Eggs In Mushrooms	34
Southern Grits Casserole	34
Strawberry Muffins	34
Spinach Casserole	35
Pumpkin Steel Cut Oatmeal	35
Cranberry Lemon Quinoa	35
Chili Cheese Quiche	35
Ham & Spinach Breakfast Bake	36
Spanish Potato And Chorizo Frittata	36
Southwest Tofu Scramble	36
Ham & Hash Brown Casserole	37
Carrot Cake Oats	37
Cheesy Shakshuka	37
Glazed Carrots	38
Breakfast Egg Pizza	38
Breakfast Pies	38
Curried Chickpea And Roasted Tomato Shakshuka	39
Egg Spinach Bites	39
Baked Eggs & Kale	39
Omelets In The Jar	40
Double Berry Dutch Baby	40
Flaxseeds Granola	40
Bacon & Egg Poppers	41
Banana Coconut Loaf	41
Sausage & Broccoli Frittata	41
Spinach Turkey Cups	42
Apricot Oatmeal	42
Spinach & Sausage Casserole	42
Grilled Broccoli	43

Savory Custards With Ham And Cheese 43	Walnut Orange Coffee Cake 47
Ham & Broccoli Frittata 44	Chicken Omelet 47
Ricotta Raspberry Breakfast Cake 44	Hearty Breakfast Muffins 48
Kale-egg Frittata 44	Double Chocolate Quinoa Bowl 48
Hearty Breakfast Skillet 45	Raspberry And Vanilla Pancake 48
Chocolate Banana Muffins 45	Apple Walnut Quinoa 49
French Dip Sandwiches 45	Prosciutto, Mozzarella Egg In A Cup 49
Brussels Sprouts Bacon Hash 46	Apple Pie Oatmeal 49
Bacon And Gruyère Egg Bites 46	Pancetta Hash With Baked Eggs 49
Sausage Wrapped Scotch Eggs 46	Applesauce Pumpkin Muffins 50
Baked Eggs In Spinach 47	Paprika Shirred Eggs 50
Paprika Hard-boiled Eggs 47	Bell Pepper Frittata 50

POULTRY RECIPES 51

Buttered Turkey 51	Turkey Rellenos 56
Healthy Chicken Stew 51	Pulled Chicken And Peach Salsa 56
Shredded Chicken Salsa 51	Garlic Turkey Breasts 56
Barbeque Chicken Drumettes 51	Riviera Chicken 56
Chicken And Quinoa Soup 52	Herby Chicken With Asparagus Sauce 57
Chicken Burrito Bowl 52	Sour Cream & Cheese Chicken 57
Chicken With Black Beans 52	Chicken & Black Bean Chowder 57
Salsa Chicken With Feta 53	Honey Garlic Chicken 58
Chicken With Crunchy Coconut Dumplings. 53	Quesadilla Casserole 58
Roasted Chicken With Potato Mash 53	Blackened Turkey Cutlets 58
Chicken Meatballs Primavera 54	Chicken With Tomatoes And Capers 59
Moo Shu Chicken 54	Pineapple Chicken Tenders 59
Tuscany Turkey Soup 55	Chicken Meatballs In Tomato Sauce 59
Chicken Bruschetta 55	Lettuce Carnitas Wraps 59
Cheesy Chicken & Zucchini Rolls 55	Chicken And Sweet Potato Corn Chowder 60

Lemon Chicken	60
Paprika Buttered Chicken	60
Cheesy Chicken & Mushrooms	61
Turkey Enchilada Casserole	61
Southwest Chicken Bake	61
Italian Turkey & Pasta Soup	62
Sticky Orange Chicken	62
Chicken Pot Pie	63
Chicken Stroganoff With Fetucini	63
Cajun Chicken & Pasta	63
Ground Turkey And Potato Chili	64
Creamy Tuscan Chicken Pasta	64
Italian Chicken Muffins	64
Stuffed Whole Chicken	65
Spicy Chicken Wings.	65
Sweet Garlicky Chicken Wings	65
Chicken Thighs With Thyme Carrot Roast	65
Bacon Ranch Chicken Bake	66
Ham-stuffed Turkey Rolls	66
Shredded Chicken With Lentils And Rice	66
Turkey & Wild Rice Casserole	67
Garlic Chicken And Bacon Pasta	67
Rosemary Lemon Chicken	67
Creamy Chicken Carbonara	68
Braised Chicken With Mushrooms And Brussel Sprouts	68
Crunchy Chicken & Almond Casserole	69
Turkey Croquettes	69
Pizza Stuffed Chicken	69
Honey Garlic Chicken And Okra	70
Chicken Piccata	70

BEEF, PORK & LAMB RECIPES 71

Beef Stew With Veggies	71
Braised Lamb Shanks	71
Pork Tenderloin With Warm Balsamic And Apple Chutney	71
Beef And Pumpkin Stew	72
Beef, Barley & Mushroom Stew	72
Baked Bacon Macaroni And Cheese	73
Spanish Lamb & Beans	73
Peppercorn Meatloaf	74
Holiday Honey Glazed Ham	74
Pork Pie	74
Bunless Burgers	75
Lamb Curry	75
Beef Pho With Swiss Chard	75
Bolognese Pizza	76
Pork Carnitas Wraps	76
Traditional Beef Stroganoff	76
Hot Dogs With Peppers	77
Beef Lasagna	77
Jamaican Pork	77
African Pork Stew	78
Pork Chops With Seasoned Butter	78
Italian Beef Steak	78
Beef And Garbanzo Bean Chili	79
Caribbean Pork Pot	79

Butter Pork Chops	79
Chinese Bbq Ribs	80
Brisket Chili Verde	80
Beef Stew With Beer	80
Meatballs With Marinara Sauce	81
Pork Chops With Gravy	81
Polish Sausage & Sauerkraut	81
Meatballs With Spaghetti Sauce	82
Beef Stroganoff	82
Steak And Chips	82
Crispy Roast Pork	83
Sausage With Celeriac And Potato Mash	83
Carne Guisada	83
Lamb Tagine	84
Beef Broccoli	84
Tender Beef & Onion Rings	85
Baked Rigatoni With Beef Tomato Sauce	85
Barbeque Sticky Baby Back Ribs With	85
Tender Butter Beef	86
Herbed Lamb Chops	86
Garlicky Pork Chops	86
Beef Bulgogi	86
Beef Congee	87
Southern Sweet Ham	87
Chipotle Beef Brisket	87
Adobo Steak	88
Lamb Chops And Potato Mash	88
One Pot Ham & Rice	88
Southern-style Lettuce Wraps	89
Swedish Meatballs With Mashed Cauliflower	89
Gingery Beef And Broccoli	89
Beef And Cabbage Stew	90
Rosemary Crusted Lamb Chops	90
Speedy Pork Stir Fry	90
Braised Short Ribs With Creamy Sauce	91
Sausage With Noodles And Braised Cabbage	91

FISH & SEAFOOD RECIPES 92

Mediterranean Cod	92
Pepper Smothered Cod	92
Glazed Salmon	92
New England Lobster Rolls	93
Tangy Catfish & Mushrooms	93
Spiced Red Snapper	93
Crab Alfredo	94
Cajun Shrimp	94
Shrimp And Chorizo Potpie	94
Crab Cakes	95
Salmon Florentine	95
Fried Salmon	95
Spicy Grilled Shrimp	95
Caribbean Catfish With Mango Salsa	96
Italian Flounder	96
Shrimp Fried Rice	96
Blackened Tilapia With Cilantro-lime Rice And Avocado Salsa	97
Creamy Crab Soup	97

Recipe	Page
Salmon With Dill Chutney	98
Shrimp & Asparagus Risotto	98
Spicy "grilled" Catfish	98
Seafood Chowder	99
Orange Glazed Cod & Snap Peas	99
Stuffed Cod	99
Salmon, Cashew & Kale Bowl	100
Salmon With Almonds, Cranberries, And Rice	100
Tuna & Avocado Patties	101
Awesome Shrimp Roast	101
Oyster Stew	101
Parmesan Tilapia	101
Panko Crusted Cod	102
Drunken Saffron Mussels	102
Flounder Veggie Soup	102
Tilapia & Tamari Garlic Mushrooms	103
Clam Fritters	103
Almond Crusted Haddock	103
Chili Mint Steamed Snapper	104
Kung Pao Shrimp	104
Pistachio Crusted Mahi Mahi	104
Shrimp & Zoodles	105
Easy Clam Chowder	105
Arroz Con Cod	105
Pistachio Crusted Salmon	106
Spicy Shrimp Pasta With Vodka Sauce	106
Crab Cake Casserole	106
Stir Fried Scallops & Veggies	107
Mackerel En Papillote With Vegetables	107
Mustard And Apricot-glazed Salmon With Smashed Potatoes	108
Tuscan Cod	108
Cod With Ginger And Scallion Sauce	109
Farfalle Tuna Casserole With Cheese	109
Coconut Cilantro Shrimp	109
Coconut Shrimp	110
Herb Salmon With Barley Haricot Verts	110
Flounder Oreganata	110
Sweet & Spicy Shrimp Bowls	111
Smoked Salmon Pilaf With Walnuts	111
Tuna Zoodle Bake	111
Curried Salmon & Sweet Potatoes	112
Garlic Shrimp And Veggies	112

VEGAN & VEGETABLE RECIPES 113

Recipe	Page
Hawaiian Tofu	113
Roasted Vegetable Salad	113
Cauliflower And Asparagus Farfalle	113
Veggie Skewers	114
Caramelized Sweet Potatoes	114
Spinach, Tomatoes, And Butternut Squash Stew	114
Creamy Spinach Soup	115
Cheesy Spicy Pasta	115
Grilled Tofu Sandwich	115
Crème De La Broc	115
Eggplant Lasagna	116
Hearty Veggie Soup	116

Recipe	Page
Eggplant With Kale	116
Mushroom Poutine	117
Garganelli With Cheese And Mushrooms	117
Spicy Kimchi And Tofu Fried Rice	117
Red Beans And Rice	118
Mashed Broccoli With Cream Cheese	118
Parsley Mashed Cauliflower	119
Cabbage With Bacon	119
Pasta Primavera	119
Roasted Squash And Rice With Crispy Tofu	120
Bok Choy And Zoddle Soup	120
Mushroom Goulash	120
Peanut Tofu & Noodles	121
Creamy Golden Casserole	121
Paneer Cutlet	121
Whole Roasted Broccoli And White Beans With Harissa, Tahini, And Lemon	122
Quick Indian-style Curry	122
Veggie Primavera	123
Cheesy Baked Spinach	123
Steamed Artichokes With Lemon Aioli	123
Spicy Cabbage Soup	123
Carrot Gazpacho	124
Crispy Kale Chips	124
Zucchinis Spinach Fry	124
Cauliflower Steaks & Veggies	124
Creamy Carrot Soup	125
Sweet Potato Noodles With Cashew Sauce	125
Grilled Cheese	125
Rosemary Sweet Potato Medallions	126
Potato Filled Bread Rolls	126
Balsamic Cabbage With Endives	126
Pasta Veggie Toss	126
Broccoli Cauliflower	127
Baby Porcupine Meatballs	127
Tomato Bisque	127
Cauliflower Chunks With Lemon Sauce	128
Italian Sausage With Garlic Mash	128
Veggie Taco Soup	128
Burrito Bowls	128
Colorful Vegetable Medley	129
Pasta With Roasted Veggies	129
Mashed Potatoes With Spinach	129
Hot & Sour Soup	130
Cheesy Chilies	130
Pomegranate Radish Mix	130
Steamed Asparagus And Pine Nuts	130
Eggplant Casserole	131
Minestrone With Pancetta	131

DESSERTS RECIPES 132

Recipe	Page
Brown Sugar And Butter Bars	132
Mini Chocolate Cheesecakes	132
Flourless Chocolate Cake	132
Classic Custard	133
Chocolate Peanut Butter And Jelly Puffs	133
Crispy Coconut Pie	133

Coconut Cream "custard" Bars 134	Coconut Rice Pudding 143
Pumpkin Custard 134	Coconut Pear Delight 143
Cherry Clafoutti 135	Brownie Bites 143
Chocolate Cake 135	Gingery Chocolate Pudding 144
Créme Brulee 135	White Chocolate Chip Cookies 144
Cinnamon Apple Cake 136	Hazelnut Cheesecake 144
Vanilla Pound Cake 136	Pecan Apple Crisp 144
Pumpkin Latte Cake 136	Irish Cream Flan 145
Coconut Lime Snack Cake 137	Banana Coconut Pudding 145
Sweet And Salty Bars 137	Spiced Poached Pears 145
Yogurt Cheesecake 137	Cranberry Cheesecake 146
Coconut Milk Crème Caramel 138	Peach Cobbler 146
Almond Banana Dessert 138	Blueberry Lemon Pound Cake 146
Carrot Raisin Cookie Bars 138	Date Orange Cheesecake 147
Banana Cinnamon Snack Cake 138	Fried Oreos 147
Chocolate Fondue 139	Mexican Chocolate Walnut Cake 147
Blackberry Crisp 139	Strawberry Cheesecake 148
Buttery Cranberry Cake 139	Hot Fudge Brownies 148
Coffee Cake 139	Sugar Cookie Pizza 148
Pineapple Cake 140	Gingerbread 149
Double Chocolate Cake 140	Vanilla Chocolate Spread 149
Vanilla Cheesecake(1) 141	Chocolate Chip Cheesecake 149
Blueberry Peach Crisp 141	Fried Snickerdoodle Poppers 150
Mocha Cake 141	Cinnamon Butternut Squash Pie 150
Sweet Potato Pie 142	Tres Leches Cake 150
Berry Apple Crisps 142	Almond Cheesecake 150
Cheat Apple Pie 142	Raspberry Crumble 151

INDEX 152

Ninja Foodi SmartLid 101

THE NINJA FOODI XL PRESSURE COOKER STEAM FRYER with SmartLid is a revolutionary new appliance that will change the way you cook. It's a multicooker with a huge difference: The lid does it all. With the SmartLid, you can Steam & Crisp, Steam & Bake, Air Fry, and Pressure Cook to make hundreds of recipes. Even better, you can cook an entire meal in one appliance—protein, vegetables, and starch. Although there are several other multicookers on the market, the Ninja Foodi SmartLid is different because you don't need to change lids depending on the functions you need. In this chapter, you'll learn about those functions and the benefits of cooking with the SmartLid so you can unleash all this cooker's potential.

WHY THE SMARTLID?

Sounds basic, but it's true: To maximize the potential of different ingredients, various cooking methods are needed. Pressure cooking cooks food quickly and makes foods such as meats very tender in a short period of time, but you won't get that wonderful crispy skin on a pressure-cooked chicken breast. Steaming cooks food gently, maintaining flavor and nutrients, but you can't achieve a crisp edge on Brussels sprouts with just steam. The SmartLid's TenderCrisp and Steam & Crisp technology cooks these foods to tender perfection by pressure cooking or steaming and then adding a crisp finish for delicious results every time.

Until now, home cooks have settled for convenience over flavor. Yes, it's easy to just throw food into a pressure cooker or steamer, but the versatility of this appliance lets you have both convenience and flavor. The lid lets you switch seamlessly between pressure cooking, steaming, and air frying. Imagine a salmon fillet that is tender and moist on the inside because it has been gently cooked with steam but with a lovely browned exterior because you finished cooking it with the air frying function.

The SmartLid is a 14-in-1 appliance that lets you change cooking techniques effortlessly by just moving a slider on the unique lid. You can steam and crisp, steam and bake, proof dough, air fry, bake, roast, broil, dehydrate, sear/sauté, steam, pressure cook, sous vide, make yogurt, and keep food warm. All that adds up to faster, better meals for you, versus Ninja Foodi SmartLid in dry mode only.

How Does the Foodi SmartLid Works?

This Innovative instant air fryer crisp pot technology ensures tender, juicy meals with a crisp, golden finish — every time.

The technology of the Foodi SmartLid is very simple. Fried foods get their crunchy texture because hot oil heats foods quickly and evenly on their surface. Oil is an excellent heat conductor, which helps with fast and simultaneous cooking across all of the ingredients. For decades cooks have used convection ovens to try to mimic the effects of frying or to cook the whole surface of the food. But the air never circulates quickly enough to achieve that delicious surface crisp we all love in fried foods.

With this mechanism, the air is circulated on high degrees, up to 200° C, to "air fry" any food such as fish, chicken or chips, etc. This technology has changed the whole idea of cooking by reducing the fat up to 80% compared to old-fashioned deep fat frying.

The Foodi SmartLid cooking releases the heat through a heating element that cooks the food in a healthier and more appropriate way. There's also an exhaust fan right above the cooking chamber, which provides the food required airflow. This way, food is cooked with constant heated air. This leads to the same heating temperature reaching every single part of the food that is being cooked. So, this is only grill and the exhaust fan that is helping the Foodi SmartLid to boost air at a constantly high speed in order to cook healthy food with less fat.

The internal pressure increases the temperature that will then be controlled by the exhaust system. Exhaust fan also releases extra filtered air to cook the food in a much healthier way. The Foodi SmartLid has no odor at all, and it is absolutely harmless, making it user and environment-friendly.

Benefits of the Foodi SmartLid

The amazing benefits include:

- Healthier, oil-free meals

- It eliminates cooking odors through internal air filters

- Makes cleaning easier due to lack of oil grease

- Foodi SmartLid is able to bake, grill, roast and fry providing more options

- A safer method of cooking compared to deep frying with exposed hot oil

- Has the ability to set and leave as most models and it includes a digital timer

The Foodi SmartLid is an all-in-one that allows cooking to be easy and quick. It also leads to a lot of possibilities once you get to know it. Once you learn the basics and become familiar with your Foodi SmartLid, you can feel free to experiment and modify the recipes in the way you prefer. You can prepare a wide number of dishes with the Foodi SmartLid, and you can adapt your favorite stove-top dish, so it becomes Air Fryer–friendly. It all boils down to variety and lots of options, right?

Cooking perfect and delicious as well as healthy meals has never been easier. You can see how this recipe collection proves itself.

Enjoy!

Snacks, Appetizers & Sides Recipes

Shallots With Mushrooms

Servings: 7
Cooking Time: 30 Minutes
Ingredients:
- 9 ounces shallot
- 8 ounces mushrooms
- ½ cup chicken stock
- 1 tablespoon paprika
- ½ tablespoon salt
- ¼ cup cream
- 1 teaspoon coriander
- ½ cup dill, chopped
- ½ cup parsley
- 1 tablespoon Erythritol

Directions:
1. Slice the shallot and chop the mushrooms.
2. Combine the chicken stock, salt, paprika, cream, coriander, and Erythritol in a mixing bowl.
3. Blend the mixture well. Chop the dill and parsley.
4. Pour the cream mixture in the Ninja Foodi's insert.
5. Set the Ninja Foodi's insert to" Sauté" mode and add sliced shallot and chopped mushrooms.
6. Blend the mixture using a wooden spoon. Close the Ninja Foodi's lid and sauté the mixture for 30 minutes.
7. Chop the parsley and dill. Once the dish is done, transfer it to serving plates.
8. Sprinkle the cooked dish with the chopped parsley and dill.
9. Do not stir again before serving it.

Nutrition Info:
- Calories: 52; Fat: 1g; Carbohydrates: 10.2g; Protein: 3g

Fried Pin Wheels

Servings: 6
Cooking Time: 50 Min
Ingredients:
- 1 sheet puff pastry
- 1 ½ cups Gruyere cheese, grated /195g
- 8 ham slices
- 4 tsp Dijon mustard /60g

Directions:
1. Place the pastry on a lightly floured flat surface. Brush the mustard over and arrange the ham slices; top with cheese. Start at the shorter edge and roll up the pastry.
2. Wrap it in a plastic foil and place in the freezer for about half an hour, until it becomes firm and comfortable to cut.
3. Meanwhile, slice the pastry into 6 rounds. Line the Ninja Foodi basket with parchment paper, and arrange the pinwheels on top.
4. Close the crisping lid and cook for 10 minutes on Air Crisp mode at 370 °F or 188°C. Leave to cool on a wire rack before serving.

Herb Roasted Mixed Nuts

Servings: 12
Cooking Time: 15 Minutes
Ingredients:
- ½ cup pecan halves
- ½ cup raw cashews
- ½ cup walnut halves
- ½ cup hazelnuts
- ½ cup Brazil nuts
- ½ cup raw almonds
- 1 tbsp. fresh rosemary, chopped
- 1 tbsp. fresh thyme, chopped
- ½ tbsp. fresh parsley, chopped
- 1 tsp garlic granules
- ½ tsp paprika
- ½ tsp salt
- ¼ tsp pepper
- ½ tbsp. olive oil

Directions:
1. Combine all ingredients in a large bowl and toss to coat thoroughly.
2. Pour the nuts in the fryer basket and place in the cooking pot. Add the tender-crisp lid and select air fry on 375°F. Cook 10 minutes, then stir the nuts around.
3. Cook another 5-10 minutes, stirring every few minutes and checking to make sure they don't burn. Serve warm.

Nutrition Info:
- Calories 229,Total Fat 21g,Total Carbs 7g,Protein 5g,Sodium 99mg.

Mini Shrimp Tacos

Servings: 8
Cooking Time: 5 Minutes
Ingredients:
- Nonstick cooking spray
- 3 tsp chili powder
- ¼ tsp salt, divided

- 24 medium shrimp, peel, devein & remove tails
- Juice of 1 lime, divided
- 1 avocado, peeled & chopped
- 1/3 cup sour cream, fat free
- 1 tsp cumin
- 2 tbsp. cilantro, chopped, divided
- 24 multigrain tortilla chip scoops

Directions:
1. Spray fryer basket with cooking spray.
2. In a large Ziploc bag, combine chili powder and 1/8 teaspoon salt. Add shrimp and toss to coat evenly.
3. Place shrimp, in a single layer, in the fryer basket. Drizzle half the lime juice over shrimp.
4. Add the tender-crisp lid and set to air fryer function on 375°F. Cook shrimp 5-8 minutes or until they are all pink, stirring halfway through cooking time.
5. In a small bowl, combine avocado and remaining salt and lime juice. Mix well.
6. In a separate small bowl, whisk together sour cream, cumin, and 1 tablespoon cilantro.
7. To assemble: place 1 teaspoon of avocado mixture and ½ teaspoon of sour cream mixture in each chip. Top with a shrimp and sprinkle of cilantro. Serve.

Nutrition Info:
- Calories 77, Total Fat 4g, Total Carbs 7g, Protein 4g, Sodium 235mg.

Sweet Pickled Cucumbers

Servings: 6
Cooking Time: 5 Min
Ingredients:
- 1 pound small cucumbers; sliced into rings /450g
- 1/4 cup green garlic, minced /32.5g
- 2 cups white vinegar /500ml
- 1 cup sugar /130g
- 1 cup water /250ml
- 2 tbsp Dill Pickle Seasoning /30g
- 2 tsp salt /10g
- 1 tsp cumin /5g

Directions:
1. Into the pot, add sliced cucumber, vinegar and pour water on top. Sprinkle sugar over cucumbers. Add cumin, dill pickle seasoning, and salt.
2. Stir well to dissolve the sugar. Seal the pressure lid, choose Pressure, set to High, and set the timer to 4 minutes. Press Start.
3. When ready, release the pressure quickly. Ladle cucumbers into a large storage container and pour cooking liquid over the top. Chill for 1 hour.

Spinach Hummus

Servings: 12
Cooking Time: 1 Hr 10 Min
Ingredients:
- 2 cups spinach; chopped /260g
- ½ cup tahini /65g
- 2 cups dried chickpeas /260g
- 8 cups water /2000ml
- 5 garlic cloves, crushed
- 5 tbsp grapeseed oil /75ml
- 2 tsp salt; divided /10g
- 5 tbsp lemon juice /75ml

Directions:
1. In the pressure cooker, mix 2 tbsp oil, water, 1 tsp or 5g salt, and chickpeas. Seal the pressure lid, choose Pressure, set to High, and set the timer to 35 minutes. Press Start. When ready, release the pressure quickly. In a small bowl, reserve ½ cup of the cooking liquid and drain chickpeas.
2. Mix half the reserved cooking liquid and chickpeas in a food processor and puree until no large chickpeas remain; add remaining cooking liquid, spinach, lemon juice, remaining tsp salt, garlic, and tahini.
3. Process hummus for 8 minutes until smooth. Stir in the remaining 3 tbsp or 45ml of olive oil before serving.

Mushrooms Stuffed With Veggies

Servings: 6
Cooking Time: 25 Minutes
Ingredients:
- 12 large mushrooms, washed
- 1 tbsp. olive oil
- 1 zucchini, grated
- ½ onion, chopped fine
- ½ red bell pepper, chopped fine
- ¼ cup bread crumbs
- ½ tsp garlic powder
- ¼ tsp salt
- ¼ tsp pepper

Directions:
1. Remove stems from mushroom and finely chop them.
2. Add oil to the cooking pot and set to sauté on medium heat.
3. Once oil is hot, add mushroom stems, zucchini, onion, and bell pepper. Cook, stirring occasionally, about 5 minutes or until vegetables are tender.
4. Stir in bread crumbs, garlic powder, salt, and pepper. Transfer mixture to a bowl.

5. Place the rack in the cooking pot and top with parchment paper.
6. Stuff each mushroom cap with vegetable mixture and place on the parchment.
7. Add the tender-crisp lid and set to air fry on 350°F. Bake 15-20 minutes or until mushrooms are tender. Serve immediately.

Nutrition Info:
- Calories 56,Total Fat 3g,Total Carbs 6g,Protein 2g,Sodium 134mg.

Mini Crab Cakes

Servings: 9
Cooking Time: 10 Minutes

Ingredients:
- Nonstick cooking spray
- 2/3 cup Italian seasoned bread crumbs
- ½ cup egg substitute
- ½ red bell pepper, chopped fine
- ½ red onion, chopped fine
- 1 stalk celery, chopped fine
- 3 tbsp. lite mayonnaise
- 2 tsp fresh lemon juice
- ½ tsp salt
- ¾ tsp pepper
- 1 tsp dried tarragon
- 2 cans lump crabmeat, drained

Directions:
1. Lightly spray fryer basket with cooking spray.
2. In a large bowl, combine all ingredients, except crab, until combined. Gently fold in crab. Form into 36 patties. Place them in a single layer in the fryer basket without overcrowding them.
3. Add the tender-crisp lid and set to air fry on 350°F. Cook patties 3-5 minutes per side until golden brown. Repeat with remaining patties. Serve warm.

Nutrition Info:
- Calories 96,Total Fat 2g,Total Carbs 8g,Protein 10g,Sodium 543mg.

Cauliflower Gratin

Servings:6
Cooking Time: 28 Minutes

Ingredients:
- 2 cups water
- 1 large head cauliflower, cut into 1-inch florets
- 3 tablespoons unsalted butter
- 3 tablespoons all-purpose flour
- 1½ cups whole milk
- 1 cup heavy (whipping) cream
- 2 tablespoons capers, drained
- 1 tablespoon fresh thyme
- Kosher salt
- Freshly ground black pepper
- ¾ cup shredded Swiss cheese
- ¼ cup grated Parmesan cheese

Directions:
1. Pour the water in the pot. Place the Reversible Rack in the lower position in the pot. Place the cauliflower on the rack. Assemble pressure lid, making sure the pressure release valve is in the SEAL position.
2. Select PRESSURE and set to HI. Set time to 5 minutes. Select START/STOP to begin.
3. When pressure cooking is complete, quick release the pressure by turning the pressure release valve to the VENT position. Carefully remove lid when the unit has finished releasing pressure.
4. Remove rack and place the cauliflower in the Ninja Multi-Purpose Pan or 8-inch baking dish. Drain the water from the pot and wipe it dry. Reinsert pot into base.
5. Select SEAR/SAUTÉ and set temperature to HI. Select START/STOP to begin. Let preheat for 5 minutes.
6. Add the butter. Once melted, add the onion and cook 3 minutes. Add the flour and cook, stirring constantly, 1 minute.
7. Add the milk, cream, capers, and thyme. Season with salt and pepper. Bring to a boil and cook, about 4 minutes.
8. Pour the sauce over the cauliflower. Place the pan onto the Reversible Rack, making sure the rack is in the lower position. Place the rack with pan in the pot. Close crisping lid.
9. Select BAKE/ROAST, set temperature to 400°F, and set time to 20 minutes. Select START/STOP to begin.
10. After 15 minutes, open lid and sprinkle the cauliflower with the Swiss and Parmesan cheeses. Close lid and continue cooking.
11. Once cooking is complete, open lid. Let the gratin sit for 10 minutes before serving.

Nutrition Info:
- Calories: 341,Total Fat: 27g,Sodium: 263mg,Carbohydrates: 16g,Protein: 11g.

Shallot Pepper Pancakes

Servings: 8
Cooking Time: 15 Minutes
Ingredients:
- 8 ounces shallot, chopped
- 2 tablespoons chives, chopped
- 1 red onion, chopped
- 1 cup coconut flour
- 2 egg
- ¼ cup sour cream
- 1 teaspoon baking soda
- 1 tablespoon lemon juice
- 1 teaspoon salt
- 1 teaspoon cilantro, chopped
- ½ teaspoon basil
- 1 tablespoon olive oil
- 1 bell pepper, chopped

Directions:
1. Chop the shallot and chives and combine them into a mixing bowl.
2. Whisk the eggs in a another bowl and add baking soda and lemon juice.
3. Stir the mixture and add the cream, salt, cilantro, basil, and coconut flour.
4. Blend the mixture well until smooth.
5. Add the vegetables to the egg mixture.
6. Stir it to the batter that forms. Set the Ninja Foodi's insert to" Sauté" mode.
7. Pour the olive oil in the Ninja Foodi's insert and preheat it.
8. Ladle the batter and cook the pancakes for 2 minutes on each side.
9. Keep the pancakes under aluminium foil to keep them warm until all the pancakes are cooked.
10. Serve the pancakes while warm.

Nutrition Info:
- Calories: 138; Fat: 6g; Carbohydrates: 7.6g; Protein: 4.7g

Cheesy Bacon Brussel Sprouts

Servings: 6
Cooking Time: 15 Minutes
Ingredients:
- Nonstick cooking spray
- 3 slices turkey bacon, chopped
- 2 tsp olive oil
- 1 lb. Brussels sprouts, trimmed & cut in half
- 2 cloves garlic, diced fine
- ¼ cup water
- 3 oz. goat cheese, soft
- 2 tbsp. skim milk
- 1 tbsp. parmesan cheese
- ¼ tsp salt
- ¼ tsp pepper
- 1 tsp paprika

Directions:
1. Spray the cooking pot with cooking spray. Set to sauté on med-high heat.
2. Add bacon and cook until crisp, transfer to paper-towel line plate.
3. Add oil and let it get hot. Add Brussel sprouts and cook, stirring frequently, 5 minutes or until they start to brown.
4. Add water, cover and cook another 5 minutes or until fork-tender. Drain any water from the pot.
5. Add goat cheese, milk, parmesan, salt, and pepper. Cook, stirring frequently, until cheese has melted.
6. Stir in bacon and cook until heated through. Sprinkle with paprika and serve.

Nutrition Info:
- Calories 106,Total Fat 6g,Total Carbs 8g,Protein 7g,Sodium 274mg.

Hand-cut French Fries

Servings:4
Cooking Time: 25 Minutes
Ingredients:
- 1 pound Russet or Idaho potatoes, cut in 2-inch strips
- 3 tablespoons canola oil

Directions:
1. Place potatoes in a large bowl and cover with cold water. Let soak for 30 minutes. Drain well, then pat with a paper towel until very dry.
2. Place Cook & Crisp Basket in pot. Close crisping lid. Select AIR CRISP, set temperature to 390°F, and set time to 5 minutes. Select START/STOP to begin preheating.
3. In a large bowl, toss the potatoes with the oil.
4. Once unit is preheated, open lid and add the potatoes to the basket. Close lid.
5. Select AIR CRISP, set temperature to 390°F, and set time to 25 minutes. Select START/STOP to begin.
6. After 10 minutes, open lid, then lift basket and shake fries or toss them with silicone-tipped tongs. Lower basket back into pot and close lid to continue cooking.
7. After 10 minutes, check for desired crispness. Continue cooking up to 5 minutes more, if necessary.
8. When cooking is complete, serve immediately with your favorite dipping sauce.

Nutrition Info:
- Calories: 171, Total Fat: 11g, Sodium: 7mg, Carbohydrates: 18g, Protein: 2g.

Pistachio Stuffed Mushrooms

Servings: 8
Cooking Time: 20 Minutes
Ingredients:
- 16 large mushrooms
- 1 tbsp. olive oil
- ½ onion, diced fine
- ¼ cup unsalted pistachios, chopped
- 1/3 cup pretzels, crushed
- 2 tbsp. sour cream, fat free
- 2 tbsp. fresh parsley, chopped
- ¼ tsp pepper
- 1/8 tsp hot pepper sauce

Directions:
1. Remove stems from mushrooms and dice them.
2. Set cooker to sauté on medium heat. Add oil and let it get hot.
3. Add the chopped mushrooms, onions, and pistachios and cook, until vegetables are tender, about 2-4 minutes. Transfer to a large bowl.
4. Add the remaining ingredients to the mushroom mixture and mix well.
5. Wipe out the cooking pot and add the rack to it. Select the air fryer function on 350°F.
6. Stuff the mushroom caps with the filling. Lay a sheet of parchment paper over the top of the rack and place mushrooms on it.
7. Add the tender-crisp lid and bake 20-25 minutes or until mushrooms are tender. Serve.
8. Preheat oven to 350 °F. Remove mushroom stems from caps; finely chop stems.

Nutrition Info:
- Calories 84, Total Fat 4g, Total Carbs 11g, Protein 3g, Sodium 26mg.

Turkey Scotch Eggs

Servings: 6
Cooking Time: 20 Min
Ingredients:
- 10 oz. ground turkey /300g
- 4 eggs, soft boiled, peeled
- 2 garlic cloves, minced
- 2 eggs, lightly beaten
- 1 white onion; chopped
- ½ cup flour /65g
- ½ cup breadcrumbs /65g
- 1 tsp dried mixed herbs /5g
- Salt and pepper to taste
- Cooking spray

Directions:
1. Mix together the onion, garlic, salt, and pepper. Shape into 4 balls. Wrap the turkey mixture around each egg, and ensure the eggs are well covered.
2. Dust each egg ball in flour, then dip in the beaten eggs and finally roll in the crumbs, until coated. Spray with cooking spray.
3. Lay the eggs into your Ninja Foodi's basket. Set the temperature to 390 °F or 199°C, close the crisping lid and cook for 15 minutes. After 8 minutes, turn the eggs. Slice in half and serve warm.

Cumin Baby Carrots

Servings: 4
Cooking Time: 25 Min
Ingredients:
- 1 ¼ lb. baby carrots /562.5g
- 1 handful cilantro; chopped
- 2 tbsp olive oil /30ml
- ½ tsp cumin powder /2.5g
- ½ tsp garlic powder /2.5g
- 1 tsp cumin seeds /5g
- 1 tsp salt /5g
- ½ tsp black pepper /2.5g

Directions:
1. Place the baby carrots in a large bowl. Add cumin seeds, cumin, olive oil, salt, garlic powder, and pepper, and stir to coat them well.
2. Put the carrots in the Ninja Foodi's basket, close the crisping lid and cook for 20 minutes on Roast mode at 370 °F or 188°C. Remove to a platter and sprinkle with chopped cilantro, to serve.

Beef Chicken Meatloaf

Servings: 9
Cooking Time: 40 Minutes
Ingredients:
- 2 cups ground beef
- 1 cup ground chicken
- 2 eggs
- 1 tablespoon salt
- 1 teaspoon black pepper
- ½ teaspoon paprika
- 1 tablespoon butter
- 1 teaspoon cilantro, chopped

- 1 tablespoon basil
- ¼ cup fresh dill, chopped

Directions:
1. Combine the ground chicken and ground beef together in a mixing bowl.
2. Add egg, salt, black pepper, paprika, butter, and cilantro.
3. Add the basil and dill and add it to the ground meat mixture and stir using your hands.
4. Place the meat mixture on aluminium foil, shape into a loaf and wrap it.
5. Place it in the Ninja Foodi's insert. Close the Ninja Foodi's lid and cook the dish in the" Sauté" mode for 40 minutes.
6. Once done, remove the meatloaf from the Ninja Foodi's insert and let it rest.
7. Remove from the foil, slice it, and serve.

Nutrition Info:
- Calories: 173; Fat: 11.5g; Carbohydrates: 0.81g; Protein: 16g

Hot Crab Dip

Servings: 8
Cooking Time: 30 Minutes

Ingredients:
- 8 oz. cream cheese, fat free, soft
- ¼ lb. crabmeat, flaked
- ½ tsp fresh lemon juice
- ½ tsp onion powder
- 1 tbsp. fresh dill, chopped
- ¼ tsp garlic powder

Directions:
1. Set to air fryer on 350°F. Place the rack in the cooking pot.
2. In a medium bowl, combine all ingredients until smooth. Transfer to a small baking dish.
3. Place the dish on the rack and add the tender-crisp lid. Bake 30-35 minutes until heated through and lightly browned on top. Serve warm.

Nutrition Info:
- Calories 78, Total Fat 1g, Total Carbs 8g, Protein 10g, Sodium 201mg.

Cheesy Onion Dip

Servings: 8
Cooking Time: 15 Minutes

Ingredients:
- 8 oz. cream cheese, soft
- 1 cup Swiss cheese, grated
- 1 cup mayonnaise
- 1 cup onion, grated

Directions:
1. In a medium bowl, combine all ingredients and mix thoroughly. Transfer to a small baking dish and cover tightly with foil.
2. Place the trivet in the cooking pot along with 1 cup of water. Place the dish on trivet.
3. Secure the lid and select pressure cooking on high. Set timer for 15 minutes.
4. When timer goes off, use quick release to remove the lid.
5. Remove the foil and add the tender-crisp lid. Set to air fryer on 400°F cook 1-2 minutes until the top is golden brown. Serve warm.

Nutrition Info:
- Calories 352, Total Fat 35g, Total Carbs 3g, Protein 6g, Sodium 290mg.

Glazed Walnuts

Servings: 4
Cooking Time: 4 Minutes

Ingredients:
- ⅓ cup of water
- 6 ounces walnuts
- 5 tablespoon Erythritol
- ½ teaspoon ground ginger
- 3 tablespoons psyllium husk powder

Directions:
1. Combine Erythritol and water together in a mixing bowl.
2. Add ground ginger and stir the mixture until the erythritol is dissolved.
3. Transfer the walnuts to the Ninja Foodi's insert and add sweet liquid.
4. Close the Ninja Foodi's lid and cook the dish in the "Pressure" mode for 4 minutes.
5. Remove the walnuts from the Ninja Foodi's insert.
6. Dip the walnuts in the Psyllium husk powder and serve.

Nutrition Info:
- Calories: 286; Fat: 25.1g; Carbohydrates: 10.4g; Protein: 10.3g

Spicy Honey Wings

Servings: 6
Cooking Time: 2 Hours

Ingredients:
- 2 tbsp. brown sugar
- 1 ½ tsp salt
- 1 tsp pepper
- 1 ½ tsp garlic powder
- 1 ½ tsp onion powder

- 1 tsp smoked paprika
- 1 tsp chili powder
- 1 tsp cumin
- 1 tsp parsley
- Nonstick cooking spray
- 4 lbs. chicken wings, pat dry
- ¾ cup hot sauce
- ½ cup honey
- 1 tbsp. butter, melted
- 1 tbsp. molasses

Directions:
1. In a small bowl, stir together brown sugar, salt, pepper, garlic powder, onion powder, paprika, chili powder, cumin, and parsley.
2. Spray the cooking pot with cooking spray. Place the wings in the pot. Sprinkle the spice mix over the chicken and rub the spices into the wings.
3. In the same bowl, whisk together hot sauce, honey, butter, and molasses. Pour over wings and toss to coat.
4. Add the lid and select slow cooking on high. Set timer for 2 hours. Cook until chicken wings are cooked through.
5. Add the tender-crisp lid and set to air fry on 450°F. Cook until wings are nicely caramelized, stirring every few minutes. Serve.

Nutrition Info:
- Calories 389,Total Fat 10g,Total Carbs 23g,Protein 50g,Sodium 781mg.

Cheesy Fried Risotto Balls

Servings:6
Cooking Time: 45 Minutes
Ingredients:
- ½ cup extra-virgin olive oil, plus 1 tablespoon
- 1 small yellow onion, diced
- 2 garlic cloves, minced
- 5 cups vegetable broth
- ½ cup white wine
- 2 cups arborio rice
- ½ cup shredded mozzarella cheese
- ½ cup shredded fontina cheese
- ½ cup grated Parmesan cheese, plus more for garnish
- 2 tablespoons chopped fresh parsley
- 1 teaspoon sea salt
- 1 teaspoon freshly ground black pepper
- 2 cups fresh bread crumbs
- 2 large eggs

Directions:

1. Select SEAR/SAUTÉ and set to MD:HI. Select START/STOP to begin. Allow the pot to preheat for 5 minutes.
2. Add 1 tablespoon of oil and the onion to the preheated pot. Cook until soft and translucent, stirring occasionally. Add the garlic and cook for 1 minute.
3. Add the broth, wine, and rice to the pot; stir to incorporate. Assemble the pressure lid, making sure the pressure release valve is in the SEAL position.
4. Select PRESSURE and set to HI. Set the time to 7 minutes. Press START/STOP to begin.
5. When pressure cooking is complete, allow pressure to naturally release for 10 minutes. After 10 minutes, quick release any remaining pressure by turning the pressure release valve to the VENT position. Carefully remove the lid when the unit has finished releasing pressure.
6. Add the mozzarella, fontina, and Parmesan cheeses, the parsley, salt, and pepper. Stir vigorously until the rice begins to thicken. Transfer the risotto to a large mixing bowl and let cool.
7. Meanwhile, clean the pot. In a medium mixing bowl, stir together the bread crumbs and the remaining ½ cup of olive oil. In a separate mixing bowl, lightly beat the eggs.
8. Divide the risotto into 12 equal portions and form each one into a ball. Dip each risotto ball in the beaten eggs, then coat in the breadcrumb mixture.
9. Arrange half of the risotto balls in the Cook & Crisp Basket in a single layer.
10. Close the crisping lid. Select AIR CRISP, set the temperature to 400°F, and set the time to 10 minutes. Select START/STOP to begin.
11. Repeat steps 9 and 10 to cook the remaining risotto balls.

Nutrition Info:
- Calories: 722,Total Fat: 33g,Sodium: 1160mg,Carbohydrates: 81g,Protein: 23g.

Herbed Cauliflower Fritters

Servings: 7
Cooking Time: 13 Minutes
Ingredients:
- 1-pound cauliflower
- 1 medium white onion
- 1 teaspoon salt
- ½ teaspoon ground white pepper
- 1 tablespoon sour cream
- 1 teaspoon turmeric
- ½ cup dill, chopped
- 1 teaspoon thyme
- 3 tablespoons almond flour

- 1 egg
- 2 tablespoons butter

Directions:
1. Wash the cauliflower and separate it into the florets.
2. Chop the florets and place them in a blender.
3. Peel the onion and dice it. Add the diced onion to a blender and blend the mixture.
4. When you get the smooth texture, add salt, ground white pepper, sour cream, turmeric, dill, thyme, and almond flour.
5. Add egg blend the mixture well until a smooth dough form.
6. Remove the cauliflower dough from a blender and form the medium balls.
7. Flatten the balls a little. Set the Ninja Foodi's insert to" Sauté" mode.
8. Add the butter to the Ninja Foodi's insert and melt it.
9. Add the cauliflower fritters in the Ninja Foodi's insert, and sauté them for 6 minutes.
10. Flip them once. Cook the dish in" Sauté" stew mode for 7 minutes.
11. Once done, remove the fritters from the Ninja Foodi's insert.
12. Serve immediately.

Nutrition Info:
- Calories: 143; Fat: 10.6g; Carbohydrates: 9.9g; Protein: 5.6g

Garlicky Tomato

Servings: 5
Cooking Time: 5 Minutes
Ingredients:
- 5 tomatoes
- ¼ cup chives, chopped
- ⅓ cup garlic clove, minced
- ½ teaspoon salt
- ½ teaspoon black pepper
- 1 tablespoon olive oil
- 7 ounces Parmesan cheese

Directions:
1. Wash the tomatoes and slice them into thick slices.
2. Place the sliced tomatoes in the Ninja Foodi's insert.
3. Combine the grated cheese and minced garlic and stir the mixture.
4. Sprinkle the tomato slices with chives, black pepper, and salt.
5. Then sprinkle the sliced tomatoes with the cheese mixture.
6. Close the Ninja Foodi's lid and cook the dish in the "Pressure" mode for 5 minutes.
7. Once done, remove the tomatoes carefully and serve.

Nutrition Info:
- Calories: 224; Fat: 14g; Carbohydrates: 12.55g; Protein: 13g

Honey Bourbon Wings

Servings: 6
Cooking Time: 11 Minutes
Ingredients:
- ¾ cup ketchup
- 1 tbsp. Liquid Smoke
- ½ cup brown sugar
- ¼ cup onion, chopped fine
- 2 cloves garlic, chopped fine
- ½ cup water
- ¼ cup bourbon
- 3 tbsp. honey
- 2 tsp paprika
- ¼ tsp cayenne pepper
- 1 tsp salt
- ½ tsp pepper
- 4-5 lb. chicken wings

Directions:
1. Set cooker to sauté on medium heat.
2. Add ketchup, liquid smoke, brown sugar, onion, and garlic to the cooking pot. Cook, stirring often, until sauce starts to thicken, about 5 minutes. Turn off the cooker.
3. Stir in water, bourbon, honey, and seasonings until combined.
4. Add the wings and stir to coat.
5. Secure the lid and set to pressure cooking on high for 5 minutes. When the timer goes off use quick release to remove the lid.
6. Line the fryer basket with foil.
7. Transfer the wings to the basket. Set cooker to sauté on medium again and cook sauce until thickened. Pour sauce into a large bowl.
8. Place the basket in the cooking pot and add the tender-crisp lid. Set to air fry on 400°F. Cook wings 6 minutes. Dunk in sauce to coat the wings, then air fry another 6 minutes. Serve with any remaining sauce for dipping.

Nutrition Info:
- Calories 636,Total Fat 13g,Total Carbs 36g,Protein 84g,Sodium 972mg.

Fried Beef Dumplings

Servings: 8
Cooking Time: 45 Min
Ingredients:
- 8 ounces ground beef /240g
- 20 wonton wrappers
- 1 carrot, grated
- 1 large egg, beaten
- 1 garlic clove, minced
- ½ cup grated cabbage /65g
- 2 tbsps olive oil /30ml
- 2 tbsps coconut aminos /30g
- ½ tbsp melted ghee /7.5ml
- ½ tbsp ginger powder /7.5g
- ½ tsp salt /2.5g
- ½ tsp freshly ground black pepper/2.5g

Directions:
1. Put the Crisping Basket in the pot. Close the crisping lid, choose Air Crisp, set the temperature to 400°F or 205°C, and the time to 5 minutes; press Start/Stop. In a large bowl, mix the beef, cabbage, carrot, egg, garlic, coconut aminos, ghee, ginger, salt, and black pepper.
2. Put the wonton wrappers on a clean flat surface and spoon 1 tbsp of the beef mixture into the middle of each wrapper.
3. Run the edges of the wrapper with a little water; fold the wrapper to cover the filling into a semi-circle shape and pinch the edges to seal. Brush the dumplings with olive oil.
4. Lay the dumplings in the preheated basket, choose Air Crisp, set the temperature to 400°F or 205°C, and set the time to 12 minutes. Choose Start/Stop to begin frying.
5. After 6 minutes, open the lid, pull out the basket and shake the dumplings. Return the basket to the pot and close the lid to continue frying until the dumplings are crispy to your desire.

Asian Chicken Nuggets

Servings: X
Cooking Time: 20 Minutes
Ingredients:
- 1 lb. chicken breasts, boneless, skinless & cut in 1-inch pieces
- 1 tsp salt
- ½ tsp pepper
- 2 eggs
- 1 cup Panko bread crumbs
- ¼ cup lite soy sauce
- ¼ cup honey
- 4 cloves garlic, diced fine
- 2 tbsp. hoisin sauce
- 1 tablespoon freshly grated ginger
- 1 tablespoon Sriracha
- 2 green onions, sliced thin
- 2 tsp sesame seeds

Directions:
1. Place the rack in the cooking pot and top with a sheet of parchment paper.
2. Sprinkle the chicken with salt and pepper.
3. In a shallow dish, beat the eggs.
4. Place the bread crumbs in a separate shallow dish. Working in batches, dip the chicken first in the eggs then bread crumbs, pressing to coat the chicken well.
5. Place the chicken on the parchment paper in a single layer. Add the tender-crisp lid and select air fry on 400 °F. Bake the chicken 10-15 minutes until golden brown and cooked through, turning over halfway through cooking time. Transfer to serving plate and keep warm.
6. Set the cooker to sauté on med-high heat. Add the soy sauce, honey, garlic, hoisin, ginger, and Sriracha, stir to combine. Cook, stirring frequently, until sauce thickens, about 2 minutes.
7. Add chicken and toss to coat. Serve immediately garnished with green onions and sesame seeds.

Nutrition Info:
- Calories 304,Total Fat 7g,Total Carbs 27g,Protein 32g,Sodium 1149mg.

Zucchini Chips

Servings: 6
Cooking Time: 10 Minutes
Ingredients:
- Nonstick cooking spray
- 1/3 cup whole wheat bread crumbs
- ¼ cup parmesan cheese, reduced fat
- ½ tsp garlic powder
- 1/8 tsp cayenne pepper
- 3 tbsp. skim milk
- 1 zucchini, cut in 1/4-inch slices

Directions:
1. Spray the rack with cooking spray and place in the cooking pot.
2. In a medium bowl, combine bread crumbs, parmesan, garlic powder, and cayenne pepper.
3. Pour milk into a shallow dish.
4. Dip the zucchini first in the milk then the crumb mixture. Lay them in a single layer on the rack.

5. Add the tender-crisp lid and set to air fry on 400°F. Cook zucchini 10 minutes, or until crisp and lightly browned. Serve immediately.

Nutrition Info:
- Calories 39, Total Fat 1g, Total Carbs 5g, Protein 2g, Sodium 111mg.

Brie Spread With Cherries & Pistachios

Servings: 10
Cooking Time: 3 Hours

Ingredients:
- ½ cup dried cherries, chopped
- ¼ cup cherry preserves
- 1 tbsp. Cognac
- 2 8 oz. wheels Brie cheese
- ½ cup pistachio nuts, toasted & chopped

Directions:
1. In a small bowl, combine cherries, preserves, and cognac, mix well.
2. Place on wheel of Brie in the cooking pot. Pour half the cherry mixture over the top. Repeat layers one more time.
3. Add the lid and select slow cooking function on low heat. Set timer for 3 hours.
4. Cook until cheese is soft, but not melted. Transfer to a serving plate and sprinkle with toasted pistachios. Serve warm.

Nutrition Info:
- Calories 224, Total Fat 15g, Total Carbs 10g, Protein 11g, Sodium 290mg.

Herby Fish Skewers

Servings: 4
Cooking Time: 75 Min

Ingredients:
- 1 pound cod loin, boneless, skinless; cubed /450g
- 2 garlic cloves, grated
- 1 lemon, juiced and zested
- 1 lemon, cut in wedges to serve
- 3 tbsp olive oil /45ml
- 1 tsp dill; chopped /5g
- 1 tsp parsley; chopped /5g
- Salt to taste

Directions:
1. In a bowl, combine the olive oil, garlic, dill, parsley, salt, and lemon juice. Stir in the cod and place in the fridge to marinate for 1 hour. Thread the cod pieces onto halved skewers.
2. Arrange into the oiled Ninja Foodi basket; close the crisping lid and cook for 10 minutes at 390 °F or 199°C. Flip them over halfway through cooking. When ready, remove to a serving platter, scatter lemon zest and serve with wedges.

Gingered Butternut Squash

Servings: 6
Cooking Time: 15 Minutes

Ingredients:
- 8 cups butternut squash, peeled, seeded, & cut in 1-inch cubes
- 1 cup water
- ½ tsp salt
- 4 tbsp. butter
- ¼ cup half n half
- 3 tbsp. honey
- ½ tsp ginger
- ¼ tsp cinnamon

Directions:
1. Add the squash, water, and salt to the cooking pot, stir.
2. Add the lid and select pressure cooking on high. Set timer for 12 minutes. When the timer goes off, use quick release to remove the lid.
3. Drain the squash and place in a large bowl.
4. Add remaining ingredients. Set cooker to saute on medium heat. Cook until butter melts, stirring occasionally
5. Once the butter melts, pour the sauce over the squash and mash with a potato masher. Serve.

Nutrition Info:
- Calories 198, Total Fat 9g, Total Carbs 31g, Protein 2g, Sodium 267mg.

Italian Pita Crisps

Servings: 8
Cooking Time: 15 Minutes

Ingredients:
- 4 whole wheat pita breads
- 1/3 cup finely chopped parsley
- 1 teaspoon Italian herb seasoning
- 1/3 cup finely grated fresh parmesan cheese

Directions:
1. With a sharp knife, cut away the outside edge of each pita. Open the pitas up into 2 halves. Cut each half into 4 wedges.
2. In a small bowl, combine parsley, seasoning, and parmesan.

3. Place pita wedges, in a single layer in the fryer basket, these will need to be cooked in batches. Sprinkle with some of the parmesan mixture.
4. Add the tender-crisp lid and set to air fryer function on 350°F. Bake 12-15 minutes or until golden brown. Repeat with remaining pitas and seasoning.

Nutrition Info:
- Calories 103,Total Fat 4g,Total Carbs 18g,Protein 4g,Sodium 303mg.

Cauliflower Nuggets

Servings: 8
Cooking Time: 10 Minutes

Ingredients:
- 8 ounces cauliflower
- 1 big red onion, chopped
- 2 carrots
- ½ cup almond flour
- ¼ cup pork rinds
- 2 eggs
- 1 teaspoon salt
- ½ teaspoon red pepper
- ⅓ teaspoon ground white pepper
- 1 tablespoon olive oil
- 1 teaspoon dried dill

Directions:
1. Peel the red onion and carrots. Chop the vegetables roughly and transfer them to the food processor.
2. Wash the cauliflower and separate it into the florets.
3. Add the cauliflower florets to a food processor and puree until smooth.
4. Add the eggs and salt. Blend the mixture for 3 minutes, then transfer to a mixing bowl.
5. Add pork rinds, red pepper, ground white pepper, and dill.
6. Blend the mixture until smooth. Form the nuggets from the vegetable mixture and dip them in the almond flour.
7. Spray the Ninja Foodi's insert with olive oil inside.
8. Place the vegetable nuggets in the Ninja Foodi's insert and cook them on the" Sauté" mode for 10 minutes.
9. Once the nuggets are cooked, remove from the Ninja Foodi's insert and serve.

Nutrition Info:
- Calories: 85; Fat: 5.1g; Carbohydrates: 5.9g; Protein: 5g

Spicy Glazed Pecans

Servings: 12
Cooking Time: 30 Minutes
Ingredients:
- Nonstick cooking spray
- 6 cups pecan halves
- 6 tbsp. butter, melted
- ¼ cup Worcestershire sauce
- 2 tbsp. hot sauce
- 1 tbsp. soy sauce
- 1 tbsp. hot curry powder
- 1 tbsp. chili powder

Directions:
1. Lightly spray the fryer basket with cooking spray.
2. In a large bowl, combine all ingredients and toss well to coat the pecans.
3. Add half the mixture to the fryer basket and place in the cooking pot. Add the tender-crisp lid and set to air fry on 250°F. Cook 20 minutes. Shake the basket and cook 10 minutes more.
4. Transfer cooked nuts to a baking sheet lined with parchment paper and spread out to cool. Repeat with remaining nut mixture. Serve warm or room temperature.

Nutrition Info:
- Calories 402,Total Fat 41g,Total Carbs 9g,Protein 5g,Sodium 220mg.

Bacon-wrapped Halloumi Cheese

Servings: 8
Cooking Time: 10 Minutes

Ingredients:
- 1-pound halloumi cheese
- 8 oz bacon, sliced
- 1 teaspoon olive oil

Directions:
1. Cut the cheese into 8 sticks.
2. Wrap every cheese stick into the sliced bacon and sprinkle with olive oil.
3. Place the wrapped sticks in the cooker basket and lower the air fryer lid.
4. Cook the snack for 4 minutes from each side. Serve it warm.

Nutrition Info:
- Calories: 365; Fat: 29.4g; Carbohydrates: 1.9g; Protein: 22.7g

Japanese Eggs

Servings: 4
Cooking Time: 20 Minutes
Ingredients:
- 1 cup Chinese master stock
- 4 eggs
- 1 teaspoon salt

Directions:
1. Pour the Chinese master stock in the Ninja Foodi's insert and Close the Ninja Foodi's lid.
2. Cook the liquid on the "Pressure" mode for 10 minutes.
3. Remove the Chinese master stock from the Ninja Foodi's insert and chill it.
4. Meanwhile, place the eggs in the Ninja Foodi's insert.
5. Add water and boil the eggs on the "Pressure" mode for 10 minutes.
6. Once eggs are done, remove from the Ninja Foodi's insert and chill well.
7. Peel the eggs and place them in the Chinese master stock.
8. Leave the eggs in the liquid for 20 minutes.
9. Remove the eggs from the liquid. Cut the eggs into halves.

Nutrition Info:
- Calories: 134; Fat: 9.7g; Carbohydrates: 2.01g; Protein: 9g

Apple Pecan Cookie Bars

Servings: 12
Cooking Time: 20 Minutes

Ingredients:
- Nonstick cooking spray
- 2/3 cup sugar
- 2 egg whites
- ½ tsp vanilla
- ½ cup flour
- 1 tsp baking powder
- 2 cups Granny Smith apples, chopped
- ¼ cup pecans, chopped

Directions:
1. Lightly spray an 8-inch baking pan with cooking spray.
2. In a large bowl, whisk together egg whites, sugar, and vanilla until frothy.
3. Whisk in flour and baking powder until combined.
4. Fold in apples and nuts and pour into pan.
5. Place the rack in the cooking pot and place the pan on it. Add the tender-crisp lid and set to air fry on 350°F. Bake 18-20 minutes or until the cookies pass the toothpick test.
6. Let cool before cutting and serving.

Nutrition Info:
- Calories 90,Total Fat 2g,Total Carbs 18g,Protein 1g,Sodium 10mg.

South Of The Border Corn Dip

Servings: 8
Cooking Time: 2 Hours

Ingredients:
- 33 oz. corn with chilies
- 10 oz. tomatoes & green chilies, diced
- 8 oz. cream cheese, cubed
- ½ cup cheddar cheese, grated
- ¼ cup green onions, chopped
- ½ tsp garlic, diced fine
- ½ tsp chili powder

Directions:
1. Place all ingredients in the cooking pot and stir to mix.
2. Add the lid and set to slow cooking function on low heat. Set timer for 2 hours. Stir occasionally.
3. Dip is done when all the cheese is melted and it's bubbly. Stir well, then transfer to serving bowl and serve warm.

Nutrition Info:
- Calories 225,Total Fat 13g,Total Carbs 24g,Protein 7g,Sodium 710mg.

Bacon Wrapped Scallops

Servings: 8
Cooking Time: 10 Minutes

Ingredients:
- 1/3 cup ketchup
- 2 tbsp. vinegar
- 1 tbsp. brown sugar
- ¼ tsp hot pepper sauce
- 13 slices turkey bacon, cut in half
- 1 lb. scallops, rinse & pat dry
- Nonstick cooking spray

Directions:
1. In a large bowl, whisk together ketchup, vinegar, brown sugar, and hot pepper sauce until smooth.
2. Wrap each scallop with a piece of bacon and use a toothpick to secure. Add to the sauce and toss to coat. Cover and refrigerate 20 minutes.
3. Place the rack in the cooking pot. Spray a small baking sheet with cooking spray. Working in batches, place scallops in a single layer on the tray and place on the rack.
4. Add the tender-crisp lid and set to air fry on 450°F. Cook scallops 4-5 minutes, then flip over and cook another 4-5 minutes or until cooked through. Serve immediately.

Nutrition Info:
- Calories 100,Total Fat 2g,Total Carbs 6g,Protein 13g,Sodium 525mg.

Chicken And Vegetable Egg Rolls

Servings: 16
Cooking Time: 10 Minutes Per Batch
Ingredients:
- 2 tablespoons sherry
- 2 tablespoons soy sauce
- 2 tablespoons beef broth
- 2 tablespoons cornstarch
- ½ teaspoon salt
- ½ teaspoon granulated sugar
- ½ teaspoon ground ginger
- 3 tablespoons canola oil
- 8 scallions, chopped
- ½ cup chopped mushrooms
- 3 cups shredded cabbage
- ½ cup shredded carrot
- ½ cup bean sprouts, washed
- 2 cups chopped cooked chicken
- 1 package egg rolls wrappers
- 1 egg, beaten
- Cooking spray
- Hot mustard, for dipping
- Sweet and sour sauce, for dipping

Directions:
1. In a small bowl, stir together the sherry, soy sauce, beef broth, cornstarch, salt, sugar, and ginger until combined and the sugar dissolves. Set aside.
2. Select SEAR/SAUTÉ and set temperature to HI. Select START/STOP to begin and allow to preheat for 5 minutes.
3. Add the canola oil to the cooking pot and allow to heat for 1 minute. Add the scallions and mushrooms and sauté for 2 to 3 minutes, stirring well, until the vegetables just begin to soften.
4. Add the cabbage, carrot, and bean sprouts, stirring to incorporate well. Decrease the temperature to MD:LO. Cook the vegetables for about 7 minutes, until cabbage and carrots are softened.
5. Stir in the chicken. Add the sauce and cook, stirring constantly, until the sauce thickens the filling, about 3 minutes. Select START/STOP to end the function. Transfer the filling to a bowl to cool. Wash the pot and return it to the cooker.
6. Place the Cook & Crisp Basket in the Foodi pot.
7. Select AIR CRISP, set the temperature to 390°F, and set the time to 5 minutes to preheat. Select START/STOP to begin.
8. Working one at a time, using a small silicone spatula, moisten the 4 sides of an egg roll wrapper with the beaten egg. Place 3 tablespoons of the filling on the center of the egg roll wrapper. Fold an edge over the mixture and tuck it under the point. Fold the edges in and continue rolling. Press the end point over the top of the roll to seal. Continue with the remaining wrappers and filling.
9. Place 3 egg rolls in the basket, making sure they don't touch each other. Coat the egg rolls in on cooking spray, then close the crisping lid.
10. Select AIR CRISP, set the temperature to 390°F, and set the time to 10 minutes. After 5 minutes, open the crisping lid, flip the egg rolls, and spritz the other side with cooking spray. Close the crisping lid and cook for the remaining 5 minutes.
11. Using tongs, carefully transfer the egg rolls to a wire rack to cool for least 6 minutes before serving.
12. Repeat step 8 with the remaining egg rolls. Keep in mind that the unit is already hot, which may decrease the cooking time. Monitor closely for doneness.
13. Serve with the hot mustard and sweet and sour sauce for dipping.

Nutrition Info:
- Calories: 166, Total Fat: 6g, Sodium: 364mg, Carbohydrates: 20g, Protein: 9g.

Sweet Potato Fries

Servings: 4
Cooking Time: 20 Minutes
Ingredients:
- Nonstick cooking spray
- ½ tsp cumin
- ½ tsp chili powder
- ½ tsp pepper
- ½ tsp salt
- ¼ tsp cayenne pepper
- 2 sweet potatoes, peeled & julienned
- 1 tbsp. extra-virgin olive oil

Directions:
1. Lightly spray fryer basket with cooking spray.
2. In a small bowl, combine cumin, chili powder, pepper, salt, and cayenne pepper.
3. Place potatoes in a large bowl and sprinkle spice mix and oil over them. Toss well to coat.
4. Place the fries, in small batches, in the basket and place in the cooking pot.
5. Add the tender-crisp lid and select air fryer on 425°F. Cook fries 15-20 minutes, until crispy on the outside and tender inside, turning halfway through cooking time. Serve immediately.

Nutrition Info:

- Calories 86,Total Fat 3g,Total Carbs 13g,Protein 1g,Sodium 327mg.

Crispy Delicata Squash

Servings:4
Cooking Time: 15 Minutes
Ingredients:
- 1 large delicata squash, seeds removed and sliced
- 1 tablespoon extra-virgin olive oil
- ¼ teaspoon sea salt

Directions:
1. Place Cook & Crisp Basket in pot. Close crisping lid. Select AIR CRISP, set temperature to 390°F, and set time to 5 minutes. Select START/STOP to begin preheating.
2. In a large bowl, toss the squash with the olive oil and season with salt.
3. Once unit has preheated, place the squash in the basket. Close crisping lid.
4. Select AIR CRISP, set temperature to 390°F, and set time to 15 minutes. Select START/STOP to begin.
5. After 7 minutes, open the lid, then lift the basket and shake the squash. Lower the basket back into pot. Close lid and continue cooking until the squash achieves your desired crispiness.

Nutrition Info:
- Calories: 75,Total Fat: 4g,Sodium: 117mg,Carbohydrates: 10g,Protein: 2g.

Horseradish Roasted Carrots

Servings:4
Cooking Time: 10 Minutes
Ingredients:
- 1 pound carrots, peeled and cut into 1-inch pieces
- ½ cup vegetable stock
- 2 tablespoons grated horseradish
- ¾ cup mayonnaise
- ½ teaspoon kosher salt
- ½ teaspoon freshly ground black pepper
- Minced parsley, for garnish

Directions:
1. Place the carrots and stock in the pot. Assemble pressure lid, making sure the pressure release valve is in the SEAL position.
2. Select PRESSURE and set to HI. Set time to 2 minutes. Select START/STOP to begin.
3. When pressure cooking is complete, quick release the pressure by turning the pressure release valve to the VENT position. Carefully remove lid when unit has finished releasing pressure.
4. In a small bowl, combine the horseradish, mayonnaise, salt, and pepper. Add mixture to the cooked carrots and stir carefully. Close crisping lid.
5. Select BROIL and set time to 6 minutes. Select START/STOP to begin.
6. After 3 minutes, open lid to check doneness. If further browning desired, close lid and continue cooking.
7. When cooking is complete, garnish with parsley and serve immediately.

Nutrition Info:
- Calories: 323,Total Fat: 30g,Sodium: 632mg,Carbohydrates: 13g,Protein: 1g.

White Bean Hummus

Servings: 8
Cooking Time: 8 Hours
Ingredients:
- 2 cups small white beans, soaked overnight
- 2 tbsp. pine nuts
- 1 tsp lemon zest, grated
- 1 tbsp. fresh lemon juice
- ¼ tsp garlic powder
- ¼ tsp salt

Directions:
1. Place beans with just enough water to cover them in the cooking pot. Add the lid and set to slow cooker function on low heat. Cook 8 hours, or until beans are tender.
2. Drain the beans, reserving some of the cooking liquid. Place beans in a food processor.
3. Wipe the cooking pot and set to sauté on low heat. Add the pine nuts and cook, stirring frequently, until lightly browned.
4. Add the lemon zest and juice, garlic powder, and salt to the beans. Pulse until almost smooth. If hummus is too thick, add reserved cooking liquid, a tablespoon at a time, until desired consistency.
5. Transfer hummus to a serving bowl and sprinkle with pine nuts. Serve.

Nutrition Info:
- Calories 169,Total Fat 1g,Total Carbs 31g,Protein 12g,Sodium 81mg.

Jalapeno Salsa

Servings: 10
Cooking Time: 7 Minutes
Ingredients:
- 8 ounces jalapeno pepper
- ¼ cup Erythritol
- 5 tablespoon water

- 2 tablespoons butter
- 1 teaspoon paprika

Directions:
1. Wash the jalapeno pepper and remove the seeds.
2. Slice it into thin circles. Sprinkle the sliced jalapeno pepper with paprika and Erythritol.
3. Put the butter and jalaeno mixture into the Ninja Foodi's insert and add water.
4. Set the Ninja Foodi's insert to" Sauté" mode.
5. Once the butter melts, add the sliced jalapeno in the Ninja Foodi's insert.
6. Close the Ninja Foodi's lid and sauté the dish for 7 minutes.
7. Once done, remove the dish from the Ninja Foodi's insert.
8. Cool it and serve.

Nutrition Info:
- Calories: 28; Fat: 2.5g; Carbohydrates: 7.5g; Protein: 0.4g

Tangy Jicama Chips

Servings: 8
Cooking Time: 10 Minutes

Ingredients:
- Nonstick cooking spray
- 1 jicama, peeled & sliced very thin
- 2 tbsp. extra virgin olive oil
- 1 ½ tsp lemon pepper seasoning

Directions:
1. Lightly spray the fryer basket with cooking spray.
2. Place the sliced jicama in a large bowl. Drizzle oil over the top and sprinkle with lemon pepper. Toss well to coat.
3. Place chips, in batches, in the basket. Place in cooker and add the tender-crisp lid. Set to air fry on 350°F. Cook 10 minutes until golden brown and crips, turning over halfway through cooking time. Repeat with remaining jicama. Serve.

Nutrition Info:
- Calories 61,Total Fat 3g,Total Carbs 7g,Protein 1g,Sodium 3mg.

Parmesan Butternut Crisps

Servings: 4
Cooking Time: 20 Minutes

Ingredients:
- 1 butternut squash, peeled, seeded & halved lengthwise
- 1 ½ tsp salt
- ½ tsp fresh rosemary, chopped
- 1/8 tsp cayenne pepper
- 2 tbsp. extra-virgin olive oil
- ¼ cup parmesan cheese, reduced fat

Directions:
1. Bring a large pot of water to a boil.
2. Cut the squash in 1/8-1/4-inch thick slices. When water is boiling, add squash and boil 1-2 minutes. Drain and rinse in cold water. Pat dry.
3. Place the rack in the cooking pot and line with parchment paper.
4. In a small bowl, combine salt, rosemary, and cayenne pepper.
5. Place the squash in a large bowl, sprinkle the spice mixture and oil over the top and toss well to coat.
6. Lay slices in a single layer on the parchment paper, these will need to be cooked in batches, and sprinkle with parmesan.
7. Add the tender-crisp lid, set to air fry on 350°F. Bake the chips 15-20 minutes or until golden brown. Store in an airtight container.

Nutrition Info:
- Calories 108,Total Fat 8g,Total Carbs 8g,Protein 2g,Sodium 971mg.

Scalloped Potatoes

Servings: 6
Cooking Time: 5 Minutes

Ingredients:
- 5 potatoes, sliced thin
- 5 tbsp. butter
- 2 cloves garlic, diced fine
- 1 cup vegetable broth
- ¾ tsp salt
- ½ tsp pepper
- 1 ½ tsp fresh parsley, diced fine
- ¼ cup cheddar cheese, grated

Directions:
1. Place potatoes in the cooking pot. Sprinkle with salt, pepper, and parsley, toss to coat.
2. Add butter, garlic, and broth to the potatoes.
3. Add the lid and select pressure cooking on high. Set timer to 5 minutes. When timer goes off use natural release to remove the lid.
4. Transfer potatoes to serving dish and top with grated cheese to garnish. Serve.

Nutrition Info:
- Calories 415,Total Fat 17g,Total Carbs 55g,Protein 12g,Sodium 587mg.

Steak And Minty Cheese

Servings: 4
Cooking Time: 15 Min
Ingredients:
- 2 New York strip steaks
- 8 oz. halloumi cheese /240g
- 12 kalamata olives
- Juice and zest of 1 lemon
- Olive oil
- 2 tbsp chopped parsley /30g
- 2 tbsp chopped mint /30g
- Salt and pepper, to taste

Directions:
1. Season the steaks with salt and pepper, and gently brush with olive oil. Place into the Ninja Foodi, close the crisping lid and cook for 6 minutes (for medium rare) on Air Crisp mode at 350 °F or 177°C. When ready, remove to a plate and set aside.
2. Drizzle the cheese with olive oil and place it in the Ninja Foodi; cook for 4 minutes.
3. Remove to a serving platter and serve with sliced steaks and olives, sprinkled with herbs, and lemon zest and juice.

Chili Chicken Dip

Servings: 8
Cooking Time: 20 Minutes
Ingredients:
- 1 tbsp. olive oil
- 1 sweet onion, chopped fine
- 2 cloves garlic, chopped fine
- 2 jalapeño peppers, seeded & chopped
- 1 Poblano pepper, seeded & chopped
- 1 cup Greek yogurt
- 8 oz. cream cheese, fat free, soft
- ½ cup cheddar cheese, reduced fat, grated
- 4 oz. green chilies, diced
- 1 tsp salt
- 2 cups chicken breasts, cooked & shredded
- 1 tbsp. chili powder
- 2 tsp cumin
- ½ tsp pepper
- 1 tsp oregano
- Nonstick cooking spray
- ¼ cup cilantro, chopped

Directions:
1. Set the cooker to sauté on medium heat. Add oil and let it get hot.
2. Add the onion, garlic, jalapeno, and poblano peppers. Cook, stirring frequently, until vegetables are tender, about 3-5 minutes. Transfer to a bowl and let cool completely.
3. In a medium bowl, beat together yogurt, and cream cheese until smooth.
4. Turn the mixer to low and add onion mixture along with remaining ingredients, except cilantro. Beat until all ingredients are combined.
5. Spray a casserole dish with cooking spray. Spread dip evenly in the dish.
6. Place the rack in the cooking pot and put the dish on it. Add the tender-crisp lid and select bake on 400°F. Bake 15 minutes until bubbly. Sprinkle with cilantro and serve.

Nutrition Info:
- Calories 189,Total Fat 7g,Total Carbs 15g,Protein 19g,Sodium 1004mg.

Artichoke Bites

Servings: 8
Cooking Time: 70 Min
Ingredients:
- ¼ cup frozen chopped kale /32.5g
- ¼ cup finely chopped artichoke hearts /32.5g
- ¼ cup goat cheese /32.5g
- ¼ cup ricotta cheese /32.5g
- 4 sheets frozen phyllo dough, thawed
- 1 lemon, zested
- 1 large egg white
- 1 tbsp olive oil /15ml
- 2 tbsps grated Parmesan cheese /30ml
- 1 tsp dried basil /5g
- ½ tsp salt /2.5g
- ½ tsp freshly ground black pepper /2.5g

Directions:
1. In a bowl, mix the kale, artichoke hearts, ricotta cheese, parmesan cheese, goat cheese, egg white, basil, lemon zest, salt, and pepper. Put the Crisping Basket in the pot. Close the crisping lid, choose Air Crisp, set the temperature to 375°F or 191°C, and the time to 5 minutes; press Start/Stop.
2. Then, place a phyllo sheet on a clean flat surface. Brush with olive oil, place a second phyllo sheet on the first, and brush with oil. Continue layering to form a pile of four oiled sheets.
3. Working from the short side, cut the phyllo sheets into 8 strips. Cut the strips in half to form 16 strips.
4. Spoon 1 tbsp of filling onto one short side of every strip. Fold a corner to cover the filling to make a triangle; continue repeatedly folding to the end of the strip, creating a triangle-

shaped phyllo packet. Repeat the process with the other phyllo bites.

5. Open the crisping lid and place half of the pastry in the basket in a single layer. Close the lid, Choose Air Crisp, set the temperature to 350°F or 177°C, and the timer to 12 minutes; press Start/Stop.

6. After 6 minutes, open the lid, and flip the bites. Return the basket to the pot and close the lid to continue baking. When ready, take out the bites into a plate. Serve warm.

Chicken Pork Nuggets

Servings: 6
Cooking Time: 20 Minutes
Ingredients:
- 2 cups ground chicken
- ½ cup dill, chopped
- 1 egg
- 2 tablespoons pork rinds
- 1 tablespoon heavy cream
- ½ cup almond flour
- 3 tablespoons butter
- 1 tablespoon canola oil
- 1 teaspoon black pepper

Directions:
1. Beat the egg in a suitable mixing bowl.
2. Add the chopped dill and ground chicken. Blend the mixture until it is smooth.
3. Sprinkle the dish with black pepper and cream.
4. Blend the nugget mixture again. Form the nuggets from the meat mixture and dip them in the almond flour and pork rinds.
5. Sprinkle the Ninja Foodi's insert with the canola oil and butter.
6. Set the Ninja Foodi's insert to "Pressure" mode. Once the butter mixture starts to melt, add the nuggets.
7. Close the Ninja Foodi's lid and cook the dish for 20 minutes.
8. Once done, check if the nuggets are cooked and remove them from the Ninja Foodi's insert.
9. Drain on a paper towel and serve.

Nutrition Info:
- Calories: 217; Fat: 15.4g; Carbohydrates: 3.1g; Protein: 17.4 g

Almond Lover's Bars

Servings: 20
Cooking Time: 30 Minutes
Ingredients:
- 2 cups almond flour, sifted
- 1 ½ cups flour
- 1 tsp baking powder
- ½ tsp salt
- 10 tbsp. butter, soft
- 1 cup sugar
- 2 eggs
- 2 tsp vanilla
- 1 tbsp. powdered sugar

Directions:
1. Line an 8-inch square baking dish with parchment paper.
2. In a medium bowl, whisk together both flours, baking powder, and salt.
3. In a large bowl, beat butter and sugar until creamy.
4. Beat in eggs and vanilla. Then stir in dry ingredients until combined. Press firmly in prepared pan.
5. Place the rack in the cooking pot and place the pan on it. Add the tender-crisp lid and set to bake on 325°F. Bake 25-30 minutes until lightly browned and the bars pass the toothpick test.
6. Let cool before cutting into bars. Sprinkle with powdered sugar before serving.

Nutrition Info:
- Calories 207, Total Fat 11g, Total Carbs 23g, Protein 3g, Sodium 83mg.

Chicken Bites

Servings: 4
Cooking Time: 8 Minutes
Ingredients:
- ½ cup Italian seasoned bread crumbs
- 2 tablespoons grated Parmesan cheese
- ¼ teaspoon sea salt
- ¼ teaspoon freshly ground black pepper
- 1 boneless, skinless chicken breast, cut into 1-inch pieces
- ½ cup unsalted butter, melted
- Cooking spray

Directions:
1. Place Cook & Crisp Basket in pot. Close crisping lid. Select AIR CRISP, set temperature to 390°F, and set time to 5 minutes. Select START/STOP to begin preheating.
2. In a medium bowl, combine the bread crumbs, Parmesan cheese, salt, and pepper. In a separate medium bowl, toss the chicken in the butter until well coated. Move a few of the chicken pieces to the breadcrumb mixture and coat. Repeat until all the chicken is coated.
3. Once unit is preheated, open lid and place the chicken bites in the basket in a single layer. Coat well with cooking spray. Close lid.

4. Select AIR CRISP, set temperature to 390°F, and set time to 8 minutes. Select START/STOP to begin.

5. After 4 minutes, open lid, then lift basket and flip the chicken bites with silicone-tipped tongs. Coat well with cooking spray. Lower basket back into pot and close lid to continue cooking.

6. After 4 minutes, check for desired crispness. Cooking is complete when the internal temperature of the chicken reads at least 165°F on a food thermometer.

Nutrition Info:
- Calories: 279,Total Fat: 25g,Sodium: 246mg,Carbohydrates: 5g,Protein: 10g.

Caponata

Servings: 10
Cooking Time: 30 Minutes
Ingredients:
- 2 tbsp. olive oil
- 1 eggplant, unpeeled & chopped
- 1 onion, chopped
- 2 tbsp. garlic powder
- ½ cup pimiento-stuffed green olives, chopped
- 3 stalks celery, chopped
- 8 oz. tomato sauce
- ¼ cup white vinegar
- 1/3 cup brown sugar, packed
- ¼ tsp hot pepper sauce

Directions:
1. Set cooker to sauté on med-high heat. Add oil and let it get hot.
2. Once oil is hot, add eggplant, onion, and garlic powder and cook 5 minutes, stirring occasionally, until eggplant starts to get soft.
3. Stir in remaining ingredients and reduce heat to low. Cook 25 minutes, or until all the vegetables are tender. Serve warm or cold.

Nutrition Info:
- Calories 87,Total Fat 3g,Total Carbs 15g,Protein 1g,Sodium 16mg.

Crispy Spiced Cauliflower Bites

Servings: 12
Cooking Time: 15 Minutes
Ingredients:
- Nonstick cooking spray
- 1 egg
- 1 tbsp. water
- 1 cup whole wheat panko bread crumbs
- 1 tbsp. garlic powder
- ½ tsp onion powder
- 1 tbsp. fresh parsley, chopped
- 6 cups cauliflower florets
- ¼ cup light mayonnaise
- 2 tbsp. sweet chili sauce
- 2 tbsp. hot sauce

Directions:
1. Lightly spray the fryer basket with cooking spray and place in the cooking pot.
2. In a small bowl, whisk together egg and water.
3. In a separate small bowl, stir together bread crumbs, garlic powder, onion powder, and parsley.
4. Dip each floret first in egg then in bread crumbs. Place in fryer basket, in batches.
5. Add the tender-crisp lid and set to air fry on 400°F. Bake cauliflower 15 minutes or until golden brown and crispy.
6. In a small bowl, whisk together mayonnaise, chili sauce, and hot sauce. When all the cauliflower is done, drizzle sauce over the top and serve.

Nutrition Info:
- Calories 77,Total Fat 3g,Total Carbs 11g,Protein 3g,Sodium 177mg.

Tiny Tostadas

Servings: 8
Cooking Time: 10 Minutes
Ingredients:
- 8 corn tortillas
- 1 cup pork, cooked & shredded
- 1 ½ tbsp. taco seasoning
- 6 tbsp. salsa
- 1 lettuce leaf, shredded
- 1 tbsp. cheddar cheese, fine grated

Directions:
1. Set to air fryer function on 400°F. Place the rack in the cooker and top with a sheet of parchment paper.
2. Cut 3 mini tortillas from each large tortilla, so you have 24. Use a jar or other round object to do this.
3. In a small bowl, combine pork and taco seasoning.
4. Place a layer of mini tortillas on the rack, you will need to make these in batches, top with 1 teaspoon of the meat mixture.
5. Add the tender-crisp lid and bake 10-12 minutes or until tortillas are golden brown. Transfer to serving plate and top with salsa, lettuce, and cheese. Repeat with remaining ingredients.

Nutrition Info:

- Calories 34,Total Fat 1g,Total Carbs 4g,Protein 2g,Sodium 84mg.

Cheesy Tomato Bruschetta

Servings: 2
Cooking Time: 15 Min
Ingredients:
- 1 Italian Ciabatta Sandwich Bread
- 2 tomatoes; chopped
- 2 garlic cloves, minced
- 1 cup grated mozzarella cheese /130g
- Olive oil to brush
- Basil leaves; chopped
- Salt and pepper to taste

Directions:
1. Cut the bread in half, lengthways, then each piece again in half. Drizzle each bit with olive oil and sprinkle with garlic. Top with the grated cheese, salt, and pepper.
2. Place the bruschetta pieces into the Ninja Foodi basket, close the crisping lid and cook for 12 minutes on Air Crisp mode at 380 °F or 194°C. At 6 minutes, check for doneness.
3. Once the Ninja Foodi beeps, remove the bruschetta to a serving platter, spoon over the tomatoes and chopped basil to serve.

Cheesy Jalapeno Boats

Servings: 12
Cooking Time: 25 Minutes
Ingredients:
- 8 oz. cream cheese, reduced fat, soft
- 1 cup cheddar cheese, reduced fat, grated
- 1 tsp garlic powder
- 2 eggs
- 2 tbsp. skim milk
- 1 cup panko bread crumbs
- ½ tsp paprika
- ½ tsp chili powder
- ½ tsp salt
- ¼ tsp pepper
- 12 jalapeno peppers, halved lengthwise, stems & seeds removed

Directions:
1. Place the rack in the cooking pot and line with parchment paper.
2. In a medium bowl, beat together cream cheese, cheddar, and garlic powder.
3. In a small bowl, whisk together eggs and milk.
4. In a shallow dish, stir together bread crumbs, paprika, chili powder, salt, and pepper.
5. Spread a tablespoon of cheese mixture in each jalapeno. Dip in egg mixture then coat with bread crumbs. Place on the parchment paper.
6. Add the tender-crisp lid and set to bake on 350°F. Cook 20-25 minutes or until golden brown. Serve immediately.
7. Bake 30 to 35 minutes, or until golden.

Nutrition Info:
- Calories 107,Total Fat 5g,Total Carbs 9g,Protein 6g,Sodium 326mg.

Buttery Chicken Meatballs

Servings: 6
Cooking Time: 90 Min
Ingredients:
- 1 pound ground chicken /450g
- 1 green bell pepper, minced
- 1 egg
- 2 celery stalks, minced
- ¼ cup hot sauce /62.5ml
- ½ cup water /125ml
- ¼ cup panko bread crumbs /32.5g
- ¼ cup crumbled queso fresco /32.5g
- 2 tbsps melted butter /30ml

Directions:
1. Choose Sear/Sauté on the pot and set to High. Choose Start/Stop to preheat the pot. Meanwhile, in a bowl, evenly combine the chicken, bell pepper, celery, queso fresco, hot sauce, breadcrumbs, and egg. Form meatballs out of the mixture.
2. Then, pour the melted butter into the pot and fry the meatballs in batches until lightly browned on all sides. Use a slotted spoon to remove the meatballs onto a plate.
3. Put the Crisping Basket in the pot. Pour in the water and put all the meatballs in the basket. Seal the pressure lid, choose Pressure, set to High, and set the timer to 5 minutes. Choose Start/Stop to begin cooking.
4. When done cooking, perform a quick pressure release and carefully open the lid. Close the crisping lid. Choose Air Crisp, set the temperature to 360°F, and set the time to 10 minutes; press Start.
5. After 5 minutes, open the lid, lift the basket and shake the meatballs. Return the basket to the pot and close the lid to continue cooking until the meatballs are crispy.

Wrapped Asparagus In Bacon

Servings: 6
Cooking Time: 30 Min
Ingredients:
- 1 lb. bacon; sliced /450g
- 1 lb. asparagus spears, trimmed /450g
- ½ cup Parmesan cheese, grated /65g
- Cooking spray
- Salt and pepper, to taste

Directions:
1. Place the bacon slices out on a work surface, top each one with one asparagus spear and half of the cheese. Wrap the bacon around the asparagus.
2. Line the Ninja Foodi basket with parchment paper. Arrange the wraps into the basket, scatter over the remaining cheese, season with salt and black pepper, and spray with cooking spray. Close the crisping lid and cook for 8 to 10 minutes on Roast mode at 370 °F or 188°C. If necessary, work in batches. Serve hot!

Breakfast Recipes

Maple Dipped Asparagus

Servings: 4
Cooking Time: 15 Minutes.
Ingredients:
- 2-pounds asparagus, trimmed
- 1/2 teaspoon black pepper
- 1 teaspoon salt
- 1/4 cup choc zero maple syrup
- 2 tablespoons olive oil
- 4 tablespoons tarragon, minced

Directions:
1. Toss asparagus with salt, oil, choc zero maple syrup, black pepper, and tarragon. Toss well.
2. Take Ninja Foodi Grill, set it over your kitchen platform, and open the Ninja Foodi's lid.
3. Set the grill grate and close the Ninja Foodi's lid.
4. Select "Grill" mode and select the "MED" temperature.
5. Set the cooking time to about 8 minutes, and then press the "Start/Stop" button to initiate preheating.
6. Set the asparagus over the grill grate.
7. Close the Ninja Foodi's lid and cook for 4 minutes.
8. Now open the Ninja Foodi's lid, flip the asparagus.
9. Close the Ninja Foodi's lid and cook for 4 more minutes.
10. Serve warm.

Nutrition Info:
- Calories: 241; Fat: 15g; Carbohydrates: 31g; Protein: 7.5g

Strawberry Oat Breakfast Bars

Servings: 16
Cooking Time: 25 Minutes
Ingredients:
- 2 cups oats
- ¼ cup oat flour
- 1 cup coconut flakes, unsweetened
- 2 tbsp. chia seeds, ground
- ½ cup almonds, chopped
- ¼ salt
- 2 bananas, mashed
- 2 tbsp. honey
- ¼ cup coconut oil, melted
- 1 cup strawberries, chopped
- 1 tsp vanilla

Directions:
1. Set to bake function on 350°F. Line an 8-inch baking dish with parchment paper.
2. In a large bowl, combine dry ingredients.
3. Stir in remaining ingredients until thoroughly combined.
4. Press mixture into prepared pan and place in cooker. Add the tender-crisp lid and bake 25 minutes until golden brown.
5. Let cool before slicing into 2-inch squares.

Nutrition Info:
- Calories 179, Total Fat 8g, Total Carbs 24g, Protein 5g, Sodium 53mg.

Pumpkin Pecan Oatmeal

Servings: 4
Cooking Time: 10 Minutes
Ingredients:
- 1 cup water
- 2 cups old fashioned oats
- 1 ¾ cup milk
- ½ cup pumpkin puree
- 1 tsp pumpkin pie spice
- ¼ tsp vanilla
- ½ cup maple syrup
- 2 tbsp. pecans, chopped

Directions:
1. Add the water, oats, milk, pumpkin, spice, vanilla, and syrup to the cooking pot. Stir to combine.
2. Secure the lid and select pressure cooking on high. Set timer for 8 minutes.
3. When timer goes off, release pressure naturally for 5 minutes, then use quick release for remaining pressure.
4. Stir oatmeal then ladle into bowls and top with pecans.

Nutrition Info:
- Calories 526,Total Fat 13g,Total Carbs 86g,Protein 17g,Sodium 54mg.

Stuffed Baked Potatoes

Servings: 4
Cooking Time: 20 Minutes
Ingredients:
- 4 large baked potatoes
- 2 tbsp. butter, melted
- 1 tsp salt
- 1 tsp black pepper
- 1 cup cheddar cheese, grated
- 6 slices bacon, cook crisp & chop
- 4 large eggs
- 2 tbsp. chives, chop

Directions:
1. Select bake function and heat cooker to 350°F.
2. Cut an opening in the top of the potatoes. With a spoon, scoop out most of the center.
3. Brush with melted butter and sprinkle with salt and pepper.
4. Divide ¾ of the cheese evenly among the potatoes. Top with ¾ of the bacon.
5. Crack one egg into each potato then top with remaining bacon, cheese and chives.
6. Place on the rack of the cooker and secure the tender-crisp lid. Set the timer for 20 minutes. Egg whites should be cooked completely but the yolk should still be soft. Serve immediately.

Nutrition Info:
- Calories 389,Total Fat 31g,Total Carbs 6g,Protein 20g,Sodium 1052mg.

Pumpkin Coconut Breakfast Bake

Servings: 8
Cooking Time: 1 Hour 15 Minutes
Ingredients:
- Butter flavored cooking spray
- 5 eggs
- ½ cup coconut milk
- 2 cups pumpkin puree
- 1 banana, mashed
- 2 dates, pitted & chopped
- 1 tsp cinnamon
- 1 cup raspberries
- ¼ cup coconut, unsweetened & shredded

Directions:
1. Lightly spray an 8-inch baking dish with cooking spray.
2. In a large bowl, whisk together eggs and milk.
3. Whisk in pumpkin until combined.
4. Stir in banana, dates, and cinnamon. Pour into prepared dish.
5. Sprinkle berries over top.
6. Place the rack in the cooking pot and place the dish on it. Add the tender-crisp lid and select bake on 350°F. Bake 20 minutes.
7. Sprinkle coconut over the top and bake another 20-25 minutes until top is lightly browned and casserole is set. Slice and serve warm.

Nutrition Info:
- Calories 113,Total Fat 5g,Total Carbs 14g,Protein 6g,Sodium 62mg.

Deviled Eggs(2)

Servings: 6
Cooking Time: 20 Min
Ingredients:
- 10 large eggs
- ¼ cup cream cheese /32.5ml
- ¼ cup mayonnaise /62.5ml
- 1 cup water /250ml
- ¼ tsp chili powder /1.25g
- salt and ground black pepper to taste

Directions:
1. Add water to the Foodi's pot. Insert the eggs into the steamer basket; place into the pot. Seal the pressure lid,

choose Pressure, set to High, and set the timer to 5 minutes. Press Start. When ready, release the pressure quickly.

2. Drop eggs into an ice bath to cool for 5 minutes. Press Start. Peel eggs and halve them.

3. Transfer yolks to a bowl and use a fork to mash; stir in cream cheese, and mayonnaise. Add pepper and salt for seasoning. Ladle yolk mixture into egg white halves.

Soft-boiled Eggs

Servings: 4
Cooking Time: 15 Min
Ingredients:
- 4 large eggs
- 1 cups water /250ml
- Salt and ground black pepper, to taste.

Directions:
1. To the pressure cooker pot, add water and place a reversible rack. Carefully place eggs on it. Seal the pressure lid, choose Pressure, set to High, and set the timer to 3 minutes. Press Start.
2. When cooking is complete, do a quick pressure release. Allow cooling completely in an ice bath. Peel the eggs and season with salt and pepper before serving.

Baked Eggs In Mushrooms

Servings: 4
Cooking Time: 15 Minutes
Ingredients:
- 4 large Portobello mushrooms, rinse & remove stems
- 4 eggs
- 1 ½ tbsp. extra virgin olive oil
- ½ tsp salt, divided
- ½ tsp black pepper, divided

Directions:
1. Set to bake function on 450°F.
2. Rub mushrooms with oil and half the salt and pepper. Place on a small baking sheet, cap side down.
3. Carefully crack an egg into each mushroom and season with remaining salt and pepper.
4. Place sheet in the cooker and secure the tender-crisp lid. Bake 12-15 minutes, or until whites of the eggs are cooked through. Serve immediately.

Nutrition Info:
- Calories 122, Total Fat 10g, Total Carbs 2g, Protein 7g, Sodium 363mg.

Southern Grits Casserole

Servings: 8
Cooking Time: 45 Minutes
Ingredients:
- 3 cups water
- 2 cups milk or heavy (whipping) cream, divided
- 2 cups stone ground grits
- Kosher salt
- Freshly ground black pepper
- 4 tablespoons unsalted butter
- 1 pound cooked breakfast sausage, casing removed and chopped
- 6 eggs
- 2 cups shredded Cheddar cheese

Directions:
1. Pour the water, 1½ cups of milk, and grits in the pot. Season with salt and pepper. Stir well. Assemble pressure lid, making sure the pressure release valve is in the SEAL position.
2. Select PRESSURE and set to HI. Set time to 10 minutes. Select START/STOP to begin.
3. When pressure cooking is complete, allow pressure to naturally release for 15 minutes. Then quick release remaining pressure by moving the pressure release valve to the VENT position. Carefully remove lid when unit has finished releasing pressure.
4. Stir in the butter and sausage.
5. In a large bowl, whisk together the eggs and remaining ½ cup of milk. Fold the eggs and cheese into the grits. Close crisping lid.
6. Select BAKE/ROAST, set temperature to 375°F, and set time to 25 minutes. Select START/STOP to begin.
7. Once cooking is complete, open lid. Let cool for 10 minutes before slicing to serve.

Nutrition Info:
- Calories: 551, Total Fat: 36g, Sodium: 692mg, Carbohydrates: 31g, Protein: 27g.

Strawberry Muffins

Servings: 12
Cooking Time: 25 Minutes
Ingredients:
- 1 ¼ cups white whole wheat flour
- 1/3 cup oats
- ½ tsp cinnamon
- ½ tsp baking soda
- 1 tsp baking powder
- ½ tsp salt
- 2/3 cup Stevia
- 3/4 cup Greek yogurt
- 1 egg
- 1/3 cup coconut oil, melted

- 1 cup strawberries, chopped

Directions:
1. Set to air fryer function on 375°F. Line 2 6-cup muffin tins with paper liners.
2. In a large bowl, combine dry ingredients.
3. In a medium bowl, whisk together yogurt, egg, and oil. Stir in berries and add to dry ingredients. Stir just until combined.
4. Fill prepared muffin tins 2/3 full. Place pans, one at a time, in the cooker and secure the tender-crisp lid. Bake 25 minutes, or until muffins pass the toothpick test. Repeat.
5. Let cool in the pan 10 minutes, then transfer to wire rack to cool completely.

Nutrition Info:
- Calories 131,Total Fat 8g,Total Carbs 27g,Protein 4g,Sodium 163mg.

Spinach Casserole

Servings: 4
Cooking Time: 5 Minutes

Ingredients:
- 4 whole eggs
- 1 tablespoons milk
- 1 tomato, diced
- ½ cup spinach
- ¼ teaspoon salt
- ¼ teaspoon black pepper

Directions:
1. Take a baking pan small enough to fit Ninja Foodi and grease it with butter.
2. Take a medium bowl and whisk in eggs, milk, salt, pepper, add veggies to the bowl and stir.
3. Pour egg mixture into the baking pan and lower the pan into the Ninja Foodi .
4. Close Air Crisping lid and Air Crisp for 325 degrees for 7 minutes.
5. Remove the pan from eggs, and enjoy hot.

Nutrition Info:
- Calories: 78; Fat: 5g; Carbohydrates: 1 g; Protein: 7 g

Pumpkin Steel Cut Oatmeal

Servings: 4
Cooking Time: 25 Min

Ingredients:
- ½ cup pumpkin seeds, toasted /65g
- 1 cup pumpkin puree /250ml
- 2 cups steel cut oats /260g
- 3 cups water /750ml
- 1 tbsp butter /15g
- 3 tbsp maple syrup /45ml
- ¼ tsp cinnamon /1.25g
- ½ tsp salt /2.5g

Directions:
1. Melt butter on Sear/Sauté. Add in cinnamon, oats, salt, pumpkin puree and water. Seal the pressure lid, choose Pressure, set to High, and set the timer to 10 minutes; press Start. When cooking is complete, do a quick release.
2. Open the lid and stir in maple syrup and top with toasted pumpkin seeds to serve.

Cranberry Lemon Quinoa

Servings: 6
Cooking Time: 20 Minutes

Ingredients:
- 16 oz. quinoa
- 4 ½ cups water
- ½ cup brown sugar, packed
- 1 tsp lemon extract
- ½ tsp salt
- ½ cup cranberries, dried

Directions:
1. Add all ingredients, except the cranberries, to the cooker and stir to mix.
2. Secure the lid and select pressure cooking on high. Set timer for 20 minutes.
3. When timer goes off, use natural release for 10 minutes. Then use quick release and remove the lid.
4. Stir in cranberries and serve.

Nutrition Info:
- Calories 284,Total Fat 4g,Total Carbs 56g,Protein 8g,Sodium 152mg.

Chili Cheese Quiche

Servings: 4
Cooking Time: 30 Minutes

Ingredients:
- Nonstick cooking spray
- 4 eggs
- 1 cup half-n- half
- 10 oz. green chilies, diced
- ½ tsp salt
- ½ tsp cumin
- 1 cup Mexican blend cheese, grated
- ¼ cup cilantro, chopped

Directions:
1. Spray a 6-inch baking pan with cooking spray.
2. In a mixing bowl, beat eggs then stir in half-n-half, chilies, salt, cumin, and half the cheese.

3. Pour into prepared pan and cover with foil.
4. Add 2 cups water to the cooking pot and add the rack. Place the pan on the rack and secure the lid.
5. Select pressure cooking on high and set timer for 20 minutes.
6. When timer goes off, release pressure naturally for 10 minutes, then use quick release.
7. Remove the foil and sprinkle remaining cheese over the top. Secure the tender-crisp lid and set to 375°F. Cook another 3-5 minutes or until cheese is melted and starts to brown. Serve garnished with cilantro.

Nutrition Info:
- Calories 300,Total Fat 23g,Total Carbs 7g,Protein 16g,Sodium 1172mg.

Ham & Spinach Breakfast Bake

Servings: 6
Cooking Time: 30 Minutes
Ingredients:
- Nonstick cooking spray
- 10 eggs
- 1 cup spinach, chopped
- 1 cup ham, chopped
- 1 cup red peppers, chopped
- 1 cup onion, chopped
- 1 tsp garlic powder
- ½ tsp onion powder
- ¼ tsp salt
- ¼ tsp pepper
- 1 cup Swiss cheese, grated

Directions:
1. Select the bake function and heat cooker to 350°F. Spray the cooking pot with cooking spray.
2. In a large bowl, whisk eggs together.
3. Add remaining ingredients and mix well.
4. Pour into cooking pot and secure the tender-crisp lid. Cook 25-30 minutes, or until eggs are set and top has started to brown.
5. Let cool 5 minutes before serving.

Nutrition Info:
- Calories 287,Total Fat 18g,Total Carbs 7g,Protein 23g,Sodium 629mg.

Spanish Potato And Chorizo Frittata

Servings:4
Cooking Time: 20 Minutes
Ingredients:
- 4 eggs
- 1 cup milk
- Sea salt
- Freshly ground black pepper
- 1 potato, diced
- ½ cup frozen corn
- 1 chorizo sausage, diced
- 8 ounces feta cheese, crumbled
- 1 cup water

Directions:
1. In a medium bowl, whisk together the eggs and milk. Season with salt and pepper.
2. Place the potato, corn, and chorizo in the Multi-Purpose Pan or an 8-inch baking pan. Pour the egg mixture and feta cheese over top. Cover the pan with aluminum foil and place on the Reversible Rack. Make sure it's in the lower position.
3. Pour the water into the pot. Assemble pressure lid, making sure the pressure release valve is in the SEAL position.
4. Select PRESSURE and set to HI. Set time to 20 minutes. Select START/STOP to begin.
5. When pressure cooking is complete, quick release the pressure by moving the pressure release valve to the VENT position. Carefully remove lid when unit has finished releasing pressure.
6. Remove the pan from pot and place it on a cooling rack for 5 minutes, then serve.

Nutrition Info:
- Calories: 361,Total Fat: 24g,Sodium: 972mg,Carbohydrates: 17g,Protein: 21g.

Southwest Tofu Scramble

Servings: 4
Cooking Time: 10 Minutes
Ingredients:
- 1 tbsp. olive oil
- 4 oz. extra firm tofu, cut in small cubes
- ¼ cup red bell pepper, diced fine
- ¼ cup red onion, diced fine
- 1 cup kale, chopped
- ½ tsp cumin
- 1 tsp chili powder
- 6 egg whites, lightly beaten
- 2 tbsp. cilantro, chopped

Directions:
1. Select sauté function on med-high heat. Add oil and heat until hot.
2. Add the tofu, pepper, onion, and kale and cook, stirring frequently, until onion is soft and kale has wilted.

3. Stir in spices. Slowly add egg whites, stirring frequently to scramble. Cook until egg whites are set, but not brown. Sprinkle with cilantro and serve immediately.

Nutrition Info:
- Calories 91, Total Fat 5g, Total Carbs 3g, Protein 10g, Sodium 97mg.

Ham & Hash Brown Casserole

Servings: 12
Cooking Time: 7 Hours

Ingredients:
- Nonstick cooking spray
- 30 oz. hash browns, shredded & frozen
- 1 lb. ham, diced
- 1 onion, diced
- 1 red bell pepper, diced
- 1 orange bell pepper, diced
- 1 ½ cups cheddar cheese, grated
- 12 eggs
- 1 cup milk
- 4 oz. green chilies, diced
- 1 tbsp. Dijon mustard
- ½ tsp garlic powder
- ½ tsp pepper
- ¼ tsp salt

Directions:
1. Spray the cooking pot with cooking spray.
2. Layer half the hash browns, ham, onions, peppers, and cheese in the pot. Repeat layers.
3. In a large bowl, whisk together the eggs, milk, green chilies, and seasonings until combined. Pour over ingredients in the cooking pot.
4. Secure the lid and set to slow cooker function on low heat. Set the timer for 7 hours. Casserole is done when the eggs are set.

Nutrition Info:
- Calories 348, Total Fat 18g, Total Carbs 22g, Protein 23g, Sodium 893mg.

Carrot Cake Oats

Servings: 8
Cooking Time: 13 Minutes

Ingredients:
- 2 cups oats
- 1 cup water
- 4 cups unsweetened vanilla almond milk
- 2 apples, diced
- 2 cups shredded carrot
- 1 cup dried cranberries
- ½ cup maple syrup
- 2 teaspoons cinnamon
- 2 teaspoons vanilla extract

Directions:
1. Place all the ingredients in the pot. Assemble pressure lid, making sure the pressure release valve is in the SEAL position.
2. Select PRESSURE and set to LO. Set time to 3 minutes. Select START/STOP to begin.
3. When pressure cooking is complete, allow pressure to naturally release for 10 minutes. Then quick release remaining pressure by moving the pressure release valve to the VENT position. Carefully remove lid when unit has finished releasing pressure.
4. Stir oats, allowing them to cool, and serve with toppings such as chopped walnuts, diced pineapple, or shredded coconut, if desired.

Nutrition Info:
- Calories: 252, Total Fat: 3g, Sodium: 112mg, Carbohydrates: 54g, Protein: 4g.

Cheesy Shakshuka

Servings: 4
Cooking Time: 50 Min

Ingredients:
- 1 small red onion; chopped
- 2 cans diced tomatoes with their juice /435ml
- ½ red bell pepper, seeded and chopped
- 1 medium banana pepper, seeded and minced
- 4 eggs
- ⅓ cup crumbled goat cheese /84g
- 2 garlic cloves; chopped
- 2 tbsp fresh cilantro; chopped /30g
- 3 tbsps ghee /45g
- ½ tsp smoked paprika /7.5g
- ½ tsp red chili flakes /2.5g
- ¼ tsp black pepper; freshly ground /1.25g
- 1 tsp salt /5g
- ½ tsp coriander, ground /2.5g

Directions:
1. Choose Sear/Sauté on you Foodi and set on Medium to preheat the inner pot; press Start. Melt the ghee and sauté the onion, bell pepper, banana pepper, and garlic. Season lightly with salt and cook for 2 minutes until the vegetables are fragrant and beginning to soften.
2. Then, stir in the tomatoes, coriander, smoked paprika, red chili flakes, and black pepper. Seal the pressure lid, choose pressure and adjust the pressure to High and the timer to 4 minutes. Press Start to continue cooking.

3. When the timer has read to the end, perform a quick pressure release. Gently crack the eggs onto the tomato sauce in different areas. Seal the pressure lid again, but with the valve set to Vent. Choose Steam and adjust the cook time to 3 minutes. Press Start to cook the eggs.

4. When ready, carefully open the pressure lid. Sprinkle with the shakshuka with goat cheese and cilantro. Dish into a serving platter and serve.

Glazed Carrots

Servings: 4
Cooking Time: 4 Minutes

Ingredients:
- 2 pounds carrots, washed, peeled and sliced
- Pepper, to taste
- 1 cup of water
- 1 tablespoon butter
- 1 tablespoon choc zero maple syrup

Directions:
1. Add carrots, water to the Instant Pot.
2. Lock and secure the Ninja Foodi's lid, then cook on "HIGH" pressure for 4 minutes.
3. Quick-release Pressure.
4. Strain carrots.
5. Add butter, maple syrup to the warm mix, stir it gently.
6. Transfer strained carrots back to the pot and stir.
7. Coat well with maple syrup.
8. Sprinkle a bit of pepper and serve.
9. Enjoy.

Nutrition Info:
- Calories: 358; Fat: 12g; Carbohydrates: 20g; Protein: 2g

Breakfast Egg Pizza

Servings: 8
Cooking Time: 28 Minutes

Ingredients:
- 12 eggs
- 1/2 cup heavy cream
- 1/2 tsp salt
- 1/4 tsp pepper
- 8 oz sausage
- 2 cups peppers sliced
- 1 cup cheese shredded

Directions:
1. Heat peppers in a bowl for 3 minutes in the microwave.
2. Place air crisper basket in the Ninja Foodi and place the bacon in it.
3. Secure the Ninja Foodi lid and Air Fry them for 10 minutes.
4. Transfer the cooked crispy bacon to a plate and keep them aside.
5. Whisk eggs with salt, pepper, and cream in a bowl.
6. Pour this mixture in a greased baking pan.
7. Place the trivet in the Ninja Food cooking pot and set the baking pan over it.
8. Secure the Ninja Foodi lid and turn the pressure valve to 'closed' position.
9. Select 'Bake/Roast' for 15 minutes at 350 °F.
10. Once done, top the egg bake with cheese and peppers.
11. Broil this pizza for 3 minutes in the broiler until the cheese melts.
12. Serve warm.

Nutrition Info:
- Calories 489; Total Fat 43.3g; Total Carbs 5g; Protein 22.2 g

Breakfast Pies

Servings: 4
Cooking Time: 20 Minutes

Ingredients:
- 1 ½ cup mozzarella cheese, grated
- 2/3 cup almond flour, sifted
- 4 eggs, beaten
- 4 tbsp. butter
- 6 slices bacon, cooked crisp & crumbled

Directions:
1. Select air fryer function and heat cooker to 400°F.
2. In a microwave safe bowl, melt the mozzarella cheese until smooth.
3. Stir in flour until well combined.
4. Roll the dough out between 2 sheets of parchment paper. Use a sharp knife to cut dough into 4 equal rectangles.
5. Heat the butter in a skillet over medium heat. Add the eggs and scramble to desired doneness.
6. Divide eggs evenly between the four pieces of dough, placing them on one side. Top with bacon.
7. Fold dough over filling and seal the edges with a fork. Poke a few holes on the top of the pies.
8. Place the pies in the fryer basket in a single layer. Secure the tender-crisp lid and bake 20 minutes, turning over halfway through. Serve immediately.

Nutrition Info:
- Calories 420,Total Fat 33g,Total Carbs 3g,Protein 28g,Sodium 663mg.

Curried Chickpea And Roasted Tomato Shakshuka

Servings: 6
Cooking Time: 30 Minutes
Ingredients:
- 2 tablespoons extra-virgin olive oil
- 2 red bell peppers, diced
- 1 small onion, diced
- 2 garlic cloves, minced
- 1 tablespoon red curry paste
- 1 tablespoon tomato paste
- 1 can crushed fire-roasted tomatoes
- 1 can chickpeas, rinsed and drained
- Kosher salt
- Freshly ground black pepper
- 6 large eggs
- 2 tablespoons chopped cilantro

Directions:
1. Select SEAR/SAUTÉ and set to HI. Select START/STOP to begin. Add the olive oil and let preheat for 5 minutes.
2. Add the bell peppers, onion, and garlic and cook for 3 minutes, stirring occasionally.
3. Add the curry and tomato pastes and cook for 2 minutes, stirring occasionally.
4. Add the crushed tomatoes, chickpeas, and season with salt and pepper and stir. Assemble pressure lid, making sure the pressure release valve is in the SEAL position.
5. Select PRESSURE and set to HI. Set time to 10 minutes. Select START/STOP to begin.
6. When pressure cooking is complete, quick release the pressure by turning the pressure release valve to the VENT position. Carefully remove the lid when the unit has finished releasing pressure.
7. With the back of a spoon, make six indents in the sauce. Crack an egg into each indent. Close crisping lid.
8. Select BAKE/ROAST, set temperature to 350°F, and set time to 10 minutes (or until eggs are cooked to your liking). Select START/STOP to begin.
9. When cooking is complete, open lid. Let cool 5 to 10 minutes, then garnish with the cilantro and serve. If desired, serve with crusty bread, chopped scallions, feta cheese, and/or pickled jalapeños.

Nutrition Info:
- Calories: 258, Total Fat: 12g, Sodium: 444mg, Carbohydrates: 27g, Protein: 11g.

Egg Spinach Bites

Servings: 6
Cooking Time: 27 Minutes
Ingredients:
- 4 slices of bacon
- 1/2 cup lite coconut milk
- 1 cup Spinach cut up
- 6 eggs

Directions:
1. Place air crisper basket in the Ninja Foodi and place the bacon in it.
2. Secure the Ninja Foodi lid and Air Fry them for 10 minutes.
3. Transfer the cooked crispy bacon to a plate and keep them aside.
4. Whisk egg with spinach, coconut milk and crispy bacon in a bowl.
5. Divide this batter in a silicone muffin tray.
6. Set the trivet in the Ninja Food then place the muffin pan over the trivet and seal the lid.
7. Secure the Ninja Foodi lid and turn the pressure valve to the 'closed' position.
8. Cook the egg bites for 17 minutes for 325 °F on Bake/Roast mode.
9. Once done, remove the lid and remove the bites from the muffin tray.
10. Serve warm.

Nutrition Info:
- Calories 211; Total Fat 18.5 g; Total Carbs 0.5 g; Protein 11.5 g

Baked Eggs & Kale

Servings: 4
Cooking Time: 25 Minutes
Ingredients:
- 1 tbsp. olive oil
- 6 cups kale, remove stems & chop
- 2 cloves garlic, diced fine
- ¼ cup ricotta cheese, fat free
- ¼ cup feta, fat free, crumbled
- 4 eggs
- 1/3 cup grape tomatoes, halved
- ¼ tsp pepper
- ½ tsp salt

Directions:
1. Add oil to the cooking pot and select sauté on medium heat.

2. Add the kale and garlic and cook until kale is wilted, about 2-3 minutes.
3. In a small bowl, combine ricotta and feta cheeses.
4. Make 4 small indents in the kale mixture and crack an egg into each one.
5. Drop the cheese mixture by tablespoons around the eggs.
6. Top with tomatoes, pepper, and salt. Secure the tender-crisp lid, set to air fryer function at 350°F and bake 20-25 minutes or until egg whites are cooked through. Serve immediately.

Nutrition Info:
- Calories 154, Total Fat 12g, Total Carbs 7g, Protein 7g, Sodium 410mg.

Omelets In The Jar

Servings: 5
Cooking Time: 8 Minutes
Ingredients:
- 10 eggs
- 1/3 cup heavy cream
- 2/3 cup of shredded cheese
- 1 green pepper, chopped
- 1 ham steak, chopped
- 1/2 lb. bacon, cooked and chopped
- 5 mason jars or other jars
- 1 cup of water

Directions:
1. Grease the mason jars with canola spray.
2. Whisk 2 eggs with 1 tbsp cream in a bowl then pour it into a jar.
3. Add 1 tbsp of ham, green peppers, and cheese to the same jar.
4. Repeat the same steps to fill remaining jars.
5. Pour 1 cup water in the Ninja Food pot and place trivet over it.
6. Set all the mason jars over the trivet.
7. Secure the Ninja Foodi lid and turn its pressure handle to 'Closed' position.
8. Select Pressure mode for 8 minutes at 350 °F.
9. Once done, release the steam naturally then remove the lid.
10. Drizzle bacon and cheese over each jar.
11. Serve fresh.

Nutrition Info:
- Calories 111; Total Fat 8.3 g; Total Carbs 1.9 g; Protein 7.4 g

Double Berry Dutch Baby

Servings: 6
Cooking Time: 25 Minutes
Ingredients:
- 1 tbsp. butter, melted
- 2 eggs
- ½ cup skim milk
- 1 tsp vanilla
- ½ cup flour
- ¼ tsp cinnamon
- 1/8 tsp salt
- 2 tbsp. sugar
- 2 tsp cornstarch
- 1/3 cup water
- ½ cup strawberries, sliced
- ½ cup blueberries

Directions:
1. Select air fryer function and heat cooker to 400°F. Pour melted butter in an 8-inch round pan and swirl to coat bottom.
2. In a medium bowl, whisk together eggs, milk, and vanilla.
3. In a small bowl, combine flour, cinnamon, and salt. Whisk into egg mixture until smooth. Pour into prepared pan.
4. Place in the cooker and secure the tender-crisp lid. Bake 18-20 minutes until golden brown and set in the center.
5. Remove pancake from the cooker and set to sauté on medium heat.
6. Add sugar, cornstarch, and water to the cooking pot and stir until smooth.
7. Stir in both berries and bring to a boil. Cook about 5 minutes, stirring frequently, until berries have softened and mixture has thickened. Spoon into pancake, slice and serve.

Nutrition Info:
- Calories 125, Total Fat 4g, Total Carbs 17g, Protein 4g, Sodium 100mg.

Flaxseeds Granola

Servings: 16
Cooking Time: 2½ Hours
Ingredients:
- ½ cup sunflower kernels
- 5 cups mixed nuts, crushed
- 2 tablespoons ground flax seeds
- ¼ cup olive oil
- ½ cup unsalted butter
- 1 teaspoon ground cinnamon
- 1 cup choc zero maple syrup

Directions:
1. Grease the Ninja Foodi's insert.

2. In the greased Ninja Foodi's insert, add sunflower kernels, nuts, flax seeds, oil, butter, and cinnamon and stir to combine.
3. Close the Ninja Foodi's lid with a crisping lid and select "Slow Cooker."
4. Set on "High" for 2½ hours.
5. Press the "Start/Stop" button to initiate cooking.
6. Stir the mixture after every 30 minutes.
7. Open the Ninja Foodi's lid and transfer the granola onto a large baking sheet.
8. Add the maple syrup and stir to combine.
9. Set aside to cool completely before serving.
10. You can preserve this granola in an airtight container.

Nutrition Info:
- Calories: 189; Fat: 10 g; Carbohydrates: 7.7 g; Protein: 4.6 g

Bacon & Egg Poppers

Servings: 6
Cooking Time: 25 Minutes
Ingredients:
- 12 slices bacon
- 4 jalapeno peppers
- 3 oz. cream cheese, soft
- 8 eggs
- ½ tsp garlic powder
- ½ tsp onion powder
- Salt & pepper, to taste
- Nonstick cooking spray
- ½ cup cheddar cheese, grated

Directions:
1. Select air fryer function and heat cooker to 375°F.
2. Heat a skillet over med-high heat and cook bacon until almost crisp but still pliable. Remove to paper towels to drain and reserve bacon fat for later.
3. Remove the seeds from 3 of the jalapenos and chop them. With the remaining jalapeno, slice into rings.
4. In a large bowl, beat together cream cheese, 1 tablespoon bacon fat, chopped jalapenos, eggs, and seasonings.
5. Spray 2 6-cup muffin tins with cooking spray. Place one slice bacon around the edges of each cup.
6. Pour egg mixture into cups, filling ¾ full then top with cheddar cheese and a jalapeno ring.
7. Place muffin pan, one at a time, in the cooker, secure the tender-crisp lid and bake 20-25 minutes, or until eggs are cooked. Repeat with other pan and serve immediately.

Nutrition Info:
- Calories 399,Total Fat 34g,Total Carbs 3g,Protein 19g,Sodium 666mg.

Banana Coconut Loaf

Servings: 8
Cooking Time: 35 Minutes
Ingredients:
- Nonstick cooking spray
- 1 ¼ cup whole wheat flour
- ½ cup coconut flakes, unsweetened
- 2 tsp baking powder
- ½ tsp baking soda
- ½ tsp salt
- 1 cup banana, mashed
- ¼ cup coconut oil, melted
- 2 tbsp. honey

Directions:
1. Select the bake function on heat cooker to 350°F. Spray an 8-inch loaf pan with cooking spray.
2. In a large bowl, combine flour, coconut, baking powder, baking soda, and salt.
3. In a separate bowl, combine banana, oil, and honey. Add to dry ingredients and mix well. Spread batter in prepared pan.
4. Secure the tender-crisp lid and bake 30-35 minutes or until loaf passes the toothpick test.
5. Remove pan from the cooker and let cool 10 minutes. Invert loaf to a wire rack and cool completely before slicing.

Nutrition Info:
- Calories 201,Total Fat 11g,Total Carbs 26g,Protein 3g,Sodium 349mg.

Sausage & Broccoli Frittata

Servings: 10
Cooking Time: 25 Minutes
Ingredients:
- 1 tbsp. olive oil
- 1 lb. country-style pork sausage
- 4 cups broccoli florets
- 1 onion, chopped
- ½ tsp salt
- ¼ tsp pepper
- 14 eggs
- ½ cup milk
- 2 cups cheddar cheese, grated

Directions:
1. Select sauté function on med-high heat.

2. Add olive oil, once it's hot, add sausage, broccoli, onions, salt, and pepper. Cook, stirring frequently, until sausage is no longer pink. Drain the fat.
3. In a large bowl, whisk together eggs, milk, and cheese. Pour over sausage mixture.
4. Set cooker to bake function on 350 °F. Secure the tender-crisp lid and set timer to 20 minutes.
5. Frittata is done when eggs are set. Let cool 5-10 minutes before serving.

Nutrition Info:
- Calories 374, Total Fat 27g, Total Carbs 4g, Protein 28g, Sodium 432mg.

Spinach Turkey Cups

Servings: 4
Cooking Time: 23 Minutes
Ingredients:
- 1 tablespoon unsalted butter
- 1-pound fresh baby spinach
- 4 eggs
- 7 ounces cooked turkey, chopped
- 4 teaspoons unsweetened almond milk
- Black pepper and salt, as required

Directions:
1. Select the "Sauté/Sear" setting of Ninja Foodi and place the butter into the pot.
2. Press the "Start/Stop" button to initiate cooking and heat for about 2-3 minutes.
3. Add the spinach and cook for about 3 minutes or until just wilted.
4. Press the "Start/Stop" button to pause cooking and drain the liquid completely.
5. Transfer the spinach into a suitable and set aside to cool slightly.
6. Set the "Air Crisp Basket" in the Ninja Foodi's insert.
7. Close the Ninja Foodi's lid with a crisping lid and select "Air Crisp."
8. Set its cooking temperature to 355 °F for 5 minutes.
9. Press the "Start/Stop" button to initiate preheating.
10. Divide the spinach into 4 greased ramekins, followed by the turkey.
11. Crack 1 egg into each ramekin and drizzle with almond milk.
12. Sprinkle with black pepper and salt.
13. After preheating, Open the Ninja Foodi's lid.
14. Place the ramekins into the "Air Crisp Basket."
15. Close the Ninja Foodi's lid with a crisping lid and select "Air Crisp."
16. Set its cooking temperature to 355 °F for 20 minutes.
17. Press the "Start/Stop" button to initiate cooking.
18. Open the Ninja Foodi's lid and serve hot.

Nutrition Info:
- Calories: 200; Fat: 10.2g; Carbohydrates: 4.5g; Protein: 23.4g

Apricot Oatmeal

Servings: 8
Cooking Time: 8 Hours
Ingredients:
- 2 cups steel-cut oats
- 1/3 cup dried apricots, chopped
- ½ cup dried cherries
- 1 teaspoon ground cinnamon
- 4 cups milk
- 4 cups water
- ¼ teaspoon liquid stevia

Directions:
1. In the Ninja Foodi's insert, place all ingredients and stir to combine.
2. Close the Ninja Foodi's lid with a crisping lid and select "Slow Cooker."
3. Set on "Low" for 6-8 hours.
4. Press the "Start/Stop" button to initiate cooking.
5. Open the Ninja Foodi's lid and serve warm.

Nutrition Info:
- Calories: 148; Fat: 3.5g; Carbohydrates: 4.2 g; Protein: 5.9 g

Spinach & Sausage Casserole

Servings: 8
Cooking Time: 7 Hours
Ingredients:
- Nonstick cooking spray
- 1 lb. pork breakfast sausage
- 1 yellow onion, diced
- 1 ½ tsp oregano
- 5 cups baby spinach, packed
- 4 cups potatoes, diced
- 1 ¼ cups Swiss cheese, grated
- ¼ cup Parmesan cheese
- 8 eggs
- 2 cups milk
- 2 tsp Dijon mustard
- 1 ½ tsp salt
- ¼ tsp black pepper

Directions:

1. Spray the cooking pot with cooking spray. Select the sauté function on med-high.
2. Add the sausage, onion, and oregano and cook, stirring to break up the sausage until no longer pink, about 8-10 minutes.
3. Stir in the spinach and cook until wilted, about 2 minutes.
4. Set the cooker to the slow cooker function on low heat.
5. Add the potatoes, 1 cup of Swiss cheese, and the parmesan cheese and mix well.
6. In a large bowl, whisk eggs, milk, mustard, salt, and pepper until smooth. Pour over ingredients in the cooking pot and stir to combine.
7. Secure the lid and set the timer for 6 hours. Casserole is done when the edges start to brown and the eggs are set. If it is not done, recover and cook another 60 minutes or until done.
8. When the casserole is set, top with remaining cheese and cover. Cook just until the cheese melts, about 5 minutes.

Nutrition Info:
- Calories 439,Total Fat 29g,Total Carbs 18g,Protein 27g,Sodium 1098mg.

Grilled Broccoli

Servings: 4
Cooking Time: 10 Minutes.
Ingredients:
- 2 heads broccoli, cut into florets
- 4 tablespoons soy sauce
- 2 tablespoons canola oil
- 4 tablespoons balsamic vinegar
- 2 teaspoons choc zero maple syrup
- Sesame seeds, to garnish
- Red pepper flakes, to garnish

Directions:
1. In a mixing bowl, add the soy sauce, balsamic vinegar, oil, and maple syrup. Whisk well and add the broccoli; toss well.
2. Take Ninja Foodi Grill, set it over your kitchen platform, and open the Ninja Foodi's lid.
3. Set the grill grate and close the Ninja Foodi's lid.
4. Press "GRILL" and select the "MAX" grill function. Adjust the timer to 10 minutes and then press the "Start/Stop" button to initiate preheating.
5. After you hear a beep, open the Ninja Foodi's lid.
6. Set the broccoli over the grill grate.
7. Close the Ninja Foodi's lid and allow it to cook until the timer reads zero.
8. Divide into serving plates.
9. Serve warm with red pepper flakes and sesame seeds on top.

Nutrition Info:
- Calories: 141; Fat: 7g; Carbohydrates: 14g; Protein: 4.5g

Savory Custards With Ham And Cheese

Servings: 4
Cooking Time: 40 Min
Ingredients:
- 4 large eggs
- 1 ounce cottage cheese; at room temperature /30g
- 2 serrano ham slices; halved widthwise
- ¼ cup caramelized white onions /32.5g
- ¼ cup half and half /62.5ml
- ¼ cup grated Emmental cheese /32.5g
- ¼ tsp salt /1.25g
- Ground black pepper to taste

Directions:
1. Preheat the inner pot by choosing Sear/Sauté and adjust to Medium; press Start. Put the serrano ham in the pot and cook for 3 to 4 minutes or until browned, turning occasionally.
2. Remove the ham onto a paper towel-lined plate. Next, use a brush to coat the inside of four 1- cup ramekins with the ham fat. Set the cups aside, then, empty and wipe out the inner pot with a paper towel, and return the pot to the base.
3. Crack the eggs into a bowl and add the cottage cheese, half and half, salt, and several grinds of black pepper. Use a hand mixer to whisk the Ingredients until co cheese lumps remain.
4. Stir in the grated emmental cheese and mix again to incorporate the cheese. Lay a piece of ham in the bottom of each custard cup. Evenly share the onions among the cups as well as the egg mixture. Cover each cup with aluminum foil.
5. Pour 1 cup or 250ml of water into the inner pot and fix the reversible rack in the pot. Arrange the ramekins on top. Lock the pressure lid in Seal position; choose Pressure, adjust to High, and set the timer to 7 minutes. Press Start.
6. After cooking, perform a quick pressure release. Use tongs to remove the custard cups from the pressure cooker. Cool for 1 to 2 minutes before serving.

Ham & Broccoli Frittata

Servings: 6
Cooking Time: 30 Minutes
Ingredients:
- 1 tbsp. butter, soft
- 1 cup red pepper, seeded & sliced
- 1 cup ham, cubed
- 2 cups broccoli florets
- 4 eggs
- 1 cup half-n- half
- 1 cup cheddar cheese, grated
- 1 tsp salt
- 2 tsp pepper
- 2 cups water

Directions:
1. Use the soft butter to grease a 6x3-inch baking dish.
2. Place the peppers in an even layer on the bottom of the dish. Top with ham then broccoli.
3. In a mixing bowl, whisk together eggs, half-n-half, salt, and pepper.
4. Stir in cheese and pour mixture over ingredients in the baking dish. Cover with foil.
5. Pour 2 cups water into the cooking pot and place the rack inside.
6. Place the baking dish on the rack and secure the lid. Select pressure cooking on high and set the timer for 20 minutes.
7. When the timer goes off, release pressure naturally for 10 minutes, then quick release.
8. Remove the baking dish and let cool at least 5 minutes. With a sharp knife, loosen the sides of the frittata then invert onto serving plate. Serve immediately.

Nutrition Info:
- Calories 401,Total Fat 29g,Total Carbs 9g,Protein 26g,Sodium 1487mg.

Ricotta Raspberry Breakfast Cake

Servings: 12
Cooking Time: 40 Minutes
Ingredients:
- Nonstick cooking spray
- 1 ¼ cups oat flour
- ½ tsp xanthan gum
- ¼ cup cornstarch
- ¼ tsp baking soda
- 1 ½ tsp baking powder
- ½ tsp salt
- ½ cup sugar
- 4 tbsp. butter, unsalted, soft
- 1 cup ricotta cheese, room temperature
- 3 eggs, room temperature, beaten
- 1 tsp vanilla
- 1 cup fresh raspberries

Directions:
1. Set to bake function on 350°F. Lightly spray an 8-inch round baking pan with cooking spray.
2. In a large bowl, combine dry ingredients.
3. Make a well in the center and add butter, ricotta, eggs, and vanilla and mix just until combined.
4. Gently fold in half the berries, being careful not to crush them.
5. Pour batter into prepared pan and sprinkle remaining berries on the top. Add the tender-crisp lid and bake 40 minutes, or until a light brown and only a few moist crumbs show on a toothpick when inserted in the center.
6. Let cool in the pan 10 minutes then transfer to a wire rack to cool completely before serving.

Nutrition Info:
- Calories 170,Total Fat 8g,Total Carbs 20g,Protein 6g,Sodium 164mg.

Kale-egg Frittata

Servings: 6
Cooking Time: 20 Min
Ingredients:
- 1 ½ cups kale; chopped /195g
- 6 large eggs
- ¼ cup grated Parmesan cheese /32.5g
- 1 cup water /250ml
- 2 tbsp heavy cream /30ml
- ½ tsp freshly grated nutmeg /2.5g
- cooking spray
- Salt and black pepper to taste

Directions:
1. In a bowl, beat eggs, nutmeg, pepper, salt, and cream until smooth; stir in Parmesan cheese and kale. Apply a cooking spray to a cake pan. Wrap aluminum foil around outside of the pan to cover completely.
2. Place egg mixture into the prepared pan. Add water into the pot of your Foodi. Set your Foodi's reversible rack over the water. Gently lay the pan onto the reversible rack.
3. Seal the pressure lid, choose Pressure, set to High, and set the timer to 10 minutes. Press Start. When ready, release the pressure quickly.

Hearty Breakfast Skillet

Servings: 4
Cooking Time: 35 Minutes
Ingredients:
- ¼ cup walnuts
- 2 tbsp. olive oil
- ½ cup onion, chopped
- 4 cups Brussel sprouts, halved
- 2 cups baby Bella mushrooms, chopped
- ¼ tsp salt
- ¼ tsp pepper
- 1 clove garlic, diced fine
- 3 tbsp. chicken broth, low sodium
- 4 eggs
- ¼ cup parmesan cheese, grated

Directions:
1. Set to sauté on medium heat. Add walnuts and cook, stirring frequently, 3-5 minutes or until golden brown. Transfer to small bowl to cool.
2. Add oil and let it get hot. Once oil is hot, add onions and Brussel sprouts and cook 5 minutes, stirring occasionally.
3. Stir in mushrooms, salt, and pepper and cook 10-12 minutes until vegetables are tender. Add garlic and cook 1 minute more.
4. Pour in broth and cook until liquid has evaporated, about 3 minutes.
5. Make 4 "well" in vegetable mixture and crack an egg in each. Add tender-crisp lid and set to air fryer function on 350°F. Bake 8-10 minutes, or until whites are cooked through.
6. Chop the walnut and sprinkle over top with parmesan cheese and serve.

Nutrition Info:
- Calories 261,Total Fat 18g,Total Carbs 14g,Protein 13g,Sodium 399mg.

Chocolate Banana Muffins

Servings: 12
Cooking Time: 25 Minutes
Ingredients:
- 1 cup almond flour, sifted
- ½ tsp baking powder
- 1/8 tsp salt
- 2 eggs
- ¼ cup Stevia
- ½ tsp almond extract
- 3 bananas, mashed
- 2 tbsp. cocoa powder, unsweetened
- 1 tbsp. almonds, sliced

Directions:
1. Select bake function and heat cooker to 325°F. Line 2 6-cup muffin tins with liners.
2. In a large bowl, combine flour, baking powder, and salt.
3. Add remaining ingredients, except almonds, and beat until thoroughly combined.
4. Spoon into liners and top with sliced almonds.
5. Place muffin tin, one at a time, in the cooker and secure the tender-crisp lid. Bake 25-30 minutes or until muffins pass the toothpick test. Serve warm.

Nutrition Info:
- Calories 87,Total Fat 5g,Total Carbs 19g,Protein 3g,Sodium 38mg.

French Dip Sandwiches

Servings: 8
Cooking Time: 1 Hr 35 Min
Ingredients:
- 2 ½ pounds beef roast /1125g
- 2 tbsp olive oil /30ml
- 1 onion; chopped
- 4 garlic cloves; sliced
- ½ cup dry red wine /125ml
- 2 cups beef broth stock /500ml
- 1 tsp dried oregano /5g
- 16 slices Fontina cheese
- 8 split hoagie rolls

Directions:
1. Generously apply pepper and salt to the beef for seasoning. Warm oil on Sear/Sauté and brown the beef for 2 to 3 minutes per side. Set aside on a plate.
2. Add onions and cook for 3 minutes, until translucent. Mix in garlic and cook for one a minute until soft.
3. To the Foodi, add red wine to deglaze. Scrape the cooking surface to remove any browned sections of the food using a wooden spoon's flat edge; mix in beef broth and take back the juices and beef to your pressure cooker. Over the meat, scatter some oregano.
4. Seal the pressure lid, choose Pressure, set to High, and set the timer to 50 minutes; press Start. Release pressure naturally for around 10 minutes. Transfer the beef to a cutting board and slice.
5. Roll the sliced beef and add a topping of onions. Each sandwich should be topped with 2 slices fontina cheese.
6. Place the sandwiches in the pot, close the crisping lid and select Air Crisp. Adjust the temperature to 360°F or 183°C and the time to 3 minutes. Press Start. When cooking is complete, the cheese should be cheese melt.

Brussels Sprouts Bacon Hash

Servings: 4
Cooking Time: 20 Minutes
Ingredients:
- 1/2 lb. brussels sprouts, sliced in half
- 4 slices bacon, chopped
- 1/2 red onion, chopped
- salt, to taste
- black pepper, to taste

Directions:
1. Toss all the ingredients into the Ninja Foodi cooking pot.
2. Secure the Ninja Foodi lid and turn its pressure handle to 'Closed' position.
3. Select mode for 20 minutes at 390 °F.
4. Once done, release the steam naturally then remove the lid.
5. Serve fresh.

Nutrition Info:
- Calories 121; Total Fat 9 g; Total Carbs 13.8 g; Protein 4.3 g

Bacon And Gruyère Egg Bites

Servings: 6
Cooking Time: 26 Minutes
Ingredients:
- 5 slices bacon, cut into ½-inch pieces
- 5 eggs
- 1 teaspoon kosher salt
- ¼ cup sour cream
- 1 cup shredded Gruyère cheese, divided
- Cooking spray
- 1 cup water
- 1 teaspoon chopped parsley, for garnish

Directions:
1. Select SEAR/SAUTÉ and set temperature to HI. Select START/STOP and let preheat for 5 minutes.
2. Add the bacon and cook, stirring frequently, about 5 minutes, or until the fat is rendered and bacon starts to brown. Transfer the bacon to a paper towel-lined plate to drain. Wipe the pot clean of any remaining fat.
3. In a medium bowl, whisk together the eggs, salt, and sour cream until well combined. Fold in ¾ cup of cheese and the bacon.
4. Spray egg molds or Ninja Silicone Mold with the cooking spray. Ladle the egg mixture into each mold, filling them halfway.
5. Pour the water in the pot. Carefully place the egg molds in the pot. Assemble pressure lid, making sure the pressure release valve is in the SEAL position.
6. Select PRESSURE and set to LO. Set time to 10 minutes. Select START/STOP to begin.
7. When pressure cooking is complete, natural release the pressure for 6 minutes, then quick release the remaining pressure by moving the pressure release valve to the VENT position.
8. Carefully remove the lid. Using mitts or a towel, carefully remove egg molds. Top with the remaining ¼ cup of cheese, then place the mold back into the pot. Close the crisping lid.
9. Select AIR CRISP, set temperature to 390°F, and set time to 5 minutes. Select START/STOP to begin.
10. Once cooking is complete, carefully remove the egg molds and set aside to cool for 5 minutes. Using a spoon, carefully remove the egg bites from the molds. Top with chopped parsley and serve immediately.

Nutrition Info:
- Calories: 230,Total Fat: 18g,Sodium: 557mg,Carbohydrates: 2g,Protein: 16g.

Sausage Wrapped Scotch Eggs

Servings: 4
Cooking Time: 55 Min
Ingredients:
- 12 ounces Italian sausage patties /360g
- 4 eggs
- 1 cup water /250ml
- 1 cup panko bread crumbs /130g
- Nonstick cooking spray; for preparing the rack
- 2 tbsps melted unsalted butter /30ml

Directions:
1. Pour 1 cup of water into the inner pot. Put the reversible rack in the pot at the bottom, and carefully place the eggs on top. Seal the pressure lid, choose Pressure, set the pressure to High, and the cook time to 3 minutes. Press Start.
2. While cooking the eggs, fill half a bowl with cold water and about a cup full of ice cubes to make an ice bath.
3. After cooking, perform a quick pressure release, and carefully open the lid. Use tongs to pick up the eggs into the ice bath. Allow cooling for 3 to 4 minutes; peel the eggs.
4. Pour the water out of the inner pot and return the pot to the base. Grease the reversible rack with cooking spray, fix the rack in the upper position, and place in the pot.
5. Cover the crisping lid; choose Air Crisp, set the temperature to 360°F or 183°C and the timer to 4 minutes. Press Start to preheat.
6. While preheating the pot, place an egg on each sausage patty. Pull the sausage around the egg and seal the edges.
7. In a small bowl, mix the breadcrumbs with the melted butter. One at a time, dredge the sausage-covered eggs in the

crumbs while pressing into the breadcrumbs for a thorough coat.

8. Open the crisping lid and place the eggs on the rack. Close the crisping lid; choose Air Crisp, adjust the temperature to 360°F or 183°C, and the cook time to 15 minutes. Press Start.

9. When the timer has ended, the crumbs should be crisp and a deep golden brown color. Remove the eggs and allow cooling for several minutes. Slice the eggs in half and serve.

Baked Eggs In Spinach

Servings: 4
Cooking Time: 20 Minutes
Ingredients:
- 2 tsp olive oil
- 2 cloves garlic, diced fine
- 4 cups baby spinach
- ½ cup parmesan cheese, reduced fat
- 4 eggs
- 1 tomato, diced fine

Directions:
1. Select sauté function on medium heat. Add oil to the pot and heat.
2. Add the spinach and garlic and cook, stirring, about 2 minutes, or until spinach has wilted. Drain off excess liquid.
3. Stir in parmesan cheese. Make 4 small indents in the spinach. Crack an egg into each indent.
4. Set to air fryer function at 350°F. Secure the tender-crisp lid and bake 15-20 minutes or until egg whites are cooked and yolks are still slightly runny.
5. Let cool 5 minutes, serve topped with tomatoes.

Nutrition Info:
- Calories 139, Total Fat 10g, Total Carbs 3g, Protein 12g, Sodium 280mg.

Paprika Hard-boiled Eggs

Servings: 3
Cooking Time: 25 Min
Ingredients:
- 6 eggs
- 1 cup water /250ml
- 1 tsp sweet paprika /5g
- Salt and ground black pepper, to taste

Directions:
1. In the Foodi, add water and place a reversible rack on top. Lay your eggs on the rack. Seal the pressure lid, choose Pressure, set to High, and set the timer to 5 minutes. Press Start.

2. Once ready, do a natural release for 10 minutes. Transfer the eggs to ice cold water to cool completely. When cooled, peel and slice. Season with salt and pepper. Sprinkle with sweet paprika before serving.

Walnut Orange Coffee Cake

Servings: 8
Cooking Time: 25 Minutes
Ingredients:
- Butter flavor cooking spray
- 1 cup Stevia
- 1/4 cup butter, unsalted, soft
- 1 egg
- 2 tsp orange zest, grated
- ½ tsp vanilla
- 1/8 tsp cinnamon
- 2 cups whole wheat flour
- 1 tsp baking soda
- ½ cup orange juice, fresh squeezed
- ½ cup water
- ½ cup walnuts, chopped

Directions:
1. Select bake function and heat cooker to 350°F. Spray a 7-inch round pan with cooking spray.
2. In a medium bowl, beat Stevia and butter until smooth.
3. Add egg, zest, vanilla, and cinnamon and mix until combined.
4. In a separate bowl, combine dry ingredients. Add to butter mixture and mix until thoroughly combined. Stir in nuts.
5. Spread batter in prepared pan and place in the cooker. Secure the tender-crisp lid and bakke 20-25 minutes, or until it passes the toothpick test.
6. Let cool in pan 10 minutes, then invert onto wire rack. Serve warm.

Nutrition Info:
- Calories 203, Total Fat 10g, Total Carbs 53g, Protein 6g, Sodium 170mg.

Chicken Omelet

Servings: 2
Cooking Time: 16 Minutes
Ingredients:
- 1 teaspoon butter
- 1 small yellow onion, chopped
- ½ jalapeño pepper, seeded and chopped
- 3 eggs
- Black pepper and salt, as required
- ¼ cup cooked chicken, shredded

Directions:
1. Select the "Sauté/Sear" setting of Ninja Foodi and place the butter into the pot.
2. Press the "Start/Stop" button to initiate cooking and heat for about 2-3 minutes.
3. Add the onion and cook for about 4-5 minutes.
4. Add the jalapeño pepper and cook for about 1 minute.
5. Meanwhile, in a suitable, add the eggs, salt, and black pepper and beat well.
6. Press the "Start/Stop" button to pause cooking and stir in the chicken.
7. Top with the egg mixture evenly.
8. Close the Ninja Foodi's lid with a crisping lid and select "Air Crisp."
9. Set its cooking temperature to 355 °F for 5 minutes.
10. Press the "Start/Stop" button to initiate cooking.
11. Open the Ninja Foodi's lid and transfer the omelette onto a plate.
12. Cut into equal-sized wedges and serve hot.

Nutrition Info:
- Calories: 153; Fat: 9.1g; Carbohydrates: 4g; Protein: 13.8g

Hearty Breakfast Muffins

Servings: 12
Cooking Time: 20 Minutes

Ingredients:
- ½ cup brown sugar
- 3 eggs
- 1/3 cup coconut oil, melted
- 1/3 cup applesauce, unsweetened
- ¼ cup orange juice
- 1 tsp vanilla
- 2 cups whole wheat flour
- 2 tsp baking soda
- 2 tsp cinnamon
- ¼ tsp salt
- 1 ½ cup carrots, grated
- 1 cup apple, grated
- ¼ cup pecans, chopped

Directions:
1. Set to bake function on 375°F. Line 2 6-cup muffin tins with paper liners.
2. In a large bowl, whisk together sugar, eggs, oil, applesauce, orange juice, and vanilla.
3. Stir in flour, baking soda, cinnamon, and salt just until combined.
4. Fold in carrots, apple, and pecans and mix well. Divide evenly among prepared muffin tins.
5. Place tins, one at a time, in the cooker and add the tender-crisp lid. Bake 20-25 minutes, or until muffins pass the toothpick test. Repeat.
6. Let cool in pan 10 minutes, then transfer to wire rack to cool completely.

Nutrition Info:
- Calories 206,Total Fat 9g,Total Carbs 28g,Protein 5g,Sodium 288mg.

Double Chocolate Quinoa Bowl

Servings: 2
Cooking Time: 15 Minutes

Ingredients:
- ½ cup quinoa
- 1 cup water
- 1 cup coconut milk
- 2 tsp honey
- 2 tsp chia seeds
- 2 tsp cocoa powder
- 1 oz. dark chocolate, chopped
- 1 tbsp. pecans, chopped
- 1 tbsp. coconut flakes

Directions:
1. Place quinoa and water in the cooking pot, stir.
2. Add the lid and select pressure cooker on high. Set timer for 10 minutes. When timer goes off, use quick release to remove the lid.
3. Set to sauté on med-low. Cook, stirring until all liquid is absorbed.
4. Stir in milk, honey, chia seeds, and cocoa powder. Cook, stirring, until heated through.
5. Ladle into bowls and top with chocolate, nuts, and coconut. Serve warm.

Nutrition Info:
- Calories 456,Total Fat 24g,Total Carbs 50g,Protein 13g,Sodium 66mg.

Raspberry And Vanilla Pancake

Servings: 4
Cooking Time: 15 Min

Ingredients:
- ½ cup frozen raspberries, thawed /65g
- 3 eggs, beaten
- 1 cup brown sugar /130g
- 2 cups all-purpose flour /260g
- 1 cup milk /250ml
- 2 tbsp maple syrup /30ml
- 1 tsp baking powder /5g
- 1 ½ tsp vanilla extract /7.5g

- Pinch of salt
- Cooking spray

Directions:
1. In a bowl, mix the sifted flour, baking powder, salt, milk, eggs, vanilla extract, sugar, and maple syrup, until smooth. Gently stir in the raspberries.
2. Grease the basket of your Ninja Foodi with cooking spray. Drop the batter into the basket. Close the crisping lid and cook for 10 minutes on Air Crisp mode at 390 °F or 199°C. Serve the pancake right away.

Apple Walnut Quinoa

Servings: 2
Cooking Time: 15 Minutes
Ingredients:
- ½ cup quinoa, rinsed
- 1 apple, cored & chopped
- 2 cups water
- ½ cup apple juice, unsweetened
- 2 tsp maple syrup
- 1 tsp cinnamon
- ¼ cup walnuts, chopped & lightly toasted

Directions:
1. Set the cooker to sauté on med-low heat. Add the quinoa and apples and cook, stirring frequently, 5 minutes.
2. Add water and apple juice and stir to mix. Secure the lid and set to pressure cooking on high. Set timer for 10 minutes.
3. When timer goes off use quick release to remove the lid. Quinoa should be tender and the liquid should be absorbed, if not cook another 5 minutes.
4. When quinoa is done, stir in syrup and cinnamon. Sprinkle nuts over top and serve.

Nutrition Info:
- Calories 348, Total Fat 12g, Total Carbs 54g, Protein 9g, Sodium 7mg.

Prosciutto, Mozzarella Egg In A Cup

Servings: 2
Cooking Time: 20 Min
Ingredients:
- 2 slices bread
- 4 tomato slices
- 2 prosciutto slices; chopped
- 2 eggs
- 2 tbsp mayonnaise /30ml
- 2 tbsp grated mozzarella /30g
- Salt and pepper, to taste
- Cooking spray

Directions:
1. Preheat the Ninja Foodi to 320 °F or 160°C. Grease two large ramekins with cooking spray. Place one bread slice in the bottom of each ramekin.
2. Arrange 1 prosciutto slice and 2 tomato slices on top of each bread slice. Divide the mozzarella between the ramekins.
3. Crack the eggs over the mozzarella. Season with salt and pepper. Close the crisping lid and cook for 10 minutes on Air Crisp mode. Top with mayonnaise.

Apple Pie Oatmeal

Servings: 8
Cooking Time: 8 Hours
Ingredients:
- 2 cups steel cut oats
- 7 cups water
- 2 apples peel, core & chop
- ¾ tsp vanilla
- ½ tsp cinnamon
- ¼ tsp ginger
- ¼ tsp nutmeg

Directions:
1. Add all the ingredients to the cooking pot and stir to combine.
2. Add the lid and set to slow cooking on low heat. Cook 6-8 hours, stirring occasionally.
3. When oatmeal is done, stir well before serving.

Nutrition Info:
- Calories 172, Total Fat 3g, Total Carbs 31g, Protein 7g, Sodium 1mg.

Pancetta Hash With Baked Eggs

Servings: 4
Cooking Time: 50 Min
Ingredients:
- 6 slices pancetta; chopped
- 2 potatoes, peeled and diced
- 4 eggs
- 1 white onion; diced
- 1 tsp freshly ground black pepper /5g
- 1 tsp garlic powder /5g
- 1 tsp sweet paprika /5g
- 1 tsp salt /5g

Directions:
1. Choose Sear/Sauté, set to Medium High, and choose Start/Stop to preheat the pot for 5 minutes.
2. Once heated, lay the pancetta in the pot, and cook, stirring occasionally; for 5 minutes, or until the pancetta is crispy.

3. Stir in the onion, potatoes, sweet paprika, salt, black pepper, and garlic powder. Close the crisping lid; choose Bake/Roast, set the temperature to 350°F or 177°C, and the time to 25 minutes. Cook until the turnips are soft and golden brown while stirring occasionally.
4. Crack the eggs on top of the hash, close the crisping lid, and choose Bake/Roast. Set the temperature to 350°F or 177°C, and the time to 10 minutes.
5. Cook the eggs and check two or three times until your desired crispiness has been achieved. Serve immediately.

Applesauce Pumpkin Muffins

Servings: 8
Cooking Time: 15 Minutes
Ingredients:
- 4 eggs
- ½ cup applesauce, unsweetened
- ½ cup pumpkin
- ½ cup coconut flour
- 2 tbsp. cinnamon
- ¼ tsp cloves
- ¼ tsp ginger
- 1/8 tsp nutmeg
- ¼ tsp salt
- 1 tsp baking soda
- 2 tsp vanilla
- 4 tbsp. coconut oil, melted
- 1 tbsp. honey

Directions:
1. Set cooker to air fryer function on 375°F. Line 2 6-cup muffin tins with paper liners.
2. Add all ingredients to a blender or food processor and blend on low just until combined.
3. Pour batter evenly into prepared tins. Place muffin pans, one at a time, in the cooker and secure the tender-crisp lid. Bake 12-15 minutes or until muffins pass the toothpick test.
4. Let cool in pans 10 minutes, then transfer to wire rack to cool completely.

Nutrition Info:
- Calories 122,Total Fat 9g,Total Carbs 11g,Protein 3g,Sodium 264mg.

Paprika Shirred Eggs

Servings: 2
Cooking Time: 20 Min
Ingredients:
- 4 eggs; divided
- 4 slices of ham
- 2 tbsp heavy cream /30ml
- 3 tbsp Parmesan cheese /45g
- ¼ tsp pepper /1.25g
- 2 tsp butter; for greasing /10g
- 2 tsp chopped chives /10g
- ¼ tsp paprika /1.25g

Directions:
1. Grease a pie pan with the butter. Arrange the ham slices on the bottom of the pan to cover it completely. Use more slices if needed.
2. Whisk one egg along with the heavy cream, salt, and pepper, in a small bowl. Pour the mixture over the ham slices. Crack the other eggs over the ham.
3. Scatter Parmesan cheese over, close the crisping lid and cook for 14 minutes on Air Crisp mode at 320 °F or 160°C. Sprinkle with paprika and garnish with chives.

Bell Pepper Frittata

Servings: 2
Cooking Time: 18 Minutes
Ingredients:
- 1 tablespoon olive oil
- 1 chorizo sausage, sliced
- 1½ cups bell peppers, seeded and chopped
- 4 large eggs
- Black pepper and salt, as required
- 2 tablespoons feta cheese, crumbled
- 1 tablespoon fresh parsley, chopped

Directions:
1. Select the "Sauté/Sear" setting of Ninja Foodi and place the butter into the pot.
2. Press the "Start/Stop" button to initiate cooking and heat for about 2-3 minutes.
3. Add the sausage and bell peppers and cook for 6-8 minutes or until golden brown.
4. Meanwhile, in a suitable bowl, add the eggs, salt, and black pepper and beat well.
5. Press the "Start/Stop" button to pasue cooking and place the eggs over the sausage mixture, followed by the cheese and parsley.
6. Close the Ninja Foodi's lid with a crisping lid and select "Air Crisp."
7. Set its cooking temperature to 355 °F for 10 minutes.
8. Press the "Start/Stop" button to initiate cooking.
9. Open the Ninja Foodi's lid and transfer the frittata onto a platter.
10. Cut into equal-sized wedges and serve hot.

Nutrition Info:
- Calories: 398; Fat: 31g; Carbohydrates: 8g; Protein: 22.9g

Poultry Recipes

Buttered Turkey

Servings: 6
Cooking Time: 25 Min
Ingredients:
- 6 turkey breasts, boneless and skinless
- 1 stick butter, melted
- 2 cups panko breadcrumbs /260g
- ½ tsp cayenne pepper /2.5g
- ½ tsp black pepper /2.5g
- 1 tsp salt /5g

Directions:
1. In a bowl, combine the panko breadcrumbs, half of the black pepper, the cayenne pepper, and half of the salt.
2. In another bowl, combine the melted butter with salt and pepper. Brush the butter mixture over the turkey breast.
3. Coat the turkey with the panko mixture. Arrange on a lined Foodi basket. Close the crisping lid and cook for 15 minutes at 390 °F or 199°C on Air Crisp mode, flipping the meat after 8 minutes.

Healthy Chicken Stew

Servings: 4
Cooking Time: 4 Hours
Ingredients:
- 1 large potato, peeled & chopped
- 2 carrots, peeled & sliced
- ½ tsp salt
- ¼ tsp pepper
- 2 cloves garlic, chopped fine
- 3 cups chicken broth, low sodium
- 2 bay leaves
- 2 chicken breasts, boneless, skinless & cut in pieces
- ½ tsp thyme
- ¼ tsp basil
- 1 tsp paprika
- 2 tbsp. cornstarch
- ½ cup water
- 1 cup green peas

Directions:
1. Add the potatoes, carrots, salt, pepper, garlic, broth, bay leaves, chicken, thyme, basil, and paprika to the cooking pot, stir to mix.
2. Add the lid and set to slow cook on high. Cook 4 hours or until vegetables and chicken are tender.
3. In a small bowl, whisk together cornstarch and water until smooth. Stir into the cooking pot along with the peas.
4. Recover and cook another 15 minutes. Stir well before serving.

Nutrition Info:
- Calories 187,Total Fat 2g,Total Carbs 25g,Protein 17g,Sodium 1038mg.

Shredded Chicken Salsa

Servings: 4
Cooking Time: 20 Minutes
Ingredients:
- 1-pound chicken breast, boneless
- ¾ teaspoon cumin
- ½ teaspoon salt
- Pinch of oregano
- Pepper to taste
- 1 cup chunky salsa

Directions:
1. Season chicken with spices and add to Ninja Foodi.
2. Cover with salsa and lock lid, cook on "HIGH" pressure for 20 minutes.
3. Quick-release pressure.
4. Add chicken to a platter and shred the chicken.
5. Serve and enjoy.

Nutrition Info:
- Calories: 125; Fat: 3g; Carbohydrates: 2g; Protein: 22g

Barbeque Chicken Drumettes

Servings: 4
Cooking Time: 30 Min
Ingredients:
- 2 lb. chicken drumettes, bone in and skin in /900g
- 1 stick butter; sliced in 5 pieces
- ½ cup chicken broth /125ml
- BBQ sauce to taste
- ½ tbsp cumin powder /7.5g
- ½ tsp onion powder /2.5g
- ¼ tsp Cayenne powder/1.25g
- ½ tsp dry mustard /2.5g
- ½ tsp sweet paprika /2.5g
- Salt and pepper, to taste
- Cooking spray

Directions:
1. Pour the chicken broth into the inner pot of Foodi P and insert the reversible rack. In a zipper bag, pour in dry

mustard, cumin powder, onion powder, cayenne powder, salt, and pepper.

2. Add the chicken, close the bag and shake to coat the chicken well with the spices. You can toss the chicken in the spices in batches too.

3. Then, remove the chicken from the bag and place on the rack. Spread the butter slices on the drumsticks. Close the lid, secure the pressure valve, and select Pressure mode on High pressure for 10 minutes. Press Start/Stop.

4. Once the timer has ended, do a quick pressure release, and open the lid. Remove the chicken onto a clean flat surface like a cutting board and brush them with the barbecue sauce using the brush. Return to the rack and close the crisping lid. Cook for 10 minutes at 400 °F or 205°C on Air Crisp mode.

Chicken And Quinoa Soup

Servings: 6
Cooking Time: 30 Min
Ingredients:
- 2 large boneless; skinless chicken breasts; cubed
- 6 ounces quinoa, rinsed /180g
- 4 ounces mascarpone cheese, at room temperature /120g
- 1 cup milk /250ml
- 1 cup heavy cream /250ml
- 1 cup red onion; chopped /130g
- 1 cup carrots; chopped /130g
- 1 cup celery; chopped /130g
- 4 cups chicken broth 1000ml
- 2 tbsp butter /30g
- 1 tbsp fresh parsley; chopped /15g
- Salt and freshly ground black pepper to taste

Directions:
1. Melt butter on Sear/Sauté. Add carrot, onion, and celery and cook for 5 minutes until tender. Add chicken broth to the pot; mix in parsley, quinoa and chicken. Add pepper and salt for seasoning.

2. Seal the pressure lid, choose Pressure, set to High, and set the timer to 5 minutes. Press Start. When ready, release the pressure quickly. Press Sear/Sauté.

3. Add mascarpone cheese to the soup and stir well to melt completely; mix in heavy cream and milk. Simmer the soup for 3 to 4 minutes until thickened and creamy.

Chicken Burrito Bowl

Servings:4
Cooking Time: 10 Minutes
Ingredients:
- 1 pound boneless, skinless chicken breasts, cut into 1-inch chunks
- 1 tablespoon chili powder
- 1½ teaspoons cumin
- 1 teaspoon sea salt
- 1 teaspoon freshly ground black pepper
- ½ teaspoon paprika
- ¼ teaspoon garlic powder
- ¼ teaspoon onion powder
- ¼ teaspoon cayenne pepper
- ¼ teaspoon dried oregano
- 1 cup chicken stock
- ¼ cup water
- 1¼ cups of your favorite salsa
- 1 can corn kernels, drained
- 1 can black beans, rinsed and drained
- 1 cup rice
- ¾ cup shredded Cheddar cheese

Directions:
1. Add the chicken, chili powder, cumin, salt, black pepper, paprika, garlic powder, onion powder, cayenne pepper, oregano, chicken stock, water, salsa, corn, and beans and stir well.

2. Add the rice to the top of the ingredients in the pot. Assemble pressure lid, making sure the pressure release valve is in the SEAL position.

3. Select PRESSURE and set to HI. Set time to 10 minutes. Select START/STOP to begin.

4. When pressure cooking is complete, quick release the pressure by moving the pressure release valve to the VENT position. Carefully remove lid when the unit has finished releasing pressure.

5. Add the cheese and stir. Serve immediately.

Nutrition Info:
- Calories: 570,Total Fat: 11g,Sodium: 1344mg,Carbohydrates: 77g,Protein: 45g.

Chicken With Black Beans

Servings: 4
Cooking Time: 25 Min
Ingredients:
- 4 boneless; skinless chicken drumsticks
- 2 green onions, thinly sliced
- 3 garlic cloves, grated
- 2 cups canned black beans/260g
- ½ cup soy sauce /125ml
- ½ cup chicken broth /125ml
- 1 piece fresh ginger, grated

- 1 tbsp sriracha /15g
- 1 tbsp sesame oil /15ml
- 1 tbsp cornstarch /15g
- 1 tbsp water /15ml
- 2 tbsp toasted sesame seeds; divided /30g
- 3 tbsp honey /45ml
- 2 tbsp tomato paste/30ml

Directions:
1. In your Foodi, mix the soy sauce, honey, ginger, tomato paste, chicken broth, sriracha, and garlic. Stir well until smooth; toss in the chicken to coat.
2. Seal the pressure lid, choose Pressure, set to High, and set the timer to 3 minutes. Press Start. Release the pressure immediately.
3. Open the lid and Press Sear/Sauté. In a small bowl, mix water and cornstarch until no lumps remain; stir into the sauce and cook for 5 minutes until thickened.
4. Stir sesame oil and 1½ tbsp or 22.5g sesame seeds through the chicken mixture; garnish with extra sesame seeds and green onions. Serve with black beans.

Salsa Chicken With Feta

Servings: 6
Cooking Time: 30 Min
Ingredients:
- 2 pounds boneless skinless chicken drumsticks /900g
- 1 cup feta cheese, crumbled /130g
- 1 ½ cups hot tomato salsa /375ml
- 1 onion; chopped
- ¼ tsp salt /1.25g

Directions:
1. Sprinkle salt over the chicken; set in the inner steel pot of Foodi. Stir in salsa to coat the chicken. Seal the pressure lid, choose Pressure, set to High, and set the timer to 15 minutes. Press Start. When ready, do a quick pressure release.
2. Press Sear/Sauté and cook for 5 to 10 minutes as you stir until excess liquid has evaporated. Top with feta cheese and serve.

Chicken With Crunchy Coconut Dumplings.

Servings: 6
Cooking Time: 70 Min
Ingredients:
- 1 pound skinless, boneless chicken breasts; cubed /450g
- 1 package refrigerated biscuits, at room temperature
- ½ cup heavy cream /125ml
- 2 cups chicken stock /500ml
- 1 white onion; chopped
- 2 carrots; diced
- 2 celery stalks; diced
- 1 tbsp ghee /15g
- 1 tsp fresh rosemary /5g
- ½ tsp salt /2.5g

Directions:
1. Choose Sear/Sauté on the pot and set to Medium High. Choose Start/Stop to preheat the pot. Melt the ghee and sauté the onion until softened, about 3 minutes.
2. Pour the carrots, celery, chicken, and stock into the pot. Season with the rosemary and salt.
3. Put the pressure lid together and lock in the Seal position. Choose Pressure, set to High, and set the time to 2 minutes. Choose Start/Stop to begin
4. When done cooking, perform a quick pressure release, and carefully open the lid.
5. Stir the heavy cream into the soup. Place the reversible rack in the higher position inside the pot, which will be over the soup and arrange the biscuits in a single layer in the rack.
6. Close the crisping lid. Choose Broil and set the time to 15 minutes. Choose Start/Stop to begin crisping. When ready, allow the biscuit and soup to rest for a few minutes and then serve.

Roasted Chicken With Potato Mash

Servings: 4
Cooking Time: 70 Min
Ingredients:
- 2 bone-in chicken breasts
- ¾ cup chicken stock /188ml
- 3 medium Yukon Gold potatoes; scrubbed
- 3 tbsp melted butter /45ml
- 2 tbsp warm heavy cream /30ml
- 2½ tsp salt /12.5g
- 4 tsp Cajun seasoning /20g

Directions:
1. Pat the chicken dry with a paper towel and carefully slide your hands underneath the skin to slightly separate the meat from the skin.
2. Then in a small bowl, combine the salt and Cajun seasoning, and rub half of the mixture under the skin and cavity of the chicken.
3. Pour the chicken stock into the inner pot of the Foodi. Fix the reversible rack in a lower position of the pot and lay the chicken, on the side in the center of the rack. Also, arrange the potatoes around the chicken.

4. Seal the pressure lid, choose pressure; adjust the pressure to High and the cook time to 13 minutes. Press Start to begin cooking the chicken. Mix the remaining spice mixture with 2 tbsps or 30ml of the melted butter, and set aside.

5. When done pressure cooking, perform a natural pressure release for 10 minutes. Remove the potatoes and chicken onto a cutting board. Pour the cooking juices into a bowl and return the rack with chicken only to the pot. Baste the outer side of the chicken with half of the spice-butter mixture.

6. Close the crisping lid and choose Air Crisp; adjust the temperature to 360°F and the cook time to 16 minutes. Press Start. After 8 minutes, open the lid and flip the chicken over. Baste this side with the remaining butter mixture and close the lid to continue cooking.

7. With a potato masher, smoothly puree the potatoes, and add the remaining salt, melted butter, heavy cream, and 2 tbsps of the reserved cooking juice; stir to combine. Taste and adjust the seasoning with salt and pepper and cover the bowl with aluminum foil to keep warm.

8. After cooking, transfer the chicken to a cutting board, leaving the rack in the pot.

9. Pour the remaining cooking sauce into the pot, choose Sear/Sauté and adjust to Medium-High. Place the bowl of potatoes on the rack to keep warm as the sauce reduces. Press Start and boil the sauce for 2 to 3 minutes or until reduced by about half.

10. Meanwhile, slice the chicken and lay the pieces on a platter. Remove the mashed potato from the pot and remove the rack. Spoon the sauce over the chicken slices and serve with the creamy potatoes.

Chicken Meatballs Primavera

Servings: 4
Cooking Time: 30 Min
Ingredients:
- 1 lb. ground chicken /450g
- ½ lb. chopped asparagus /225g
- 1 cup chopped tomatoes /130g
- 1 cup chicken broth /250ml
- 1 red bell pepper, seeded and sliced
- 2 cups chopped green beans /260g
- 1 egg, cracked into a bowl
- 2 tbsp chopped basil + extra to garnish /30g
- 1 tbsp olive oil + ½ tbsp olive oil /22.5ml
- 6 tsp flour /30g
- 1 ½ tsp Italian Seasoning /7.5g
- Salt and black pepper to taste

Directions:

1. In a mixing bowl, add the chicken, egg, flour, salt, pepper, 2 tbsps of basil, 1 tbsp of olive oil, and Italian seasoning. Mix them well with hands and make 16 large balls out of the mixture. Set the meatballs aside.

2. Select Sear/Sauté mode. Heat half tsp of olive oil, and add peppers, green beans, and asparagus. Cook for 3 minutes, stirring frequently.

3. After 3 minutes, use a spoon the veggies onto a plate and set aside. Pour the remaining oil in the pot to heat and then fry the meatballs in it in batches. Fry them for 2 minutes on each side to brown them lightly.

4. After, put all the meatballs back into the pot as well as the vegetables. Also, pour the chicken broth over it.

5. Close the lid, secure the pressure valve, and select Pressure mode on High pressure for 10 minutes. Press Start/Stop. Do a quick pressure release. Close the crisping lid and select Air Crisp. Cook for 5 minutes at 400 °F or 205°C, until nice and crispy.

6. Dish the meatballs with sauce into a serving bowl and garnish it with basil. Serve with over cooked pasta.

Moo Shu Chicken

Servings: 4
Cooking Time: 20 Minutes
Ingredients:
- 1 tbsp. sesame oil
- 1 cup mushrooms, sliced
- 2 cups cabbage, shredded
- ½ cup green onion, sliced thin
- 3 cups chicken, cooked & shredded
- 2 eggs, lightly beaten
- ¼ cup hoisin sauce
- 2 tbsp. tamari
- 2 tsp sriracha sauce

Directions:

1. Add the oil to the cooking pot and set to sauté on med-high heat.

2. Add the mushrooms and cook 5-6 minutes, stirring frequently, until mushrooms have browned and liquid has evaporated.

3. Add cabbage and green onion, cook, stirring, 2 minutes.

4. Stir in chicken and cook 3-5 minutes until heated through.

5. Add the eggs and cook, stirring to scramble, until eggs are cooked.

6. Stir in remaining ingredients. Reduce heat and simmer until heated through. Serve immediately.

Nutrition Info:

- Calories 378, Total Fat 25g, Total Carbs 15g, Protein 23g, Sodium 1067mg.

Tuscany Turkey Soup

Servings: 4
Cooking Time: 40 Min
Ingredients:
- 1 pound hot turkey sausage /450g
- 4 Italian bread slices
- 3 celery stalks; chopped
- 3 garlic cloves; chopped
- 1 can cannellini beans, rinsed /450g
- 9 ounces refrigerated tortellini /270g
- 1 Parmesan cheese rind
- 1 red onion; chopped
- ½ cup dry white wine /125ml
- 4 cups chicken broth /1000ml
- 2 cups chopped spinach /260g
- ½ cup grated Parmesan cheese /130g
- 2 tbsp melted butter /30ml
- 2 tbsp olive oil /30ml
- ½ tsp fennel seeds /2.5g
- 1 tsp salt /5g
- Cooking spray

Directions:
1. On the Foodi, choose Sear/Sauté and adjust to Medium. Press Start to preheat the inner pot. Heat olive oil and cook the sausage for 4 minutes, while stirring occasionally until golden brown.
2. Stir in the celery, garlic, and onion, season with the salt and cook for 2 to 3 minutes, stirring occasionally. Pour in the wine and bring the mixture to a boil until the wine reduces by half. Scrape the bottom of the pot to let off any browned bits. Add the chicken stock, fennel seeds, tortellini, Parmesan rind, cannellini beans, and spinach.
3. Lock the pressure lid into place and to seal. Select Pressure; adjust the pressure to High and the cook time to 5 minutes; press Start. Brush the butter on the bread slices, and sprinkle with half of the cheese. Once the timer is over, perform a natural pressure release for 5 minutes.
4. Grease the reversible rack with cooking spray and fix in the upper position of the pot. Lay the bread slices on the rack.
5. Close the crisping lid and Choose Broil. Adjust the cook time to 5 minutes; press Start.
6. When the bread has browned and crisp, transfer from the rack to a cutting board and let cool for a couple of minutes. Cut the slices into cubes.
7. Ladle the soup into bowls and sprinkle with the remaining cheese. Share the croutons among the bowls and serve.

Chicken Bruschetta

Servings: 4
Cooking Time: 9 Minutes
Ingredients:
- 2 tablespoons balsamic vinegar
- 1/3 cup olive oil
- 2 teaspoons garlic cloves, minced
- 1 teaspoon black pepper
- ½ teaspoon salt
- ½ cup sun-dried tomatoes, in olive oil
- 2 pounds chicken breasts, quartered, boneless
- 2 tablespoons fresh basil, chopped

Directions:
1. Take a suitable and whisk in vinegar, oil, garlic, pepper, salt.
2. Fold in tomatoes, basil and add breast; mix well.
3. Transfer to fridge and let it sit for 30 minutes.
4. Add everything to Ninja Foodi and lock lid, cook on "HIGH" pressure for 9 minutes
5. Quick-release pressure.
6. Serve and enjoy.

Nutrition Info:
- Calories: 480; Fat: 26g; Carbohydrates: 4g; Protein: 52g

Cheesy Chicken & Zucchini Rolls

Servings: 4
Cooking Time: 15 Minutes
Ingredients:
- Nonstick cooking spray
- 2 chicken breasts, boneless & skinless
- ½ tsp salt
- ¼ tsp pepper
- 2 zucchini, sliced very thin
- 4 slices provolone cheese, fat free
- ½ cup bread crumbs

Directions:
1. Spray the fryer basket with cooking spray.
2. Cut the chicken in half horizontally. Place pieces between 2 sheets of plastic wrap and pound out to ¼-inch thick.
3. Lay the chicken pieces, one at a time, on a plate and season with salt and pepper.
4. Place slices of zucchini and cheese on the chicken. Roll up and secure with a toothpick.

5. Place the bread crumbs in a shallow dish. Coat chicken rolls with bread crumbs and place in the basket.
6. Add the tender-crisp lid and set to air fry on 375°F. Cook 15 minutes until golden brown on the outsides and cooked through on the inside, turning over halfway through cooking time. Serve immediately.

Nutrition Info:
- Calories 166,Total Fat 2g,Total Carbs 12g,Protein 23g,Sodium 472mg.

Turkey Rellenos

Servings: 4
Cooking Time: 20 Minutes
Ingredients:
- Nonstick cooking spray
- 4 poblano chilies
- ½ lb. hot Italian turkey sausage, casings removed
- 1 cup cottage cheese, reduced fat, drained
- ½ cup mozzarella cheese, grated

Directions:
1. Lightly spray fryer basket with cooking spray and place in the cooking pot.
2. Split the chilies with a knife and remove the seeds, do not remove the stems. Place in the basket.
3. Add the tender-crisp lid and set to broil. Cook chilies until skin chars on all sides. Transfer to a large Ziploc bag and seal. When the chilies have cooled, carefully remove the skin.
4. Remove the fryer basket and set to cooker to sauté on med-high heat. Cook sausage until no longer pink. Transfer to a medium bowl.
5. Add the cottage cheese to the sausage and mix well.
6. Spoon the sausage mixture into the chilies and lay them in the basket, spit side up. Sprinkle the mozzarella cheese over.
7. Add the basket back to the pot and set to bake on 350°F. Bake 15 minutes until the cheese is melted and bubbly. Serve immediately.

Nutrition Info:
- Calories 179,Total Fat 7g,Total Carbs 9g,Protein 20g,Sodium 977mg.

Pulled Chicken And Peach Salsa

Servings: 4
Cooking Time: 40 Min
Ingredients:
- 4 boneless; skinless chicken thighs
- 15 ounces canned peach chunks /450g
- 2 cloves garlic; minced
- 14 ounces canned diced tomatoes /420g
- ½ tsp cumin /2.5g
- ½ tsp salt /2.5g
- Cheddar shredded cheese
- Fresh chopped mint leaves

Directions:
1. Strain canned peach chunks. Reserve the juice and set aside. In your Foodi, add chicken, tomatoes, cumin, garlic, peach juice, and salt.
2. Seal the pressure lid, choose Pressure, set to High, and set the timer to 15 minutes. Press Start. When ready, do a quick pressure release.
3. Shred chicken with the use of two forks. Transfer to a serving plate. Add peach chunks to the cooking juices and mix until well combined.
4. Pour the peach salsa over the chicken, top with chopped mint leaves and shredded cheese. Serve immediately.

Garlic Turkey Breasts

Servings: 4
Cooking Time: 17 Minutes
Ingredients:
- ½ teaspoon garlic powder
- 4 tablespoons butter
- ¼ teaspoon dried oregano
- 1-pound turkey breasts, boneless
- 1 teaspoon pepper
- ½ teaspoon salt
- ¼ teaspoon dried basil

Directions:
1. Season turkey on both sides generously with garlic, dried oregano, dried basil, black pepper and salt.
2. Select "Sauté" mode on your Ninja Foodi and stir in butter; let the butter melt.
3. Add turkey breasts and sauté for 2 minutes on each side.
4. Lock the lid and select the "Bake/Roast" setting; bake for 15 minutes at 355 °F.
5. Serve and enjoy once done.

Nutrition Info:
- Calories: 223; Fat: 13g; Carbohydrates: 5g; Protein: 19g

Riviera Chicken

Servings: 4
Cooking Time: 20 Minutes
Ingredients:
- Nonstick cooking spray
- 4 chicken breast halves, boneless & skinless
- 1/8 tsp salt
- 1/8 tsp pepper

- 14 ½ oz. tomatoes with basil, garlic, and oregano, diced
- ½ cup black olives, sliced
- 1 tbsp. lemon zest, grated fine
- 2 cloves garlic, chopped fine

Directions:
1. Spray the cooking pot with cooking spray and set to sauté on med-high heat.
2. Season chicken with salt and pepper and add to the pot. Cook 5-7 minutes per side, until no longer pink. Transfer chicken to a plate and reduce heat to medium.
3. Add remaining ingredients to the pot and cook 4 minutes or until hot, stirring occasionally. Return the chicken to the pot and cook until heated through. Serve immediately.

Nutrition Info:
- Calories 175,Total Fat 5g,Total Carbs 5g,Protein 27g,Sodium 371mg.

Herby Chicken With Asparagus Sauce

Servings: 4
Cooking Time: 1 Hr
Ingredients:
- 1 Young Whole Chicken /1575g
- 8 ounces asparagus, trimmed and chopped /240g
- 1 onion; chopped
- 1 cup chicken stock /250ml
- 4 fresh thyme; minced
- 3 fresh rosemary; minced
- 4 garlic cloves; minced
- 2 lemons, zested and quartered
- 1 fresh thyme sprig
- 1 tbsp flour /15g
- 1 tbsp soy sauce /15ml
- 2 tbsp olive oil /30ml
- 1 tsp olive oil /5ml
- Cooking spray
- salt and freshly ground black pepper to taste
- Chopped parsley to garnish

Directions:
1. Rub all sides of the chicken with garlic, rosemary, black pepper, lemon zest; minced thyme, and salt. Into the chicken cavity, insert lemon wedges.
2. Warm oil on Sear/Sauté. Add in onion and asparagus, and cook for 5 minutes until softened. Mix in chicken stock, 1 thyme sprig, black pepper, soy sauce, and salt.
3. Into the inner pot, set trivet over asparagus mixture. On top of the trivet, place your chicken with breast-side up.
4. Seal the pressure lid, choose Pressure, set to High, and set the timer to 20 minutes. Press Start. Once ready, do a quick release. Remove the chicken to a serving platter.
5. In the inner pot, sprinkle flour over asparagus mixture and blend the sauce with an immersion blender until desired consistency. Top the chicken with asparagus sauce and garnish with parsley.

Sour Cream & Cheese Chicken

Servings: 8
Cooking Time: 25 Minutes
Ingredients:
- Nonstick cooking spray
- 1 cup sour cream
- 2 tsp garlic powder
- 1 tsp seasoned salt
- ½ tsp pepper
- 1 ½ cups parmesan cheese, divided
- 3 lbs. chicken breasts, boneless

Directions:
1. Spray the cooking pot with cooking spray.
2. In a medium bowl, combine sour cream, garlic powder, seasoned salt, pepper, and 1 cup parmesan cheese, mix well.
3. Place the chicken in the cooking pot. Spread the sour cream mixture over the top and sprinkle with remaining parmesan cheese.
4. Add the tender-crisp lid and set to bake on 375°F. Bake chicken 25-30 minutes until cooked through.
5. Set cooker to broil and cook another 2-3 minutes until top is lightly browned. Serve immediately.

Nutrition Info:
- Calories 377,Total Fat 21g,Total Carbs 3g,Protein 41g,Sodium 737mg.

Chicken & Black Bean Chowder

Servings: 6
Cooking Time: 6 Hours
Ingredients:
- 15 oz. black beans, rinsed & drained
- 3 chicken breasts, boneless & skinless
- 1 cup corn, frozen
- 16 oz. salsa
- 4 cups chicken broth, low sodium
- 4 oz. green chilies, diced
- ¼ cup cilantro, chopped
- 1 lime, cut in wedges

Directions:
1. Place all ingredients, except cilantro and limes, in the cooking pot, stir to mix well.

2. Add the lid and set to slow cook on low. Cook 5-6 hours until chicken is tender.
3. Transfer chicken to a cutting board and shred. Return to the pot and increase temperature to high. Cook 30 minutes.
4. Ladle into bowls and serve garnished with cilantro and a lime wedge.

Nutrition Info:
- Calories 350,Total Fat 8g,Total Carbs 29g,Protein 42g,Sodium 749mg.

Honey Garlic Chicken

Servings: 4
Cooking Time: 30 Min

Ingredients:
- 4 boneless; skinless chicken breast; cut into chunks
- 4 garlic cloves, smashed
- 1 onion; diced
- ½ cup honey /125ml
- 1 tbsp cornstarch /15g
- 1 tbsp water /15ml
- 2 tbsp lime juice /30ml
- 3 tbsp soy sauce /45ml
- 2 tsp sesame oil /10ml
- 1 tsp rice vinegar /5ml
- Salt and black pepper to taste

Directions:
1. Mix garlic, onion and chicken in your Foodi. In a bowl, combine honey, sesame oil, lime juice, soy sauce, and rice vinegar; pour over the chicken mixture.
2. Seal the pressure lid, choose Pressure, set to High, and set the timer to 15 minutes. Press Start. When ready, release the pressure quickly.
3. Mix water and cornstarch until well dissolved; stir into the sauce. Press Scar/Sauté. Simmer the sauce and cook for 2 to 3 minutes as you stir until thickened.

Quesadilla Casserole

Servings: 8
Cooking Time: 30 Minutes

Ingredients:
- Nonstick cooking spray
- 2 cups chicken, cooked & shredded
- ½ cup sour cream, fat free
- 1 cup cheddar cheese, reduced fat, grated, divided
- 2 tsp cumin, divided
- 1 tbsp. chili powder, divided
- 1 tsp salt
- ¼ tsp pepper, divided
- 1 cup corn
- 15 oz. black beans, drained & rinsed
- 4 large whole grain tortillas

Directions:
1. Spray the cooking pot with cooking spray.
2. In a large bowl, combine chicken, sour cream, half the cheese, half the cumin, half the chili powder, salt, and half the pepper and mix well.
3. In a separate bowl, combine the corn, beans, and remaining spices, mix well.
4. Lay 2 of the tortillas in the bottom of the cooking pot. Spread half the chicken mixture over the tortillas and top with half the bean mixture. Repeat. Sprinkle the remaining cheese over the top.
5. Add the tender-crisp lid and set to bake on 400°F. Bake 25-30 minutes until cheese is melted and casserole is hot. Serve immediately.

Nutrition Info:
- Calories 354,Total Fat 13g,Total Carbs 35g,Protein 23g,Sodium 533mg.

Blackened Turkey Cutlets

Servings: 4
Cooking Time: 5 Minutes

Ingredients:
- Nonstick cooking spray
- 2 tsp paprika
- 1 tsp thyme
- ½ tsp sugar
- ½ tsp onion powder
- ½ tsp garlic powder
- ½ tsp salt
- ½ tsp pepper
- ¼ tsp cayenne pepper
- 4 turkey breast cutlets, boneless & skinless

Directions:
1. Spray the fryer basket with cooking spray.
2. In a small bowl, combine everything but the turkey and mix well. Rub both sides of the cutlets with the seasoning mixture and place in the basket.
3. Add the tender-crisp lid and set to air fry on 350°F. Cook 4-5 minutes per side or until turkey is cooked through. Serve immediately.

Nutrition Info:
- Calories 134,Total Fat 2g,Total Carbs 1g,Protein 27g,Sodium 419mg.

Chicken With Tomatoes And Capers

Servings: 4
Cooking Time: 45 Min
Ingredients:
- 4 chicken legs
- 1 onion; diced
- 2 garlic cloves; minced
- ⅓ cup red wine /84ml
- 2 cups diced tomatoes /260g
- ⅓ cup capers /44g
- ¼ cup fresh basil /32.5g
- 2 pickles; chopped
- 2 tbsp olive oil /30ml
- sea salt and fresh ground black pepper to taste

Directions:
1. Sprinkle pepper and salt over the chicken. Warm oil on Sear/Sauté. Add in onion and cook for 3 minutes until fragrant; add in garlic and cook for 30 seconds until softened.
2. Mix the chicken with vegetables and cook for 6 to 7 minutes until lightly browned.
3. Add red wine to the pan to deglaze, scrape the pan's bottom to get rid of any browned bits of food; stir in tomatoes. Seal the pressure lid, choose Pressure, set to High, and set the timer to 12 minutes; press Start.
4. When ready, release the pressure quickly. To the chicken mixture, add basil, capers and pickles. Serve the chicken in plates covered with the tomato sauce mixture.

Pineapple Chicken Tenders

Servings: 4
Cooking Time: 15 Minutes
Ingredients:
- 1 lb. chicken tenders
- ½ cup stir-fry sauce
- 1 tbsp. olive oil
- ½ red bell pepper, chopped
- ½ yellow bell pepper, chopped
- ½ green bell pepper, chopped
- ¼ cup green onions, sliced
- 8 oz. pineapple chunks or tidbits, juice reserved

Directions:
1. Combine chicken and stir fry sauce in a large Ziploc bag. Seal and turn to coat the chicken. Refrigerate 20 minutes.
2. Add the oil to the cooking pot and set to sauté on med-high heat.
3. Add the chicken and cook 6-8 minutes or until cooked through. Transfer chicken to a plate and keep warm.
4. Add the peppers to the pot and cook 4-5 minutes until tender-crisp.
5. Add the green onions, pineapple, 1 tablespoon pineapple juice and 2 teaspoons marinade and cook, stirring about 1 minute. Spoon over chicken and serve immediately.

Nutrition Info:
- Calories 253,Total Fat 7g,Total Carbs 19g,Protein 29g,Sodium 694mg.

Chicken Meatballs In Tomato Sauce

Servings: 5
Cooking Time: 35 Min
Ingredients:
- 1 pound ground chicken /450g
- 1 egg
- 15 ounces canned tomato sauce /450g
- ¼ cup bread crumbs /32.5g
- ¼ cup Pecorino cheese /32.5g
- 1 cup chicken broth /250ml
- ⅓ cup crumbled blue cheese /44g
- 3 tbsp red hot sauce /45ml
- 1 tbsp ranch dressing /15g
- 2 tbsp olive oil /30ml
- 1 tsp dried basil /5g
- A handful of parsley; chopped
- salt and ground black pepper to taste

Directions:
1. In a bowl, mix ground chicken, egg, pecorino, basil, pepper, salt, ranch dressing, blue cheese, 3 tbsp or 45ml hot sauce, and bread crumbs; shape the mixture into meatballs.
2. Warm oil on Sear/Sauté. Add in the meatballs and cook for 2 to 3 minutes until browned on all sides. Add in tomato sauce and broth. Seal the pressure lid, choose Pressure, set to High, and set the timer to 7 minutes. Press Start.
3. When ready, release the pressure quickly. Remove meatballs carefully and place to a serving plate; top with parsley and serve.

Lettuce Carnitas Wraps

Servings: 6
Cooking Time: 50 Min
Ingredients:
- 2 pounds chicken thighs, boneless; skinless /900g
- 12 large lettuce leaves
- 2 cups canned pinto beans, rinsed and drained /260g
- 1 cup pineapple juice /250ml
- ⅓ cup water /88ml
- ¼ cup soy sauce /62.5ml
- 3 tbsp cornstarch /45g

- 2 tbsp maple syrup /30ml
- 2 tbsp canola oil /30ml
- 1 tbsp rice vinegar /15ml
- 1 tsp chili-garlic sauce /5ml
- salt and freshly ground black pepper to taste

Directions:
1. Warm oil on Sear/Sauté. In batches, sear chicken in the oil for 5 minutes until browned. Set aside in a bowl. Into your pot, mix chili-garlic sauce, pineapple juice, soy sauce, vinegar, maple syrup, and water; stir in chicken to coat.
2. Seal the pressure lid, choose Pressure, set to High, and set the timer to 7 minutes. Press Start. Release pressure naturally for 10 minutes. Shred the chicken with two forks. Take ¼ cup liquid from the pot to a bowl; stir in cornstarch to dissolve.
3. Mix the cornstarch mixture with the mixture in the pot and return the chicken.
4. Select Sear/Sauté and cook for 5 minutes until the sauce thickens; add pepper and salt for seasoning. Transfer beans into lettuce leaves; apply a topping of chicken carnitas and serve.

Chicken And Sweet Potato Corn Chowder

Servings: 8
Cooking Time: 40 Min
Ingredients:
- 4 boneless; skinless chicken breast; diced
- 19 ounces corn kernels, frozen /570g
- 1 sweet potato, peeled and cubed
- 4 ounces canned diced green chiles, drained /120g
- 3 garlic cloves; minced
- 2 cups cheddar cheese, shredded /260g
- 2 cups creme fraiche /500ml
- 1 cup chicken stock /250ml
- Cilantro leaves; chopped
- 2 tsp chili powder /10g
- 1 tsp ground cumin /5g
- Salt and black pepper to taste

Directions:
1. Mix chicken, corn, chili powder, cumin, chicken stock, sweet potato, green chiles, and garlic in the pot of the Foodi. Seal the pressure lid, choose Pressure, set to High, and set the timer to 10 minutes. Press Start.
2. When ready, release the pressure quickly. Set the chicken to a cutting board and use two forks to shred it. Return to pot and stir well into the liquid.
3. Stir in cheese and creme fraiche; season with pepper and salt. Cook for 2 to 3 minutes until cheese is melted. Place chowder into plates and top with cilantro.

Lemon Chicken

Servings: 4
Cooking Time: 18 Minutes
Ingredients:
- 4 bone-in, skin-on chicken thighs
- Black pepper and salt to taste
- 2 tablespoons butter
- 2 teaspoons garlic, minced
- ½ cup herbed chicken stock
- ½ cup heavy whip cream
- ½ a lemon, juiced

Directions:
1. Season the four chicken thighs generously with black pepper and salt.
2. Set your Ninja Foodi to sauté mode and add oil, let it heat up.
3. Add thigh, Sauté on both sides for 6 minutes.
4. Remove thigh to a platter and keep it on the side.
5. Add garlic, cook for 2 minutes.
6. Whisk in chicken stock, heavy cream, lemon juice and gently stir.
7. Bring the mix to a simmer and reintroduce chicken.
8. Lock and secure the Ninja Foodi's lid and cook for 10 minutes on "HIGH" pressure.
9. Release pressure over 10 minutes.
10. Serve and enjoy.

Nutrition Info:
- Calories: 294; Fat: 26g; Carbohydrates: 4g; Protein: 12g

Paprika Buttered Chicken

Servings: 6
Cooking Time: 45 Min
Ingredients:
- 3.5-pound whole chicken /1575g
- ½ onion, thinly sliced
- 2 cloves garlic; minced
- 1 cup chicken stock /250ml
- ½ cup white wine /125ml
- 3 tbsp butter, melted /45ml
- ½ tsp paprika /2.5g
- ½ tsp ground black pepper /2.5g
- ½ tsp dried thyme /2.5g
- 1 tsp salt /5g

Directions:

1. Into the Foodi, add onion, chicken stock, white wine, and garlic. Over the mixture, place the reversible rack. Apply pepper, salt, and thyme to the chicken; lay onto reversible rack breast-side up.

2. Seal the pressure lid, choose Pressure, set to High, and set the timer to 26 minutes. Press Start. When ready, release the pressure quickly.

3. While pressure releases, preheat oven broiler. In a bowl, mix paprika and butter.

4. Remove the reversible rack with chicken from your pot. Get rid of onion and stock.

5. Onto the chicken, brush butter mixture and take the reversible rack back to the pot. Cook under the broiler for 5 minutes until chicken skin is crispy and browned.

6. Set chicken to a cutting board to cool for about 5 minutes, then carve and transfer to a serving platter.

Cheesy Chicken & Mushrooms

Servings: 4
Cooking Time: 30 Minutes
Ingredients:
- Nonstick cooking spray
- 1 ½ cups mushrooms, sliced
- ¼ cup ham, chopped
- 4 chicken breasts, boneless & skinless
- ½ tsp garlic powder
- ¼ tsp pepper
- 1 can cream of chicken soup, reduced fat
- ¾ cup skim milk
- ½ tsp thyme
- ½ tsp onion powder
- ¼ cup mozzarella cheese, grated

Directions:
1. Spray the cooking pot with cooking spray.
2. Set to sauté on med-high heat. Add the mushrooms and ham and cook, stirring occasionally, until mushrooms start to brown, about 5-7 minutes. Transfer to a bowl.
3. Season both sides of the chicken with garlic powder and pepper. Place in the pot. Spoon the mushroom mixture over the top.
4. In a medium bowl, whisk together soup, milk, thyme, and onion powder. Pour over mushrooms and top with cheese.
5. Add the tender-crisp lid and set to bake on 350°F. Cook 25-30 minutes until chicken is cooked through. Serve.

Nutrition Info:
- Calories 243, Total Fat 9g, Total Carbs 9g, Protein 32g, Sodium 987mg.

Turkey Enchilada Casserole

Servings: 6
Cooking Time: 70 Min
Ingredients:
- 1 pound boneless; skinless turkey breasts /450g
- 2 cups shredded Monterey Jack cheese; divided /260g
- 2 cups enchilada sauce /500ml
- 1 yellow onion; diced
- 2 garlic cloves; minced
- 1 can pinto beans, drained and rinsed /450g
- 1 bag frozen corn /480g
- 8 tortillas, each cut into 8 pieces
- 1 tbsp butter /15g
- ¼ tsp salt /1.25g
- ¼ tsp freshly ground black pepper /1.25g

Directions:
1. Choose Sear/Sauté on the pot and set to Medium High. Choose Start/Stop to preheat the pot. Melt the butter and cook the onion for 3 minutes, stirring occasionally. Stir in the garlic and cook until fragrant, about 1 minute more.
2. Put the turkey and enchilada sauce in the pot, and season with salt and black pepper. Stir to combine. Seal the pressure lid, choose Pressure, set to High, and set the time to 15 minutes. Choose Start/Stop.
3. When done cooking, perform a quick pressure release and carefully open the lid. Shred the turkey with two long forks while being careful not to burn your hands. Mix in the pinto beans, tortilla pieces, corn, and half of the cheese to the pot. Sprinkle the remaining cheese evenly on top of the casserole.
4. Close the crisping lid. Choose Broil and set the time to 5 minutes. Press Start/Stop to begin broiling. When ready, allow the casserole to sit for 5 minutes before serving.

Southwest Chicken Bake

Servings: 8
Cooking Time: 20 Minutes
Ingredients:
- 1 tablespoon extra-virgin olive oil
- 2 boneless, skinless chicken breasts, cut into 1-inch cubes
- ½ red onion, diced
- ½ red bell pepper, diced
- 1 cup white rice
- 1 can fire-roasted tomatoes with chiles
- 1 can black beans, rinsed and drained
- 1 can corn, rinsed
- 1 packet taco seasoning

- 2 cups chicken broth
- Kosher salt
- Freshly ground black pepper
- 2 cups shredded Cheddar cheese

Directions:
1. Select SEAR/SAUTÉ and set to MD:HI. Select START/STOP to begin. Let preheat for 5 minutes.
2. Place the olive oil and chicken into the pot and cook, stirring occasionally, until the chicken is cooked through, 2 to 3 minutes. Add the onion and bell pepper and cook until softened, about 2 minutes.
3. Add the rice, tomatoes, beans, corn, taco seasoning, broth, salt, and pepper and stir. Assemble pressure lid, making sure the pressure release valve is in the SEAL position.
4. Select PRESSURE and set to HI. Set time to 7 minutes. Select START/STOP to begin.
5. When complete, quick release the pressure by turning the pressure release valve to the VENT position. Carefully remove lid when unit has finished releasing pressure.
6. Add the cheese on top of the mixture. Close crisping lid.
7. Select BROIL and set time to 8 minutes. Select START/STOP to begin.
8. When cooking is complete, serve along with your choice of toppings, such as chopped cilantro, diced avocado, diced fresh tomatoes, sour cream, and sliced scallions.

Nutrition Info:
- Calories: 333,Total Fat: 17g,Sodium: 630mg,Carbohydrates: 27g,Protein: 25g.

Italian Turkey & Pasta Soup

Servings: 8
Cooking Time: 10 Minutes
Ingredients:
- 1 lb. ground turkey sausage
- 1 onion, chopped fine
- 5 cloves garlic, chopped fine
- 1 green bell pepper, chopped fine
- 1 tbsp. Italian seasoning
- 2 15 oz. cans tomatoes, diced
- 2 8 oz. cans tomato sauce
- 4 cups chicken broth, low sodium
- 3 cups whole wheat pasta
- ¼ cup parmesan cheese
- ¼ cup mozzarella cheese, grated

Directions:
1. Add the sausage, onions, and garlic to the cooking pot. Set to sauté on med-high and cook, breaking sausage up, until meat is no longer pink and onions are translucent. Drain off excess fat.
2. Stir in bell pepper, Italian seasoning, tomatoes, tomato sauce, broth, and pasta, mix well.
3. Add the lid and set to pressure cook on high. Set the timer for 5 minutes. Once the timer goes off, use the natural release for 5-10 minutes, then quick release to remove the pressure.
4. Stir the soup and ladle into bowls. Serve garnished with parmesan and mozzarella cheeses.

Nutrition Info:
- Calories 294,Total Fat 8g,Total Carbs 37g,Protein 22g,Sodium 841mg.

Sticky Orange Chicken

Servings: 4
Cooking Time: 30 Min
Ingredients:
- 2 chicken breasts; cubed
- 1 cup diced orange /130g
- ⅓ cup soy sauce /188ml
- ⅓ cup chicken stock /188ml
- ⅓ cup hoisin sauce /188ml
- 3 cups hot cooked quinoa /390g
- ½ cup honey /125ml
- ½ cup orange juice /125ml
- 1 garlic clove; minced
- 2 tsp cornstarch /10g
- 2 tsp water /10ml

Directions:
1. Arrange the chicken to the bottom of the Foodi's pot. In a bowl, mix honey, soy sauce, garlic, hoisin sauce, chicken stock, and orange juice, until the honey is dissolved; pour the mixture over the chicken.
2. Seal the pressure lid, choose Pressure, set to High, and set the timer to 7 minutes. Press Start. When ready, release the pressure quickly. Take the chicken from the pot and set to a bowl. Press Sear/Sauté.
3. In a small bowl, mix water with cornstarch; pour into the liquid within the pot and cook for 3 minutes until thick. Stir diced orange and chicken into the sauce until well coated. Serve with quinoa.

Chicken Pot Pie

Servings: 8
Cooking Time: 25 Minutes
Ingredients:
- Nonstick cooking spray
- 1 tbsp. light butter
- ½ cup onion, chopped
- 8 oz. mushrooms, chopped
- 1 ½ cup frozen mixed vegetables, thawed
- 3 cups chicken, cooked & chopped
- ½ tsp thyme
- ½ tsp salt
- ¼ tsp pepper
- 1 cup chicken broth, low sodium
- ½ cup evaporated milk, fat free
- 2 tbsp. flour
- 4 slices refrigerated crescent rolls, low fat

Directions:
1. Spray an 8-inch deep dish pie plate with cooking spray.
2. Add the butter to the cooking pot and set to sauté on med-high to melt.
3. Add onions and mushrooms and cook 3-5 minutes until they start to soften. Add vegetables, chicken, thyme, salt, and pepper and stir to mix. Bring to a simmer and cook 5-6 minutes.
4. In a small bowl, whisk together milk and flour until smooth. Stir into the chicken mixture and cook 3-5 minutes until thickened. Pour into prepared pie plate.
5. Add the rack to the cooking pot. Arrange slices of dough on top of the chicken mixture with widest part of dough on the outside edge.
6. Place the pie on the rack and add the tender-crisp lid. Set to bake on 375°F. Bake 20-25 minutes until crust is golden brown and filling is hot and bubbly. Serve.

Nutrition Info:
- Calories 203,Total Fat 6g,Total Carbs 17g,Protein 21g,Sodium 197mg.

Chicken Stroganoff With Fetucini

Servings: 4
Cooking Time: 35 Min
Ingredients:
- 2 large boneless skinless chicken breasts
- 8 ounces fettucini /240g
- ½ cup sliced onion /65g
- ½ cup dry white wine /125ml
- 1 cup sautéed mushrooms /130g
- ¼ cup heavy cream /62.5ml
- 1 ½ cups water /375ml
- 2 cups chicken stock /500ml
- 2 tbsp butter /30g
- 1 tbsp flour /15g
- 2 tbsp chopped fresh dill to garnish /30g
- ½ tsp Worcestershire sauce /2.5ml
- 1½ tsp salt /7.5g

Directions:
1. Season the chicken on both sides with salt and set aside. Choose Sear/Sauté and adjust to Medium. Press Start to preheat the pot. Melt the butter and sauté the onion until brown, about 3 minutes.
2. Mix in the flour to make a roux, about 2 minutes and gradually pour in the dry white wine while stirring and scraping the bottom of the pot to release any browned bits. Allow the white wine to simmer and to reduce by two-thirds.
3. Pour in the water, chicken stock, 1 tbsp or 15g of salt, and fettucini. Mix and arrange the chicken on top of the fettucini.
4. Lock the pressure lid to Seal. Choose Pressure; adjust the pressure to High and the cook time to 5 minutes; press Start. When done pressure-cooking, perform a quick pressure release.
5. Transfer the chicken breasts to a cutting board to cool slightly, and then cut into bite-size chunks. Return the chicken to the pot and stir in the Worcestershire sauce and mushrooms. Add the heavy cream and cook until the mixture stops simmering. Ladle the stroganoff into bowls and garnish with dill.

Cajun Chicken & Pasta

Servings: 8
Cooking Time: 20 Minutes
Ingredients:
- 2 tsp olive oil
- ½ cup onion, chopped fine
- ¼ cup red bell pepper, chopped fine
- ¼ cup green bell pepper, chopped fine
- 3 cloves garlic, chopped fine
- 1 cup Andouille sausage, cut in 1-inch pieces
- 1 tbsp. Cajun seasoning
- 2 cup chicken, cooked & shredded
- 16 oz. whole wheat penne pasta, cooked
- 1 ½ cups skim milk
- ½ cup parmesan cheese, low fat
- 1 tbsp. cornstarch
- ¼ cup chicken broth, low sodium

Directions:

1. Add the oil to the cooking pot and set to sauté on med-high heat.
2. Add the onion, peppers, and garlic and cook until they soften.
3. Add the sausage and cook 5 minutes, until heated through, stirring occasionally.
4. Add the Cajun seasoning and chicken and cook, stirring occasionally until heated through.
5. Stir in the pasta and milk and bring to a simmer. Cook 5 minutes.
6. In a small bowl, whisk together cornstarch and broth until smooth. Add to the pot and cook, stirring until sauce thickens.
7. Stir in parmesan cheese and serve.

Nutrition Info:
- Calories 359,Total Fat 10g,Total Carbs 42g,Protein 23g,Sodium 457mg.

Ground Turkey And Potato Chili

Servings: 6
Cooking Time: 55 Min

Ingredients:
- 1 pound ground turkey /450g
- 2 bell peppers; chopped
- 6 potatoes, peeled and sliced
- 1 small onion; diced
- 2 garlic cloves; minced
- 1 cups tomato puree /250ml
- 1 cups diced tomatoes /130g
- 1 cup chicken broth /250ml
- 1cup carrots; chopped /130g
- 1 cups fresh or frozen corn kernels, roasted /130g
- 1 tbsp olive oil /15ml
- 1 tbsp ground cumin /15g
- 1 tbsp chili powder /15g
- salt and fresh ground black pepper

Directions:
1. Warm the olive on Sear/Sauté and stir-fry onions and garlic until soft, for about 3 minutes. Press Start. Stir in turkey and cook until thoroughly browned, about 5-6 minutes. Add the remaining ingredients, and stir to combine.
2. Seal the pressure lid, choose Pressure, set to High, and set the timer to 25 minutes; press Start. Once ready, do a quick release. Set on Sear/Sauté. Cook uncovered for 15 more minutes. Serve warm.

Creamy Tuscan Chicken Pasta

Servings:8
Cooking Time: 6 Minutes

Ingredients:
- 32 ounces chicken stock
- 1 jar oil-packed sun-dried tomatoes, drained
- 2 teaspoons Italian seasoning
- 3 garlic cloves, minced
- 1 pound chicken breast, cubed
- 1 box penne pasta
- 4 cups spinach
- 1 package cream cheese, cubed
- 1 cup shredded Parmesan cheese
- Kosher salt
- Freshly ground black pepper

Directions:
1. Place the chicken stock, sun-dried tomatoes, Italian seasoning, garlic, chicken breast, and pasta and stir. Assemble pressure lid, making sure the pressure release valve is in the SEAL position.
2. Select PRESSURE and set to HI. Set time to 6 minutes. Select START/STOP to begin.
3. When pressure cooking is complete, quick release the pressure by turning the pressure release valve to the VENT position. Carefully remove lid when unit has finished releasing pressure.
4. Add the spinach and stir, allowing it to wilt with the residual heat. Add the cream cheese, Parmesan cheese, salt and pepper and stir until melted. Serve.

Nutrition Info:
- Calories: 429,Total Fat: 21g,Sodium: 567mg,Carbohydrates: 32g,Protein: 29g.

Italian Chicken Muffins

Servings: 4
Cooking Time: 25 Minutes

Ingredients:
- Nonstick cooking spray
- 4 chicken breast halves, boneless & skinless
- ½ tsp salt, divided
- ½ tsp pepper, divided
- 1/3 cup part-skim ricotta cheese
- ¼ cup mozzarella cheese, grated
- 2 tbsp. parmesan cheese
- ½ tsp Italian seasoning
- ½ tsp garlic powder
- 2 tbsp. whole-wheat panko bread crumbs
- 1 tbsp. light butter, melted
- Paprika for sprinkling

Directions:

1. Place the rack in the cooking pot. Spray 4 cups of a 6-cup muffin tin.
2. Lay chicken between 2 sheets of plastic wrap and pound to ¼-inch thick. Season with ¼ teaspoon of salt and pepper.
3. In a medium bowl, combine ricotta, mozzarella, parmesan, Italian seasoning, garlic powder, and remaining salt and pepper, mix well. Spoon evenly onto centers of chicken. Wrap chicken around filling and place, seam side down, in prepared muffin cups.
4. In a small bowl, stir together bread crumbs and butter, sprinkle over the chicken then top with paprika.
5. Place muffin tin on rack and add the tender-crisp lid. Set to bake on 350°F. Cook chicken 25-30 minutes or until chicken is cooked through. Serve immediately.

Nutrition Info:
- Calories 224, Total Fat 8g, Total Carbs 4g, Protein 31g, Sodium 485mg.

Stuffed Whole Chicken

Servings: 6
Cooking Time: 8 Hours
Ingredients:
- 1 cup mozzarella cheese
- 4 whole garlic cloves, peeled
- 1 whole chicken 2 pounds, cleaned and pat dried
- Black pepper and salt, to taste
- 2 tablespoons fresh lemon juice

Directions:
1. Stuff the chicken cavity with garlic cloves and mozzarella cheese.
2. Season chicken generously with black pepper and salt.
3. Transfer chicken to your Ninja Foodi and drizzle lemon juice.
4. Lock and secure the Ninja Foodi's lid and set to "Slow Cooker" mode, let it cook on LOW for 8 hours.
5. Once done, serve and enjoy.

Nutrition Info:
- Calories: 309; Fat: 12g; Carbohydrates: 1.6g; Protein: 45g

Spicy Chicken Wings.

Servings: 2
Cooking Time: 25 Min
Ingredients:
- 10 chicken wings
- ½ tbsp honey /15ml
- 2 tbsp hot chili sauce /30ml
- ½ tbsp lime juice /7.5ml
- ½ tsp kosher salt /2.5g
- ½ tsp black pepper /2.5g

Directions:
1. Mix the lime juice, honey, and chili sauce. Toss the mixture over the chicken wings.
2. Put the wings in the fryer's basket, close the crisping lid and cook for 25 minutes on Air Crisp mode at 350 °F or 177°C. Shake the basket every 5 minutes.

Sweet Garlicky Chicken Wings

Servings: 4
Cooking Time: 20 Min
Ingredients:
- 16 chicken wings
- 4 garlic cloves; minced
- ¾ cup potato starch /98g
- ¼ cup butter /32.5g
- ¼ cup honey /62.5ml
- ½ tsp salt /2.5g

Directions:
1. Rinse and pat dry the wings, and place them in a bowl. Add the starch to the bowl, and mix to coat the chicken.
2. Place the chicken in a baking dish that has been previously coated lightly with cooking oil. Close the crisping lid and cook for 5 minutes on Air Crisp mode at 370 °F or 188°C.
3. Meanwhile, whisk the rest of the ingredients together in a bowl. Pour the sauce over the wings and cook for another 10 minutes.

Chicken Thighs With Thyme Carrot Roast

Servings: 4
Cooking Time: 50 Min
Ingredients:
- 4 bone-in, skin-on chicken thighs
- 1 ½ cups chicken broth /375ml
- 1 cup basmati rice /130g
- 2 carrots; chopped
- 2 tbsp melted butter /30ml
- 2 tsp chopped fresh thyme /10g
- 2 tsp chicken seasoning /10g
- 1 tsp salt; divided /5g

Directions:
1. Pour the chicken broth and rice in the pot. Then, put the reversible rack in the pot. Arrange the chicken thighs on the rack, skin side up, and arrange the carrots around the chicken.

2. Put the pressure lid together and lock in the Seal position. Choose Pressure, set to High, and the time to 2 minutes. Choose Start/Stop to begin cooking the chicken.
3. When done cooking, perform a quick pressure release, and carefully open the lid. Brush the carrots and chicken with the melted butter. Season the chicken with the chicken seasoning and half of the salt. Also, season the carrots with the thyme and remaining salt.
4. Close the crisping lid; choose Broil and set the time to 10 minutes. Choose Start/Stop to begin crisping. When done cooking, check for your desired crispiness, and the turn the Foodi off. Spoon the rice into serving plates, and serve the chicken and carrots over the rice.

Bacon Ranch Chicken Bake

Servings:6
Cooking Time: 30 Minutes
Ingredients:
- 1 pound chicken breast, cut in 1-inch cubes
- 2 tablespoons extra-virgin olive oil
- 3 tablespoons ranch seasoning mix, divided
- 4 strips bacon, chopped
- 1 small onion, chopped
- 2 garlic cloves, minced
- 1 cup long-grain white rice
- 2 cups chicken broth
- ½ cup half-and-half
- 2 cups shredded Cheddar cheese, divided
- 2 tablespoons chopped fresh parsley

Directions:
1. Select SEAR/SAUTÉ and set to HI. Select START/STOP to begin. Let preheat for 5 minutes.
2. In a large bowl, toss the chicken with the olive oil and 2 tablespoons of ranch seasoning mix.
3. Add the bacon to the pot and cook, stirring frequently, for about 6 minutes, or until crispy. Using a slotted spoon, transfer the bacon to a paper towel-lined plate to drain.
4. Add the onion and cook for about 5 minutes. Add the garlic and cook for 1 minute more. Add the chicken and stir, cooking until chicken is cooked through, about 3 minutes.
5. Add the rice, chicken broth, and remaining ranch mix. Assemble pressure lid, making sure the pressure release valve is in the SEAL position.
6. Select PRESSURE and set to HI. Set time to 7 minutes. Select START/STOP to begin.
7. When complete, quick release the pressure by turning the valve to the VENT position. Carefully remove lid when unit has finished releasing pressure.
8. Stir in half-and-half and 1 cup of Cheddar cheese. Top with the remaining 1 cup of cheese. Close crisping lid.
9. Select BROIL and set time to 8 minutes. Select START/STOP to begin. When cooking is complete, serve garnished with fresh parsley.

Nutrition Info:
- Calories: 512,Total Fat: 27g,Sodium: 999mg,Carbohydrates: 28g,Protein: 35g.

Ham-stuffed Turkey Rolls

Servings: 8
Cooking Time: 20 Minutes
Ingredients:
- 4 tablespoons fresh sage leaves
- 8 ham slices
- 8 6 ounces each turkey cutlets
- Black pepper and salt to taste
- 2 tablespoons butter, melted

Directions:
1. Season turkey cutlets with black pepper and salt.
2. Roll turkey cutlets and wrap each of them with ham slices tightly.
3. Coat each roll with butter and gently place sage leaves evenly over each cutlet.
4. Transfer them to your Ninja Foodi.
5. Lock and secure the Ninja Foodi's lid and select the "Bake/Roast" mode, bake for 10 minutes a 360 °F.
6. Open the Ninja Foodi's lid and gently give it a flip, Lock and secure the Ninja Foodi's lid again and bake for 10 minutes more.
7. Once done, serve and enjoy.

Nutrition Info:
- Calories: 467; Fat: 24g; Carbohydrates: 1.7g; Protein: 56g

Shredded Chicken With Lentils And Rice

Servings: 4
Cooking Time: 45 Min
Ingredients:
- 4 boneless; skinless chicken thighs
- 1 garlic clove; minced
- 1 small yellow onion; chopped
- 1 cup white rice /130g
- ½ cup dried lentils/65g
- 3 cups chicken broth; divided /750ml
- 1 tsp olive oil /5ml
- Chopped fresh parsley for garnish

- Salt and ground black pepper to taste

Directions:
1. Set your Foodi to Sear/Sauté, set to Medium High, and choose Start/Stop to preheat the pot. Warm oil. Add in onion and garlic and cook for 3 minutes until soft; add in broth, rice, lentils, and chicken.
2. Season with pepper and salt. Seal the pressure lid, choose Pressure, set to High, and set the timer to 15 minutes. Press Start.
3. Once ready, do a quick release. Remove and shred the chicken in a large bowl. Set the lentils and rice into serving plates, top with shredded chicken and parsley and serve.

Turkey & Wild Rice Casserole

Servings: 6
Cooking Time: 25 Minutes

Ingredients:
- Nonstick cooking spray
- 6 oz. pkg. long grain-wild rice mix, prepared according to directions
- 2 cups turkey, cooked & cubed
- 10 oz. cream of mushroom soup, fat free
- 4 oz. jar pimentos, diced, undrained
- ¼ cup water
- ½ tsp onion powder
- ¼ tsp pepper

Directions:
1. Add the rack to the cooking pot. Spray an 8x8-inch baking pan with cooking spray.
2. In a large bowl, combine all ingredients to mix well. Pour into prepared pan.
3. Place the pan on the rack and add the tender-crisp lid. Set to bake on 350°F. Bake 25 minutes until casserole is hot and bubbly. Serve.

Nutrition Info:
- Calories 207, Total Fat 4g, Total Carbs 25g, Protein 19g, Sodium 285mg.

Garlic Chicken And Bacon Pasta

Servings: 4
Cooking Time: 10 Minutes

Ingredients:
- 3 strips bacon, chopped
- ½ pound boneless, skinless chicken breast, cut into ½-pieces
- 1 teaspoon dried basil
- 1 teaspoon dried oregano
- ¼ teaspoon sea salt
- 1 tablespoon unsalted butter
- 3 garlic cloves, minced
- 1 cup chicken stock
- 1½ cups water
- 8 ounces dry penne pasta
- ½ cup half-and-half
- ½ cup grated Parmesan cheese, plus more for serving

Directions:
1. Select SEAR/SAUTÉ and set to HI. Select START/STOP to begin. Let preheat for 5 minutes.
2. Add the bacon and cook, stirring frequently, for about 5 minutes or until crispy. Using a slotted spoon, transfer the bacon to a paper towel-lined plate to drain.
3. Season the chicken with the basil, oregano, and salt, coating all the pieces.
4. Add the butter, chicken, and garlic and sauté for 2 minutes, until the chicken begins to brown and the garlic is fragrant.
5. Add the chicken stock, water, and penne pasta. Assemble pressure lid, making sure the pressure release valve is in the SEAL position.
6. Select PRESSURE and set to HI. Set time to 3 minutes. Select START/STOP to begin.
7. When pressure cooking is complete, allow pressure to naturally release for 2 minutes. After 2 minutes, quick release remaining pressure by moving the pressure release valve to the VENT position. Carefully remove lid when unit has finished releasing pressure.
8. Add the half-and-half, cheese, and bacon, and stir constantly to thicken the sauce and melt the cheese. Serve immediately, with additional Parmesan cheese to garnish.

Nutrition Info:
- Calories: 458, Total Fat: 18g, Sodium: 809mg, Carbohydrates: 45g, Protein: 30g.

Rosemary Lemon Chicken

Servings: 2
Cooking Time: 60 Min

Ingredients:
- 2 chicken breasts
- 2 rosemary sprigs
- ½ lemon; cut into wedges
- 1 tbsp oyster sauce /15ml
- 3 tbsp brown sugar /45g
- 1 tbsp soy sauce /15ml
- ½ tbsp olive oil /7.5ml
- 1 tsp minced ginger /5g

Directions:
1. Place the ginger, soy sauce, and olive oil, in a bowl. Add the chicken and coat well. Cover the bowl and

refrigerate for 30 minutes. Transfer the marinated chicken to the Foodi basket.

2. Close the crisping lid and cook for about 6 minutes on Air Crisp mode at 370 F. or 188°C

3. Mix the oyster sauce, rosemary and brown sugar in a small bowl. Pour the sauce over the chicken. Arrange the lemon wedges in the dish. Return to the Foodi and cook for 13 more minutes on Air Crisp mode.

Creamy Chicken Carbonara

Servings:4
Cooking Time: 15 Minutes
Ingredients:
- 4 strips bacon, chopped
- 1 medium onion, diced
- 1½ pounds chicken breast, cut into ¾ inch-cubes
- 6 garlic cloves, minced
- 2 cups chicken stock
- 8 ounces dry spaghetti, with noodles broken in half
- 2 cups freshly grated Parmesan cheese, plus more for serving
- 2 eggs
- Sea salt
- Freshly ground black pepper

Directions:
1. Select SEAR/SAUTÉ and set to HI. Select START/STOP to begin. Let preheat for 5 minutes.
2. Add the bacon and cook, stirring frequently, for about 6 minutes, or until crispy. Using a slotted spoon, transfer the bacon to a paper towel-lined plate to drain. Leave any bacon fat in the pot.
3. Add the onion, chicken, and garlic and sauté for 2 minutes, until the onions start to become translucent and the garlic is fragrant.
4. Add the chicken stock and spaghetti noodles. Assemble pressure lid, making sure the pressure release valve is in the SEAL position.
5. Select PRESSURE and set to HI. Set time to 6 minutes. Select START/STOP to begin.
6. When pressure cooking is complete, allow pressure to naturally release for 5 minutes. After 5 minutes, quick release remaining pressure by moving the pressure release valve to the VENT position. Carefully remove lid when unit has finished releasing pressure.
7. Add the cheese and stir to fully combine. Close the crisping lid, leaving the unit off, to keep the heat inside and allow the cheese to melt.
8. Whisk the eggs until full beaten.
9. Open lid, select SEAR/SAUTÉ, and set to LO. Select START/STOP to begin. Add the eggs and stir gently to incorporate, taking care to ensure the eggs are not scrambling while you work toward your desired sauce consistency. If your pot gets too warm, turn unit off.
10. Add the bacon back to the pot and season with salt and pepper. Stir to combine. Serve, adding more cheese as desired.

Nutrition Info:
- Calories: 732,Total Fat: 28g,Sodium: 1518mg,Carbohydrates: 47g,Protein: 70g.

Braised Chicken With Mushrooms And Brussel Sprouts

Servings: 4
Cooking Time: 40 Min
Ingredients:
- 4 chicken thighs, bone-in skin-on
- ½ small onion; sliced
- ¼ cup heavy cream /62.5ml
- 1 cup frozen halved Brussel sprouts; thawed /130g
- ½ cup dry white wine /125ml
- ⅓ cup chicken stock /188ml
- 1 cup sautéed Mushrooms /130g
- 1 bay leaf
- 1 tbsp olive oil /15ml
- 1 tsp salt or to taste; divided /5g
- ¼ tsp dried rosemary /1.25g
- Freshly ground black pepper

Directions:
1. Season the chicken on both sides with half of the salt. On your pot, Choose Sear/Sauté and adjust to Medium-High. Press Start to preheat the inner pot.
2. Heat olive oil and add the chicken thighs. Fry for 4 to 5 minutes or until browned. Turn and lightly sear the other side, about 1 minute. Use tongs to remove the chicken into a plate and spoon out any thick coating of oil in the pot.
3. Sauté the onion in the pot and season with the remaining salt. Cook for about 2 minutes to soften and just beginning to brown for 2 minutes. Stir in the white wine and bring to a boil for 2 to 3 minutes or until reduced by about half.
4. Mix in the chicken stock, brussel sprouts, bay leaf, rosemary, and several grinds of black pepper. Arrange the chicken thighs on top with skin-side up.
5. Seal the pressure lid, choose Pressure; adjust the pressure to High and the cook time to 5 minutes. Press Start to begin cooking.
6. When the timer is over, perform a quick pressure release and carefully open the lid. Remove the bay leaf. Remove the

chicken onto the reversible rack, and stir the mushrooms into the sauce. Carefully set the rack in the upper position of the pot.

7. Close the crisping lid and Choose Bake/Roast; adjust the temperature to 375°F or 191°C and the cook time to 12 minutes. Press Start to commence browning.

8. When ready, open the lid and transfer the chicken to a platter. Stir the heavy cream into the sauce and adjust the taste with salt and pepper. Spoon the sauce and vegetables around the chicken and serve.

Crunchy Chicken & Almond Casserole

Servings: 6
Cooking Time: 30 Minutes
Ingredients:
- Nonstick cooking spray
- 3 cups chicken breast, cooked & chopped
- ¾ cup mozzarella cheese, grated
- 10 ¾ oz. condensed cream of chicken soup, low fat
- ¼ cup skim milk
- 1 cup red bell pepper, chopped
- ¼ cup celery, chopped
- ¼ cup green onions, sliced
- ¼ tsp pepper
- ¼ cup cornflakes, crushed
- ¼ cup almonds, sliced

Directions:
1. Spray the cooking pot with cooking spray.
2. In a large bowl, combine chicken, cheese, soup, milk, bell pepper, celery, green onions, and pepper. Pour into the pot.
3. In a small bowl, combine cornflakes and almonds, sprinkle over the top of the chicken mixture.
4. Add the tender-crisp lid and set to bake on 400°F. Bake 30 minutes until casserole is hot and bubbly. Turn off the heat and let sit 10 minutes before serving.

Nutrition Info:
- Calories 266,Total Fat 13g,Total Carbs 7g,Protein 28g,Sodium 526mg.

Turkey Croquettes

Servings: 10
Cooking Time: 20 Minutes
Ingredients:
- Nonstick cooking spray
- 2 ½ cups turkey, cooked
- 1 stalk celery, chopped
- 2 green onions, chopped
- ½ cup cauliflower, cooked
- ½ cup broccoli, cooked
- 1 cup stuffing, cooked
- 1 cup cracker crumbs
- 1 egg, lightly beaten
- 1/8 tsp salt
- 1/8 tsp pepper
- 1 cup French fried onions, crushed

Directions:
1. Spray the fryer basket with cooking spray.
2. Add the turkey, celery, onion, cauliflower, and broccoli to a food processor and pulse until finely chopped. Transfer to a large bowl.
3. Stir in stuffing and 1 cup of the cracker crumbs until combined.
4. Add the egg, salt and pepper and stir to combine. Form into 10 patties.
5. Place the crushed fried onions in a shallow dish. Coat patties on both sides in the onions and place in the basket. Lightly spray the tops with cooking spray.
6. Add the tender-crisp lid and set to air fry on 375°F. Cook 5-7 minutes until golden brown. Flip over and spray with cooking spray again, cook another 5-7 minutes. Serve immediately.

Nutrition Info:
- Calories 133,Total Fat 4g,Total Carbs 16g,Protein 9g,Sodium 449mg.

Pizza Stuffed Chicken

Servings: 4
Cooking Time: 20 Minutes
Ingredients:
- Nonstick cooking spray
- 2 chicken breasts, boneless & skinless
- 2 tbsp. parmesan cheese, divided
- ½ tsp oregano
- 12 slices turkey pepperoni
- ½ cup mozzarella cheese, grated, divided
- 3 tbsp. whole-wheat bread crumbs
- 4 tbsp. marinara sauce, low sodium

Directions:
1. Place the rack in the cooking pot. Spray the fryer basket with cooking spray.
2. Cut each breast in half horizontally. Place between 2 sheets of plastic wrap and pound out to ¼-inch thick.
3. Sprinkle 1 tablespoon of parmesan and the oregano over chicken. Top each cutlet with 3 slices of pepperoni and 1 tablespoon mozzarella. Roll up.

4. In a shallow dish, combine bread crumbs and remaining parmesan, mix well. Coat chicken rolls in bread crumbs and place, seam side down, in the fryer basket. Lightly spray with cooking spray.

5. Add the tender-crisp lid and set to air fry on 400 °F. Cook 15 minutes.

6. Open the lid and top each chicken roll with 1 tablespoon marinara sauce and remaining mozzarella. Cook 5-7 minutes until chicken is cooked through and cheese is melted. Serve immediately.

Nutrition Info:
- Calories 268,Total Fat 8g,Total Carbs 7g,Protein 41g,Sodium 800mg.

Honey Garlic Chicken And Okra

Servings: 4
Cooking Time: 25 Min
Ingredients:
- 4 boneless; skinless chicken breasts; sliced
- 4 spring onions, thinly sliced
- 6 garlic cloves, grated
- ⅓ cup honey /84ml
- 1 cup rice, rinsed /130g
- ¼ cup tomato puree /62.5ml
- ½ cup soy sauce /125ml
- 2 cups water /500ml
- 2 cups frozen okra /260g
- 1 tbsp cornstarch /15g
- 2 tbsp rice vinegar /30ml
- 1 tbsp olive oil /15ml
- 1 tbsp water /15ml
- 2 tsp toasted sesame seeds /10g
- ½ tsp salt /2.5g

Directions:
1. In the inner pot of the Foodi, mix garlic, tomato puree, vinegar, soy sauce, ginger, honey, and oil; toss in chicken to coat. In an ovenproof bowl, mix water, salt and rice. Set the reversible rack on top of chicken. Lower the bowl onto the reversible rack.

2. Seal the pressure lid, choose Pressure, set to High, and set the timer to 10 minutes; press Start. Release pressure naturally for 5 minutes, release the remaining pressure quickly.

3. Use a fork to fluff the rice. Lay okra onto the rice. Allow the okra steam in the residual heat for 3 minutes. Take the trivet and bowl from the pot. Set the chicken to a plate.

4. Press Sear/Sauté. In a small bowl, mix 1 tbsp of water and cornstarch until smooth; stir into the sauce and cook for 3 to 4 minutes until thickened.

5. Divide the rice, chicken, and okra between 4 bowls. Drizzle sauce over each portion; garnish with spring onions and sesame seeds.

Chicken Piccata

Servings: 4
Cooking Time: 4 Hours
Ingredients:
- Nonstick cooking spray
- ¼ cup flour
- 1 tsp garlic powder
- ½ tsp salt
- ¼ tsp pepper
- 2 chicken breasts, boneless, skinless & halved horizontally
- 2 cups chicken broth, low sodium
- 1 tbsp. fresh lemon juice
- ½ cup heavy cream

Directions:
1. Spray the cooking pot with cooking spray.
2. In a small bowl, combine flour, garlic powder, salt, and pepper, mix well.
3. Coat chicken in flour mixture on all sides. Set the cooker to sear and add the chicken, brown on both sides. Pour in broth.
4. Add the lid and set to slow cook on low. Cook 4 hours or until chicken is cooked through.
5. Stir in lemon juice and cream. Season with salt and pepper and increase temperature to high. Cook another 10 minutes until sauce has thickened slightly.
6. Transfer chicken to serving plates and top with sauce. Serve.

Nutrition Info:
- Calories 248,Total Fat 10g,Total Carbs 8g,Protein 31g,Sodium 1071mg.

Beef, Pork & Lamb Recipes

Beef Stew With Veggies

Servings: 6
Cooking Time: 1 Hr 15 Min
Ingredients:
- 2 pounds beef chuck; cubed /900g
- 1 cup dry red wine /250ml
- 3 cups carrots; chopped /390g
- ¼ cup flour /32.5g
- 2 cups beef stock /500ml
- 4 cups potatoes; diced /520g
- 1 onion; diced
- 3 garlic cloves; minced
- 2 celery stalks; chopped
- 3 tomatoes; chopped
- 2 bell pepper, thinly sliced
- 1 tbsp dried Italian seasoning /15g
- 2 tbsp olive oil /30ml
- 2 tbsp butter /30g
- 2 tsp salt; divided /10g
- 1 tsp paprika /5g
- 1 tsp ground black pepper/5g
- 2 tsp Worcestershire sauce /10ml
- A handful of fresh parsley; chopped
- salt and ground black pepper to taste

Directions:
1. In a bowl, mix black pepper, beef, flour, paprika, and 1 tsp salt. Toss the ingredients and ensure the beef is coated. Warm butter and oil on Sear/Sautét. Add in beef and cook for 8- 10 minutes until browned. Set aside on a plate.
2. To the same fat, add garlic, onion, and celery, bell peppers, and cook for 4-5 minutes until tender.
3. Deglaze with wine, scrape the bottom to get rid of any browned beef bits. Pour in remaining salt, beef stock, Worcestershire sauce, and Italian seasoning. Return beef to the pot; add carrots, tomatoes, and potatoes.
4. Seal the pressure lid, choose Pressure, set to High, and set the timer to 35 minutes. Press Start. Release pressure naturally for 10 minutes. Taste and adjust the seasonings as necessary. Serve on plates and scatter over the parsley.

Braised Lamb Shanks

Servings:4
Cooking Time: 4 Hours 15 Minutes
Ingredients:
- 2 bone-in lamb shanks, 2 to 2½ pounds each
- Kosher salt
- Freshly ground black pepper
- 2 tablespoons canola oil
- 2 Yukon gold potatoes, cut into 1-inch pieces
- 2 carrots, cut into 2-inch pieces
- 2 parsnips, peeled and cut into 2-inch pieces
- 1 bag frozen pearl onions
- 1 bottle red wine
- 1 cup chicken stock
- 1 tablespoon chopped fresh rosemary

Directions:
1. Select SEAR/SAUTÉ and set to HI. Select START/STOP to begin. Let preheat for 5 minutes.
2. Season the lamb shanks with salt and pepper.
3. Add the oil and lamb. Cook for 5 minutes on one side, then turn and cook for an additional 5 minutes. Remove the lamb and set aside.
4. Add the potatoes, carrots, parsnips, and pearl onions. Cook for 5 minutes, stirring occasionally.
5. Stir in the red wine, chicken stock, and rosemary. Add the lamb back to the pot and press down on the shanks to ensure they are mostly submerged in liquid. Assemble pressure lid, making sure the pressure release valve is in the VENT position.
6. Select SLOW COOK and set to HI. Set time to 4 hours. Select START/STOP to begin.
7. When cooking is complete, remove lid and serve.

Nutrition Info:
- Calories: 791,Total Fat: 34g,Sodium: 591mg,Carbohydrates: 47g,Protein: 51g.

Pork Tenderloin With Warm Balsamic And Apple Chutney

Servings:4
Cooking Time: 23 Minutes
Ingredients:
- 1 pound pork tenderloin
- 2½ tablespoons minced rosemary, divided
- 2½ tablespoons minced thyme, divided
- Kosher salt
- Freshly ground black pepper
- 2 tablespoons extra-virgin olive oil
- 1 small white onion
- 1 tablespoon minced garlic
- ¾ cup apple juice

- 2 apples, cut into ½-inch cubes
- 2½ tablespoons balsamic vinegar
- 1 tablespoon honey
- 2½ teaspoons cornstarch
- 3 tablespoons unsalted butter, cubed

Directions:
1. Select SEAR/SAUTÉ and set to HI. Select START/STOP to begin. Let preheat for 5 minutes.
2. Season the pork with 1 tablespoon of rosemary, 1 tablespoon of thyme, salt, and pepper.
3. Once unit is preheated, add the olive oil. Once hot, add the pork and sear for 3 minutes on each side. Once seared, place the pork on a plate and set aside.
4. Add the onion, garlic, and apple juice. Stir, scraping the bottom of the pot to remove any brown bits. Add apples and vinegar and stir. Return the pork to the pot, nestling it in the apple mixture. Assemble pressure lid, making sure the pressure release valve is in the SEAL position.
5. Select PRESSURE and set to HI. Set time to 7 minutes. Select START/STOP to begin.
6. When pressure cooking is complete, allow pressure to naturally release for 14 minutes. After 14 minutes, quick release the pressure by turning the pressure release valve to the VENT position. Carefully remove lid when unit has finished releasing pressure.
7. Remove the pork from the pot, place it on a plate, and cover with aluminum foil.
8. Slightly mash the apples with a potato masher. Stir the honey into the mixture.
9. Remove ¼ cup of cooking liquid from the pot and mix it with the cornstarch until smooth. Pour this mixture into the pot and stir until thickened. Add the butter, 1 tablespoon of rosemary, and 1 tablespoon of thyme and stir until the butter is melted.
10. Slice the pork and serve it with the chutney. Garish with the remaining ½ tablespoon of rosemary and ½ tablespoon of thyme.

Nutrition Info:
- Calories: 406,Total Fat: 20g,Sodium: 107mg,Carbohydrates: 33g,Protein: 24g.

Beef And Pumpkin Stew

Servings: 6
Cooking Time: 35 Min
Ingredients:
- 2 pounds stew beef; cut into 1-inch chunks /900g
- 3 carrots; sliced
- 1 onion; chopped
- 3 whole cloves
- 1 bay leaf
- ½ butternut pumpkin; sliced
- 1 cup red wine /250ml
- 2 tbsp cornstarch /30g
- 2 tbsp canola oil /30ml
- 3 tbsp water /45ml
- 1 tsp garlic powder /5g
- 1 tsp salt /5g

Directions:
1. Warm oil on Sear/Sauté. Add beef and brown for 5 minutes on each side. Deglaze the pot with wine, scrape the bottom to get rid of any browned beef bits. Add in onion, salt, bay leaf, cloves, and garlic powder. Seal the pressure lid, choose Pressure, set to High, and set the timer to 15 minutes. Press Start.
2. When ready, release the pressure quickly. Add in pumpkin and carrots without stirring. Seal the pressure lid again, choose Pressure, set to High, and set the timer to 5 minutes. Press Start.
3. When ready, release the pressure quickly. In a bowl, mix water and cornstarch until cornstarch dissolves completely; mix into the stew. Allow the stew to simmer while uncovered on Keep Warm for 5 minutes until you attain the desired thickness.

Beef, Barley & Mushroom Stew

Servings: 8
Cooking Time: 1 Hour 15 Minutes
Ingredients:
- 2 tbsp. butter, unsalted
- 2 lbs. beef chuck, cubed
- 1 tsp salt
- 3 cups onions, chopped
- 1 lb. mushrooms, sliced
- 1 quart beef broth, low sodium
- 3 cups water
- 2 tsp marjoram
- 1 cup pearl barley
- 1 cup carrot, chopped
- 3 cups turnips, peeled & chopped
- ½ tsp pepper
- ½ cup sour cream
- 8 small sprigs fresh dill

Directions:
1. Add the butter to the cooking pot and set to sauté on medium heat.

2. Working in batches, cook the beef until brown on all sides, seasoning with salt as it cooks. Transfer browned beef to a bowl.
3. Add the onions and cook, stirring up brown bits from the bottom of the pot, about 5-6 minutes or until they begin to brown.
4. Add the mushrooms and increase heat to med-high. Cook 2-3 minutes.
5. Add the beef back to the pot and stir in marjoram, broth, and water, stir to mix.
6. Add the lid and set to pressure cook on high. Set timer for 30 minutes. When timer goes off use quick release to remove the pressure.
7. Stir in barley, turnips, and carrots. Add the lid and pressure cook on high another 30 minutes. When the timer goes off, use quick release to remove the pressure.
8. Ladle into bowls and garnish sour cream and dill. Serve immediately.

Nutrition Info:
- Calories 67,Total Fat 2g,Total Carbs 5g,Protein 7g,Sodium 162mg.

Baked Bacon Macaroni And Cheese

Servings:6
Cooking Time: 30 Minutes

Ingredients:
- 4 strips bacon, chopped
- 5 cups water
- 1 box elbow pasta
- 2 tablespoons unsalted butter
- 1 tablespoon ground mustard
- 1 can evaporated milk
- 8 ounces Cheddar cheese, shredded
- 8 ounces Gouda, shredded
- Sea salt
- Freshly ground black pepper
- 2 cups panko or Italian bread crumbs
- 1 stick (½ cup) butter, melted

Directions:
1. Select SEAR/SAUTÉ and set temperature to HI. Select START/STOP to begin. Let preheat for 5 minutes.
2. Add the bacon and cook, stirring frequently, for about 6 minutes or until crispy. Using a slotted spoon, transfer the bacon to a paper towel-lined plate to drain.
3. Add the water, pasta, 2 tablespoons of butter, and mustard. Assemble pressure lid, making sure the pressure release valve is in the SEAL position.
4. Select PRESSURE and set to LO. Set time to 0 minutes. Select START/STOP to begin.
5. When pressure cooking is complete, allow pressure to naturally release for 10 minutes. After 10 minutes, quick release remaining pressure by moving the pressure release valve to the VENT position. Carefully remove lid when unit has finished releasing pressure.
6. Add the evaporated milk, Cheddar cheese, Gouda cheese and the bacon. Season with salt and pepper. Stir well to melt the cheeses and ensure all ingredients are combined.
7. In a medium bowl, stir together the bread crumbs and melted butter. Cover the pasta evenly with the mixture. Close crisping lid.
8. Select AIR CRISP, set temperature to 360°F, and set time to 7 minutes. Select START/STOP to begin.
9. When cooking is complete, serve immediately.

Nutrition Info:
- Calories: 721,Total Fat: 45g,Sodium: 1213mg,Carbohydrates: 44g,Protein: 35g.

Spanish Lamb & Beans

Servings: 8
Cooking Time: 6 Hours

Ingredients:
- 2 tbsp. olive oil, divided
- 2 onions, sliced
- ½ red hot pepper, chopped fine
- 1 chorizo sausage, chopped
- 2 lbs. lamb, cubed
- 2 cups beef broth, low sodium
- 2 cups water
- 4 cloves garlic, chopped fine
- 2 tsp Worcestershire sauce
- 2 tbsp. balsamic vinegar
- ¼ tsp oregano
- ¼ tsp pepper
- 3 tbsp. tomato paste
- 1 zucchini, sliced
- 2 carrots, sliced
- 15 oz. cannellini beans, drained & rinsed

Directions:
1. Add half the oil to the cooking pot and set to sauté on med-high heat.
2. Add the onions and cook 3 minutes, stirring occasionally. Add the pepper and chorizo and cook 5-6 minutes or until chorizo is cooked through. Transfer to a bowl.
3. Add remaining oil to the pot and let it get hot. Add the lamb and cook until browned on the outside.

4. Return the chorizo mixture along with the broth, water, garlic, Worcestershire, vinegar, oregano, and pepper, stir to mix.
5. Add the lid and set to slow cook on low. Cook 4 hours.
6. Add the tomato paste, zucchini, carrots, and beans, stir to combine. Recover and cook another 2 hours until lamb and vegetables are tender. Serve.

Nutrition Info:
- Calories 710,Total Fat 54g,Total Carbs 21g,Protein 36g,Sodium 890mg.

Peppercorn Meatloaf

Servings: 8
Cooking Time: 35 Min
Ingredients:
- 4 lb. ground beef /1800g
- 10 whole peppercorns, for garnishing
- 1 onion; diced
- 1 cup breadcrumbs /130g
- 1 tbsp parsley /15g
- 1 tbsp Worcestershire sauce /15ml
- 3 tbsp ketchup /45ml
- 1 tbsp basil /15g
- 1 tbsp oregano /15g
- ½ tsp salt /2.5g
- 1 tsp ground peppercorns /5g

Directions:
1. Place the beef in a large bowl. Add all of the ingredients except the whole peppercorns and the breadcrumbs. Mix with your hand until well combined. Stir in the breadcrumbs.
2. Put the meatloaf on a lined baking dish. Insert in the Foodi, close the crisping lid and cook for 25 minutes on Air Crisp mode at 350 °F or 177°C.
3. Garnish the meatloaf with the whole peppercorns and let cool slightly before serving.

Holiday Honey Glazed Ham

Servings: 10
Cooking Time: 30 Min
Ingredients:
- 1 ham, bone-in /2250g
- ¼ cup brown sugar /32.5g
- ½ cup apple cider /125ml
- ¼ cup honey /62.5ml
- 1 pinch ground cloves
- 2 tbsp orange juice /30ml
- 1 tbsp Dijon mustard /15ml
- 2 tbsp pineapple juice (optional) /30ml
- ¼ tsp grated nutmeg /32.5g
- ½ tsp ground cinnamon /2.5g

Directions:
1. Set on Sear/Sauté, set to Medium High, and choose Start/Stop to preheat the pot. Press Start. Mix in apple cider, mustard, pineapple juice, cloves, cinnamon, brown sugar, honey, orange juice, and nutmeg; cook until sauce becomes warm and the sugar and spices are completely dissolved.
2. Lay ham into the sauce. Seal the pressure lid, choose Pressure, set to High, and set the timer to 10 minutes; press Start. When ready, release the pressure quickly.
3. As the ham cooks, preheat the oven's broiler. Line aluminum foil to a baking sheet. Transfer the ham to the prepared baking sheet. On Sear/Sauté, cook the remaining liquid for 4 to 6 minutes until you have a thick and syrupy glaze. Brush the glaze onto ham.
4. Set the glazed ham in the preheated broiler and bake for 3 to 5 minutes until the glaze is caramelized. Place the ham on a cutting board and slice. Transfer to a serving bowl and drizzle glaze over the ham.

Pork Pie

Servings:8
Cooking Time: 45 Minutes
Ingredients:
- 2 tablespoons extra-virgin olive oil
- 1 pound ground pork
- 1 yellow onion, diced
- 1 can black beans, drained
- 1 cup frozen corn kernels
- 1 can green chiles
- 2 tablespoons chili powder
- 1 box cornbread mix
- 1½ cups milk
- 1 cup shredded Cheddar cheese

Directions:
1. Select SEAR/SAUTÉ and set temperature to MED. Select START/STOP to begin. Let preheat for 3 minutes.
2. Add the olive oil, pork, and onion. Brown the pork, stirring frequently to break the meat into smaller pieces, until cooked through, about 5 minutes.
3. Add the beans, corn, chiles, and chili powder and stir. Simmer, stirring frequently, about 10 minutes.
4. In a medium bowl, combine the cornbread mix, milk, and cheese. Pour it over simmering mixture in an even layer. Close crisping lid.
5. Select BAKE/ROAST, set temperature to 360°F, and set time for 25 minutes. Select START/STOP to begin.
6. After 20 minutes, use wooden toothpick to check if cornbread is done. If the toothpick inserted into the

cornbread does not come out clean, close lid and cook for the remaining 5 minutes.
7. When cooking is complete, open lid. Let cool for 10 minutes before slicing and serving.
Nutrition Info:
- Calories: 491,Total Fat: 24g,Sodium: 667mg,Carbohydrates: 47g,Protein: 24g.

Bunless Burgers

Servings:4
Cooking Time: 10 Minutes
Ingredients:
- ¼ teaspoon onion powder
- ¼ teaspoon garlic powder
- ¼ teaspoon Italian seasoning
- Dash Himalayan pink salt
- 1 pound ground beef

Directions:
1. Place the Cook & Crisp Basket into the cooking pot. Select AIR CRISP, set the temperature to 375°F, and set the time to 5 minutes to preheat. Select START/STOP to begin.
2. In a small bowl, stir together the onion powder, garlic powder, Italian seasoning, and salt.
3. Divide the ground beef into 4 equal portions and shape each into a patty. Season both side of the patties with the seasoning mix and place them on a sheet of parchment paper.
4. Once the unit is preheated, add the burgers to the basket, working in batches as needed. Close the crisping lid.
5. Select AIR CRISP, set the temperature to 375°F, and set the time to 8 to 10 minutes. Select START/STOP to begin. Cook the burgers until cooking is complete; no need to flip the burgers!

Nutrition Info:
- Calories: 172,Total Fat: 8g,Sodium: 82mg,Carbohydrates: 0g,Protein: 23g.

Lamb Curry

Servings: 6
Cooking Time: 6 Hours
Ingredients:
- ¼ cup flour
- 2 lbs. lamb shoulder, cubed
- ½ tsp salt
- ½ tsp pepper
- 2 tbsp. olive oil
- 1 onion, chopped
- 2 cloves garlic, chopped fine
- 2-inch piece fresh ginger, peeled, grated
- 1 hot red chili, chopped fine
- ¼ cup Indian madras curry paste
- 1 ¼ cups light coconut milk
- ¾ cups vegetable broth, low sodium
- 1 cinnamon stick
- 1 bay leaf
- 2 tbsp. cilantro, chopped

Directions:
1. Place flour in a large Ziploc bag. Season lamb with salt and pepper and add to the flour. Seal and turn to coat.
2. Add oil to the cooking pot and set to sauté on med-high. Cook lamb, in batches until browned on the outside. Transfer to a bowl.
3. Add onion, garlic, and ginger to the pot. Cook, stirring frequently, 4-5 minutes until tender.
4. Stir in chili and curry paste and cook 1 minute more. Add the milk and broth and bring to a boil.
5. Return the lamb to the pot along with the cinnamon stick and bay leaf. Add the lid and set to slow cook on low. Cook 6 hours or until lamb is tender. Discard the bay leaf and cinnamon stick. Serve over hot cooked rice garnished with cilantro.

Nutrition Info:
- Calories 407,Total Fat 25g,Total Carbs 13g,Protein 33g,Sodium 373mg.

Beef Pho With Swiss Chard

Servings: 6
Cooking Time: 1 Hr 10 Min
Ingredients:
- 2 pounds Beef Neck Bones /900g
- 10 ounces sirloin steak /300g
- 8 ounces rice noodles /240g
- 1 yellow onion, quartered
- A handful of fresh cilantro; chopped
- 2 scallions; chopped
- 2 jalapeño peppers; sliced
- ¼ cup minced fresh ginger /32.5g
- 9 cups water /2250ml
- 2 cups Swiss chard; chopped /260g
- 2 tsp coriander seeds /10g
- 2 tsp ground cinnamon /10g
- 2 tsp ground cloves /10g
- 2 tbsp coconut oil /30ml
- 3 tbsp sugar /45g
- 2 tbsp fish sauce /30ml
- 2 ½ tsp kosher salt /12.5g
- Freshly ground black pepper to taste

Directions:

1. Melt the oil on Sear/Sauté. Add ginger and onions and cook for 4 minutes until the onions are softened. Stir in cloves, cinnamon and coriander seeds and cook for 1 minute until soft. Add in water, salt, beef meat and bones.
2. Seal the pressure lid, choose Pressure, set to High, and set the timer to 30 minutes. Press Start. Release pressure naturally for 10 minutes.
3. Transfer the meat to a large bowl; cover with it enough water and soak for 10 minutes. Drain the water and slice the beef. In hot water, soak rice noodles for 8 minutes until softened and pliable; drain and rinse with cold water. Drain liquid from cooker into a separate pot through a fine-mesh strainer; get rid of any solids.
4. Add fish sauce and sugar to the broth; transfer into the Foodi and simmer on Sear/Sauté. Place the noodles in four separate soup bowls. Top with steak slices, scallions, swiss chard; sliced jalapeño pepper, cilantro, red onion, and pepper. Spoon the broth over each bowl to serve.

Bolognese Pizza

Servings: 4
Cooking Time: 70 Min
Ingredients:
- ½ lb. ground pork, meat cooked and crumbled /225g
- 1 cup shredded mozzarella cheese /130g
- ½ cup canned crushed tomatoes /65g
- 1 yellow bell pepper; sliced; divided
- 4 pizza crusts
- 1 tbsp chopped fresh basil, for garnish /15g
- 1 tsp red chili flakes; divided /5g
- Cooking spray

Directions:
1. Place the reversible rack in the pot. Close the crisping lid; choose Air Crisp, set the temperature to 400°F or 205°C, and the time to 5 minutes.
2. Grease one side of a pizza crust with cooking spray and lay on the preheated rack, oiled side up. Close the crisping lid. Choose Air Crisp, set the temperature to 400°F, and set the time to 4 minutes. Choose Start/Stop to begin baking.
3. Remove the crust from the rack and flip so the crispy side is down. Top the crust with 2 tbsps of crushed tomatoes, a quarter of bell pepper, 2 ounces or 60g of ground pork, ¼ cup or 32.5g of mozzarella cheese, and ¼ tbsp or 1.25g of red chili flakes.
4. Close the crisping lid. Choose Broil and set the time to 3 minutes. Choose Start/Stop to continue baking. When done baking and crispy as desired, remove the pizza from the rack. Repeat with the remaining pizza crusts and ingredients. Top each pizza with some basil and serve.

Pork Carnitas Wraps

Servings: 12
Cooking Time: 1 Hr 15 Min
Ingredients:
- 1 boneless pork shoulder /2250g
- 12 corn tortillas, warmed
- 1 avocado; sliced
- 1 onion; sliced
- 2 garlic cloves; minced
- 2 jalapeños; sliced
- 2 oranges, juiced
- 2 limes, juiced
- Fresh cilantro leaves; chopped
- 2 tbsp sweet smoked paprika /30g
- 1 tbsp dried oregano /15g
- 1 tbsp salt /15g
- 2 tsp grapeseed oil /10ml
- 2 tsp ground black pepper /10g

Directions:
1. Warm oil on Sear/Sauté. Add in pork and cook for 5 minutes until golden brown. Transfer the pork to a plate. Add garlic and onions to the inner pot and cook for 2 to 3 minutes until soft.
2. Add lime and orange juices into the pot to deglaze, scrape the bottom to get rid of any browned bits of food.
3. Stir in pepper, paprika, salt and oregano. Return the pork to pot; stir to coat in seasoning and liquid. Seal the pressure lid, choose Pressure, set to High, and set the timer to 35 minutes. Press Start. When ready, release the pressure quickly.
4. Press Sear/Sauté. When the liquid starts to simmer, use two forks to shred the pork. Cook for 10 more minutes until liquid is reduced by half. Serve in warmed tortillas topped with jalapeños, avocado slices and cilantro.

Traditional Beef Stroganoff

Servings: 6
Cooking Time: 1 Hr 15 Min
Ingredients:
- 2 pounds beef stew meat /900g
- 8 ounces sour cream /240g
- 2 garlic cloves; minced
- 1 onion; chopped
- 3 cups fresh mushrooms; chopped /390g
- 1 cup long-grain rice, cooked /130g
- 1 cup beef broth /250ml
- ¼ cup flour /32.5g
- 2 tbsp olive oil /30ml

- 1 tbsp chopped fresh parsley /15g
- salt and ground black pepper to taste

Directions:
1. In a large bowl, combine salt, pepper and flour. Add beef and massage to coat beef in flour mixture. Warm oil on Sear/Sauté. Brown the beef for 4 to 5 minutes. Add garlic and onion and cook for 3 minutes until fragrant. Add beef broth to the pot.
2. Seal the pressure lid, choose Pressure, set to High, and set the timer to 35 minutes. Press Start. When ready, release the pressure quickly.
3. Open the lid and stir mushrooms and sour cream into the beef mixture. Seal the pressure lid again, choose Pressure, set to High, and set the timer to 2 minutes. Press Start.
4. When ready, release the pressure quickly. Season the stroganoff with pepper and salt; scoop over cooked rice before serving.

Hot Dogs With Peppers

Servings: 6
Cooking Time: 15 Min

Ingredients:
- 6 sausages pork sausage links
- 1 green bell pepper; sliced into strips
- 1 red bell pepper; sliced into strips
- 1 yellow bell pepper; sliced into strips
- 2 spring onions; sliced
- 1 ½ cups beer /375ml
- 6 hot dog rolls
- 1 tbsp olive oil /15ml

Directions:
1. Warm oil on Sear/Sauté. Add in sausage links and sear for 5 minutes until browned; set aside on a plate. Into the Foodi, pile peppers. Lay the sausages on top. Add beer into the pot.
2. Seal the pressure lid, choose Pressure, set to High, and set the timer to 5 minutes. Press Start. When ready, release the pressure quickly. Serve sausages in buns topped with onions and peppers.

Beef Lasagna

Servings: 4
Cooking Time: 10-15 Minutes

Ingredients:
- 2 small onions
- 2 garlic cloves, minced
- 1-pound ground beef
- 1 large egg
- 1 and 1/2 cups ricotta cheese
- 1/2 cup parmesan cheese
- 1 jar 25 ounces0 marinara sauce
- 8 ounces mozzarella cheese, sliced

Directions:
1. Select "Sauté" mode on your Ninja Foodi and stir in beef, brown the beef.
2. Add onion and garlic.
3. Add parmesan, ricotta, egg in a small dish and keep it on the side.
4. Stir in sauce to browned meat, reserve half for later.
5. Sprinkle mozzarella and half of ricotta cheese into the browned meat.
6. Top with remaining meat sauce.
7. For the final layer, add more mozzarella cheese and the remaining ricotta.
8. Stir well.
9. Cover with a foil transfer to Ninja Foodi.
10. Lock and secure the Ninja Foodi's lid, then cook on "HIGH" pressure for 8-10 minutes.
11. Quick-release pressure.
12. Drizzle parmesan cheese on top.
13. Enjoy.

Nutrition Info:
- Calories: 365; Fats: 25g; Carbohydrates: 6g; Protein: 25g

Jamaican Pork

Servings: 4
Cooking Time: 25 Minutes

Ingredients:
- 1 tbsp. butter
- 1 tsp curry powder
- 2 bananas, sliced ½-inch thick
- 1 lb. pork tenderloin, cubed
- ½ tsp salt
- ½ cup pineapple juice, unsweetened
- ¼ cup onion, chopped fine
- ¼ cup coconut flakes, unsweetened

Directions:
1. Add butter to the cooking pot and set to sauté on medium heat.
2. Once the butter has melted, stir in curry powder until foamy.
3. Add bananas and cook until golden brown, about 3-5 minutes. Transfer to a plate.
4. Add pork and cook until golden brown, about 6-8 minutes. Season with salt.

5. Stir in pineapple juice and onion. Cover, reduce heat, and simmer 10 minutes until pork is tender.

6. Stir in coconut and bananas and toss gently to combine. Serve over cooked rice.

Nutrition Info:
- Calories 247,Total Fat 7g,Total Carbs 21g,Protein 25g,Sodium 100mg.

African Pork Stew

Servings: 6
Cooking Time: 8 Hours

Ingredients:
- 14½ oz. yellow hominy, drained
- 3 cups red beans, drained & rinsed
- 1 onion, chopped
- 2 tbsp. garlic, chopped fine
- 2 bay leaves
- 1 tsp Adobo powder
- 2 lbs. pork loin, cubed
- 2 potatoes, peeled & cubed
- 1 lb. smoked sausage, sliced
- 1 can diced tomatoes
- 2 tbsp. olive oil
- 3 slices bacon, chopped

Directions:

1. Add all the ingredients to the cooking pot and stir to combine.

2. Add the lid and set to slow cook on low. Cook 6-8 hours or until meat and vegetables are tender.

3. Discard the bay leaves, stir well and serve.

Nutrition Info:
- Calories 784,Total Fat 37g,Total Carbs 55g,Protein 55g,Sodium 1185mg.

Pork Chops With Seasoned Butter

Servings: 4
Cooking Time: 15 Minutes

Ingredients:
- ¼ cup butter, soft
- 2 tbsp. Dijon mustard
- 1 clove garlic, chopped fine
- Nonstick cooking spray
- 4 pork chops, 1 ¼-inch thick
- 4 slices bacon, thick-cut

Directions:

1. In a small bowl, combine butter, mustard, and garlic until thoroughly combine. Wrap in waxed paper and form into the shape of a stick of butter. Refrigerate until ready to use.

2. Spray the rack with cooking spray and add it to the pot.

3. Season chops with salt and pepper. Wrap a slice of bacon around each chop and secure with a toothpick. Place them on the rack.

4. Add the tender-crisp lid and set to broil. Cook chops 6-7 minutes, turn the chops over and cook another 5-6 minutes. Turn off the heat and let rest 3 minutes.

5. To serve, place the chops on serving plates. Slice the seasoned butter into 4 pieces and place one on each chop. Serve immediately.

Nutrition Info:
- Calories 450,Total Fat 40g,Total Carbs 1g,Protein 33g,Sodium 362mg.

Italian Beef Steak

Servings: 8
Cooking Time: 4 Hours

Ingredients:
- Nonstick cooking spray
- 2 lbs. round steak, cut in 1-inch pieces
- ½ tsp salt
- ¼ tsp pepper
- 1 onion, sliced thin
- 1 tsp oregano
- 1 tsp basil
- 1 tsp rosemary
- ½ tsp thyme
- 4 cloves garlic, chopped fine
- ½ cup balsamic vinegar
- 28 oz. tomatoes, diced & undrained

Directions:

1. Spray the cooking pot with cooking spray.

2. Season the beef with salt and pepper and add it to the cooking pot.

3. Top the beef with onion and herbs to cover it evenly. Sprinkle the garlic overall then add the vinegar and tomatoes, do not stir.

4. Add the lid and set to slow cook on high. Cook 4 hours or until beef is tender. Stir to mix and serve over pasta or rice.

Nutrition Info:
- Calories 200,Total Fat 9g,Total Carbs 9g,Protein 26g,Sodium 218mg.

Beef And Garbanzo Bean Chili

Servings: 10
Cooking Time: 45 Min
Ingredients:
- 1 pound garbanzo beans; soaked overnight, rinsed /900g
- 2 ½ pounds ground beef /1150g
- 1 can tomato puree /180ml
- 1 small jalapeño with seeds; minced
- 6 garlic cloves; minced
- 2 onions, finely chopped
- 2 ½ cups beef broth /625ml
- ¼ cup chili powder /32.5g
- 2 tbsp ground cumin /30g
- 1 tbsp olive oil /15ml
- 1 tsp garlic powder /5g
- ¼ tsp cayenne pepper /1.25g
- 1 tsp dried oregano /5g
- 2 tsp salt /10g
- 1 tsp smoked paprika /5g

Directions:
1. Add the garbanzo beans to the Foodi and pour in cold water to cover 1 inch. Seal the pressure lid, choose Pressure, set to High, and set the timer to 20 minutes. Press Start. When ready, release the pressure quickly.
2. Drain beans and rinse with cold water. Set aside. Wipe clean the Foodi and set to Sear/Sauté, set to Medium High, and choose Start/Stop to preheat the pot. Press Start. Warm olive oil, add in onion, and cook for 3 minutes until soft.
3. Add jalapeño, ground beef, and minced garlic, and stir-fry for 5 minutes until everything is cooked through. Stir in chili powder, kosher salt, garlic powder, paprika, cumin, oregano, and cayenne pepper, and cook until soft, about 30 seconds. Pour beef broth, garbanzo beans, and tomato paste into the pot.
4. Seal the pressure lid, choose Pressure, set to High, and set the timer to 20 minutes; press Start. When ready, release pressure naturally for about 10 minutes. Open the lid, press Sear/Sauté, and cook as you stir until desired consistency is attained. Spoon chili into bowls and serve.

Caribbean Pork Pot

Servings: 6
Cooking Time: 15 Minutes
Ingredients:
- 1 tbsp. olive oil
- 1 ½ lb. pork tenderloin, cut in ¾-inch cubes
- 20 oz. chunked pineapple in juice, drained with liquid reserved
- 8 oz. water chestnuts, drained & sliced
- 1 cup fresh broccoli florets
- 1 red bell pepper, cut in ¾-inch strips
- 2 tbsp. soy sauce, low sodium
- 1 tbsp. vinegar
- 1 tbsp. ketchup
- 2 tbsp. cornstarch
- 2 tbsp. sugar

Directions:
1. Add the oil to the cooking pot and set to sauté on med-high heat.
2. Add the pork and cook 4-5 minutes until no longer pink, stirring frequently.
3. Add the pineapple, water chestnuts, broccoli, and bell pepper and cook, stirring frequently, 6-8 minutes or until vegetables are tender-crisp.
4. In a small bowl, whisk together reserved pineapple juice, soy sauce, vinegar, ketchup, cornstarch, and sugar until smooth. Stir into pork mixture and cook 4 minutes until sauce has thickened. Serve immediately.

Nutrition Info:
- Calories 266, Total Fat 6g, Total Carbs 41g, Protein 26g, Sodium 263mg.

Butter Pork Chops

Servings: 4
Cooking Time: 10 Minutes
Ingredients:
- 4 pork chops
- Black pepper and salt, to taste
- 2 tablespoons butter
- 2 teaspoons garlic, minced
- 1/2 cup herbed chicken stock
- 1/2 cup heavy whip cream
- 1/2 a lemon, juiced

Directions:
1. Season the four pork chops with black pepper and salt.
2. Select "Sauté" mode on Ninja Foodi and add oil to heat up.
3. Add pork chops and sauté both sides until the golden, total for 6 minutes.
4. Remove thighs to a platter and keep it on the side.
5. Add garlic and cook for 2 minutes.
6. Whisk in chicken stock, heavy cream, lemon juice and bring the sauce to simmer and reintroduce the pork chops.
7. Lock and secure the Ninja Foodi's lid and cook for 10 minutes on "HIGH" pressure.
8. Release pressure naturally over 10 minutes.
9. Serve warm and enjoy.

Nutrition Info:
- Calories: 294; Fat: 26g; Carbohydrates: 4g; Protein: 12g

Chinese Bbq Ribs

Servings: 6
Cooking Time: 8 Hours
Ingredients:
- 4 tbsp. hoisin sauce
- 4 tbsp. oyster sauce
- 2 tbsp. soy sauce, low sodium
- 2 tbsp. rice wine
- 2 lbs. pork ribs, cut in 6 pieces
- Nonstick cooking spray
- 2-inch piece fresh ginger, grated
- 3 green onions, sliced
- 2 tbsp. honey

Directions:
1. In a large bowl, whisk together hoisin sauce, oyster sauce, soy sauce, and rice wine. Add the ribs and turn to coat. Cover and refrigerate overnight.
2. Spray the cooking pot with cooking spray.
3. Add the ribs and marinade. Top with ginger and green onions. Add the lid and set to slow cook on low. Cook 6-8 hours or until ribs are tender.
4. Transfer ribs to a serving plate. Spray the rack with the cooking spray and place in the pot. Lay the ribs, in a single layer, on the rack and brush with honey.
5. Add the tender-crisp lid and set to broil. Cook 3-4 minutes to caramelize the ribs. Serve.

Nutrition Info:
- Calories 135,Total Fat 4g,Total Carbs 6g,Protein 17g,Sodium 419mg.

Brisket Chili Verde

Servings:4
Cooking Time: 19 Minutes
Ingredients:
- 1 tablespoon vegetable oil
- ½ white onion, diced
- 1 jalapeño pepper, diced
- 1 teaspoon garlic, minced
- 1 pound brisket, cooked
- 1 can green chile enchilada sauce
- 1 can fire-roasted diced green chiles
- Juice of 1 lime
- 1 teaspoon seasoning salt
- ½ teaspoon ground chipotle pepper

Directions:
1. Select SEAR/SAUTÉ and set temperature to HI. Select START/STOP to begin and allow to preheat for 5 minutes.
2. Add oil to the pot and allow to heat for 1 minute. Add the onion, jalapeño, and garlic. Sauté for 3 minutes or until onion is translucent.
3. Add the brisket, enchilada sauce, green chiles, lime juice, salt, and chipotle powder. Mix well.
4. Assemble the pressure lid, making sure the pressure release valve is in the SEAL position.
5. Select PRESSURE and set to HI. Set the time to 15 minutes. Select START/STOP to begin.
6. When cooking is complete, quick release the pressure by turning the pressure release valve to the VENT position. Carefully remove the lid when the unit has finished releasing pressure.

Nutrition Info:
- Calories: 427,Total Fat: 16g,Sodium: 1323mg,Carbohydrates: 30g,Protein:41g.

Beef Stew With Beer

Servings: 4
Cooking Time: 60 Min
Ingredients:
- 2 lb. beef stewed meat; cut into bite-size pieces /900g
- 1 packet dry onion soup mix
- 2 cloves garlic; minced
- 2 cups beef broth /500ml
- ¼ cup flour /32.5g
- 1 medium bottle beer
- 3 tbsp butter/45g
- 2 tbsp Worcestershire sauce /30ml
- 1 tbsp tomato paste /15g
- Salt and black pepper to taste

Directions:
1. In a zipper bag, add beef, salt, all-purpose flour, and pepper. Close the bag up and shake it to coat the meat well with the mixture. Select Sear/Sauté mode on the Foodi. Melt the butter, and brown the beef on both sides, for 5 minutes.
2. Pour the broth to deglaze the bottom of the pot. Stir in tomato paste, beer, Worcestershire sauce, and the onion soup mix.
3. Close the lid, secure the pressure valve, and select Pressure mode on High pressure for 25 minutes. Press Start/Stop to start cooking.
4. Once the timer is done, do a natural pressure release for 10 minutes, and then a quick pressure release to let out any remaining steam.
5. Open the pressure lid and close the crisping lid. Cook on Broil mode for 10 minutes. Spoon the beef stew into serving

bowls and serve with over a bed of vegetable mash with steamed greens.

Meatballs With Marinara Sauce

Servings: 6
Cooking Time: 35 Min
Ingredients:
- 1½ pounds ground beef /675g
- 1 egg
- 3 cups marinara sauce /750ml
- ⅓ cup warm water /88ml
- ¾ cup grated Parmigiano-Reggiano cheese /98g
- ½ cup bread crumbs /65g
- ½ cup capers /65g
- 2 tbsp fresh parsley /30g
- ¼ tsp dried oregano /1.25g
- ¼ tsp garlic powder /1.25g
- 1 tsp olive oil /5ml
- salt and ground black pepper to taste

Directions:
1. In a large bowl, mix ground beef, garlic powder, pepper, oregano, bread crumbs, egg, and salt; shape into meatballs. Warm the oil on Sear/Sauté. Add meatballs to the oil and brown for 2-3 minutes and all sides.
2. Pour water and marinara sauce over the meatballs. Seal the pressure lid, choose Pressure, set to High, and set the timer to 10 minutes. Press Start.
3. When ready, release the pressure quickly. Serve in large bowls topped with capers and Parmigiano-Reggiano cheese.

Pork Chops With Gravy

Servings: 5
Cooking Time: 10 Minutes
Ingredients:
- 5 pork chops
- 1 tablespoon olive oil
- 1 teaspoon salt
- 1/2 teaspoon pepper
- 1/2 teaspoon garlic powder
- 2 cups beef broth
- 1 packet ranch dressing mix
- 10-1/2 oz. cream of chicken soup
- 1 packet brown gravy mix
- 2 tablespoons corn starch
- 2 tablespoons water

Directions:
1. Season both sides of the pat dried pork chops with salt, pepper and garlic powder.
2. Pour the olive oil into the Ninja Foodi. Set it to sauté.
3. Brown the pork chops on both sides. Remove and set aside.
4. Pour the beef broth to deglaze the pot.
5. Stir in the rest of the ingredients except the corn starch. Seal the pot.
6. Set it to pressure. Cook at "HIGH" pressure for 8 minutes. Release the pressure naturally.
7. Remove the pork chops. Turn the pot to sauté. Stir in the corn starch.
8. Simmer to thicken. Pour the gravy over the pork chops.

Nutrition Info:
- Calories: 357; Fat: 26.8g; Carbohydrate 6g; Protein: 21.6g

Polish Sausage & Sauerkraut

Servings: 6
Cooking Time: 7 Hours
Ingredients:
- 2 tbsp. olive oil
- 1 onion, chopped
- ½ lb. bacon, chopped
- ½ lb. smoked Polish sausage, cut in 1-inch pieces
- 1 head cabbage, chopped
- 1 lb. sauerkraut, rinsed & drained
- 1 cup beef broth, low sodium
- 2 bay leaves
- 1 cup dry red wine

Directions:
1. Add the oil to the cooking pot and set to sauté on medium heat.
2. Add the onions and cook, stirring occasionally, until onions are golden. Use a slotted spoon to transfer onions to a bowl.
3. Add bacon to the pot and cook 2-3 minutes. Add sausage and cook until nicely browned, about 5 minutes. Use a slotted spoon to transfer meat to the bowl with onions. Drain off any remaining fat.
4. Add the cabbage, sauerkraut, and broth to the pot and mix well. Add the lid and set to slow cook on low. Cook 4 hours.
5. Stir in the onion mixture, bay leaves, and wine. Recover and cook another 2-3 hours until vegetables are tender. Discard bay leaves, stir and serve.

Nutrition Info:
- Calories 390,Total Fat 27g,Total Carbs 16g,Protein 15g,Sodium 1607mg.

Meatballs With Spaghetti Sauce

Servings: 6
Cooking Time: 20 Min
Ingredients:
- 2 lb. ground beef /900g
- 1 cup grated Parmesan cheese /130g
- 4 cups spaghetti sauce /1000ml
- 1 cup breadcrumbs /130g
- 1 cup water /250ml
- 2 cloves garlic; minced
- 2 eggs, cracked into a bowl
- 1 onion, finely chopped
- 3 tbsp milk /45ml
- 1 tbsp olive oil /15ml
- 1 tsp dried oregano /5g
- Salt and pepper, to taste

Directions:
1. In a bowl, add beef, onion, breadcrumbs, parmesan, eggs, garlic, milk, salt, oregano, and pepper. Mix well with hands and shape bite-size balls.
2. Open the pot, and add the spaghetti sauce, water and the meatballs. Close the lid, secure the pressure valve, and select Steam mode on High pressure for 6 minutes. Press Start/Stop.
3. Once the timer is done, do a natural pressure release for 5 minutes, then do a quick pressure release to let out any extra steam, and open the lid. Dish the meatball sauce over cooked pasta and serve.

Beef Stroganoff

Servings:6
Cooking Time: 55 Minutes
Ingredients:
- 2 tablespoons unsalted butter
- 1 yellow onion, diced
- 4 cups cremini mushrooms, sliced
- 2 pounds beef stew meat, cut in 1- to 2-inch cubes
- 2 teaspoons freshly ground black pepper
- 2 sprigs fresh thyme
- 2 tablespoons soy sauce
- 2 cups chicken stock
- 1 package egg noodles
- 2 tablespoons cornstarch
- 2 tablespoons water
- ½ cup sour cream

Directions:
1. Select SEAR/SAUTÉ and set to MED. Select START/STOP to begin. Let preheat for 3 minutes.
2. Add the butter, onion, and mushrooms and sauté for 5 minutes.
3. Add the beef, black pepper, thyme, soy sauce, and chicken stock. Simmer for 2 to 3 minutes. Assemble pressure lid, making sure the pressure release valve is in the SEAL position.
4. Select PRESSURE and set to HI. Set time to 10 minutes. Select START/STOP to begin.
5. When pressure cooking is complete, quick release the pressure by turning the pressure release valve to the VENT position. Carefully remove lid when unit has finished releasing pressure.
6. Add the egg noodles. Stir well. Assemble pressure lid, making sure the pressure release valve is in the SEAL position.
7. Select PRESSURE and set to HI. Set time to 5 minutes. Select START/STOP to begin.
8. In a small bowl, mix the cornstarch and water until smooth.
9. When pressure cooking is complete, quick release the pressure by turning the pressure release valve to the VENT position. Carefully remove lid when unit has finished releasing pressure.
10. Stir in cornstarch until incorporated. Stir in the sour cream. Serve immediately.

Nutrition Info:
- Calories: 448,Total Fat: 16g,Sodium: 605mg,Carbohydrates: 35g,Protein: 41g.

Steak And Chips

Servings: 4
Cooking Time: 50 Min
Ingredients:
- 4 potatoes; cut into wedges
- 4 rib eye steaks
- 1 tbsp olive oil /15ml
- 1 tsp sweet paprika /5g
- 1 tsp salt; divided /5g
- 1 tsp ground black pepper /5g
- Cooking spray

Directions:
1. Put the Crisping Basket in the pot. Close the crisping lid. Choose Air Crisp, set the temperature to 390°F or 199°C, and set the time to 5 minutes. Press Start. Meanwhile, rub all over with olive oil. Put the potatoes in the preheated Crisping Basket and season with ½ tsp or 2.5g of salt and ½ tsp or 2.5g of black pepper and sweet paprika.
2. Close the crisping lid. Choose Air Crisp, set the temperature to 400°F or 205°C, and set the time to 35 minutes. Choose Start/Stop to begin baking.

3. Season the steak on both sides with the remaining salt and black pepper. When done cooking, remove potatoes to a plate.
4. Grease the Crisping Basket with cooking spray and put the steaks in the basket.
5. Close the crisping lid. Choose Air Crisp, set the temperature to 400°F or 205°C, and set the time to 8 minutes. Choose Start/Stop to begin grilling.
6. When ready, check the steaks for your preferred doneness and cook for a few more minutes if needed. Take out the steaks from the basket and rest for 5 minutes. Serve the steaks with the potato wedges and the steak sauce.

Crispy Roast Pork

Servings: 4
Cooking Time: 50 Min
Ingredients:
- 4 pork tenderloins
- ¾ tsp garlic powder /3.75g
- 1 tsp five spice seasoning /5g
- ½ tsp white pepper /2.5g
- 1 tsp salt /5g
- Cooking spray

Directions:
1. Place the pork, white pepper, garlic powder, five seasoning, and salt into a bowl and toss to coat. Leave to marinate at room temperature for 30 minutes.
2. Place the pork into the Foodi basket, greased with cooking spray, close the crisping lid and cook for 20 minutes at 360 °F or 183°C. After 10 minutes, turn the tenderloins. Serve hot.

Sausage With Celeriac And Potato Mash

Servings: 4
Cooking Time: 45 Min
Ingredients:
- 4 potatoes, peeled and diced
- 4 pork sausages
- 1 onion
- 2 cups vegetable broth /500ml
- 1 cup celeriac; chopped /130g
- ¼ cup milk /62.5ml
- ½ cup water /125ml
- 1 tbsp heavy cream /15ml
- 1 tbsp olive oil /15ml
- 2 tbsp butter /30g
- 1 tsp Dijon mustard /5g
- ½ tsp dry mustard powder /2.5g
- Fresh flat-leaf parsley; chopped
- salt and ground black pepper to taste

Directions:
1. Warm oil on Sear/Sauté. Add in sausages and cook for 1 to 2 minutes for each side until browned. Set the sausages to a plate. To the same pot, add onion and cook for 3 minutes until fragrant.
2. Add sausages on top of onions and pour water and broth over them. Place a trivet over onions and sausages. Put potatoes and celeriac in the steamer basket and transfer it to the trivet.
3. Seal the pressure lid, choose Pressure, set to High, and set the timer to 11 minutes. Press Start. When ready, release the pressure quickly.
4. Transfer potatoes and celeriac to a bowl and set sausages on a plate and cover them with aluminum foil. Using a potato masher, mash potatoes and celeriac together with black pepper, milk, salt and butter until mash becomes creamy and fluffy. Adjust the seasonings.
5. Set your Foodi to Sear/Sauté. Add the onion mixture and bring to a boil. Cook for 5 to 10 minutes until the mixture is reduced and thickened. Into the gravy, stir in dry mustard, salt, pepper, mustard and cream. Place the mash in 4 bowls in equal parts, top with a sausage or two, and gravy. Add parsley for garnishing.

Carne Guisada

Servings: 4
Cooking Time: 45 Minutes
Ingredients:
- 3 pounds beef stew
- 3 tablespoon seasoned salt
- 1 tablespoon oregano chilli powder
- 1 tablespoon cumin
- 1 pinch crushed red pepper
- 2 tablespoons olive oil
- 1/2 medium lime, juiced
- 1 cup beef bone broth
- 3 ounces tomato paste
- 1 large onion, sliced

Directions:
1. Trim the beef stew to taste into small bite-sized portions.
2. Toss the beef stew pieces with dry seasoning.
3. Select "Sauté" mode on your Ninja Foodi and stir in oil; allow the oil to heat up.
4. Add seasoned beef pieces and brown them.
5. Combine the browned beef pieces with the rest of the ingredients.

6. Lock the Ninja foodi's lid and cook on "HIGH" pressure for 3 minutes.
7. Release the pressure naturally.
8. Enjoy.

Nutrition Info:
- Protein: 33g; Carbohydrates: 11g; Fats: 12g; Calories: 274

Lamb Tagine

Servings: 8
Cooking Time: 55 Minutes

Ingredients:
- 1 cup couscous
- 2 cups water
- 3 tablespoons extra-virgin olive oil, divided
- 2 yellow onions, diced
- 3 garlic cloves, minced
- 2 pounds lamb stew meat, cut into 1- to 2-inch cubes
- 1 cup dried apricots, sliced
- 2 cups chicken stock
- 2 tablespoons ras el hanout seasoning
- 1 can chickpeas, drained
- Kosher salt
- Freshly ground black pepper
- 1 cup toasted almonds, for garnish

Directions:
1. Place the couscous in the pot and pour in the water. Assemble pressure lid, making sure the pressure release valve is in the SEAL position.
2. Select PRESSURE and set to HI. Set time to 5 minutes. Select START/STOP to begin.
3. When pressure cooking is complete, quick release the pressure by turning the pressure release valve to the VENT position. Carefully remove lid when unit has finished releasing pressure.
4. Stir 1 tablespoon of oil into the couscous, then transfer the couscous to a bowl.
5. Select SEAR/SAUTÉ and set to MD:HI. Select START/STOP to begin. Let preheat for 3 minutes
6. Add the remaining 2 tablespoons of oil, onion, garlic, and lamb. Sauté for 7 to 10 minutes, stirring frequently.
7. Add the apricots, chicken stock, and ras el hanout. Stir to combine. Assemble pressure lid, making sure the pressure release valve is in the SEAL position.
8. Select PRESSURE and set to HI. Set time to 30 minutes. Select START/STOP to begin.
9. When pressure cooking is complete, quick release the pressure by turning the pressure release valve to the VENT position. Carefully remove lid when unit has finished releasing pressure.
10. Stir in the chickpeas.
11. Select SEAR/SAUTÉ and set to MD:LO. Select START/STOP to begin. Let the mixture simmer for 10 minutes. Season with salt and pepper.
12. When cooking is complete, ladle the tagine over the couscous. Garnish with the toasted almonds.

Nutrition Info:
- Calories: 596, Total Fat: 21g, Sodium: 354mg, Carbohydrates: 65g, Protein: 39g.

Beef Broccoli

Servings: 6
Cooking Time: 16 Minutes

Ingredients:
- 1-1/2 lb. beef chuck roast boneless, trimmed and sliced
- Black pepper and salt to taste
- 2 teaspoons olive oil
- 1 onion, chopped
- 4 cloves garlic, minced
- 3/4 cup beef broth
- 1/2 cup soy sauce
- 1/3 cup erythritol
- 2 tablespoons sesame oil
- 1 lb. broccoli florets
- 3 tablespoons water
- 3 tablespoons corn starch

Directions:
1. Season the beef strips with black pepper and salt.
2. Stir in the olive oil to the Ninja Foodi. Switch it to sauté.
3. Add the onion and saute for 1 minute. Stir in the garlic and cook for 30 seconds.
4. Stir in the beef and cook in batches until brown on both sides.
5. Deglaze the pot with broth and soy sauce.
6. Stir in the erythritol and sesame oil. Cover the pot.
7. Set it to pressure. Cook at "HIGH" pressure for 12 minutes.
8. Release the pressure naturally. Stir in the broccoli. Seal the pot.
9. Cook at "HIGH" pressure for 3 minutes. Release the pressure quickly.
10. Mix corn starch with water and add to the pot.
11. Simmer until the sauce has thickened.
12. Serve warm.

Nutrition Info:
- Calories: 563; Fat: 38.1g; Carbohydrate: 10.7g; Protein: 34.1g

Tender Beef & Onion Rings

Servings: 6
Cooking Time: 25 Minutes
Ingredients:
- 2 lb. chuck roast, cubed
- ¼ cup soy sauce, low sodium
- 1 tbsp. lemon juice
- ½ tsp pepper
- 1 cup water
- 3 tbsp. olive oil
- 3 cloves garlic, chopped fine
- 1 onion, sliced & separated in rings

Directions:
1. In a large bowl, combine beef, soy sauce, lemon juice, and pepper, mix well. Cover and let sit 1 hour.
2. Add the beef mixture to the cooking pot. Stir in water. Add the lid and set to pressure cook on high. Set timer for 20 minutes. When the timer goes off, use natural release to remove the pressure.
3. Use a slotted spoon to transfer beef to a bowl.
4. Set cooker to sauté on medium heat. Cook until sauce reduces and thickens, about 3-4 minutes.
5. Stir in oil and garlic. Add the beef back to the pot and cook until sauce turns a light brown, about 4-5 minutes. Add the onion rings and cook 2 minutes, or until onions are almost soft. Serve.

Nutrition Info:
- Calories 529,Total Fat 29g,Total Carbs 4g,Protein 62g,Sodium 1059mg.

Baked Rigatoni With Beef Tomato Sauce

Servings: 4
Cooking Time: 75 Min
Ingredients:
- 2 pounds ground beef /900g
- 2 cans tomato sauce /720ml
- 16-ounce dry rigatoni /480g
- 1 cup cottage cheese /130g
- 1 cup shredded mozzarella cheese /130g
- ½ cup chopped fresh parsley /65g
- 1 cup water /250ml
- 1 cup dry red wine /250ml
- 1 tbsp butter /15g
- ½ tsp garlic powder /2.5g
- ½ tsp salt /2.5g

Directions:

1. Choose Sear/Sauté and set to High. Choose Start/Stop to preheat the pot. Melt the butter, add the beef and cook for 5 minutes, or until browned and cooked well. Stir in the tomato sauce, water, wine, and rigatoni; season with the garlic powder and salt.
2. Put the pressure lid together and lock in the Seal position. Choose Pressure, set to Low, and set the time to 2 minutes. Choose Start/Stop to begin cooking.
3. When the timer is done, perform a natural pressure release for 10 minutes, then a quick pressure release and carefully open the lid. Stir in the cottage cheese and evenly sprinkle the top of the pasta with the mozzarella cheese. Close the crisping lid.
4. Choose Broil, and set the time to 3 minutes. Choose Start/Stop to begin. Cook for 3 minutes, or until the cheese has melted, slightly browned, and bubbly. Garnish with the parsley and serve immediately.

Barbeque Sticky Baby Back Ribs With

Servings: 6
Cooking Time: 40 Min
Ingredients:
- 1 reversible rack baby back ribs; cut into bones
- 1/3 cup ketchup /88ml
- 1 cup barbecue sauce /250ml
- ½ cup apple cider /125ml
- 1 tbsp mustard powder /15g
- 1 tbsp smoked paprika /15g
- 2 tbsp olive oil /30ml
- 1 tbsp dried oregano/15g
- ½ tsp ground black pepper /2.5g
- ½ tsp salt /2.5g

Directions:
1. In a bowl, thoroughly combine salt, mustard powder, smoked paprika, oregano, and black pepper. Rub the mixture over the ribs. Warm oil on Sear/Sauté.
2. Add in the ribs and sear for 1 to 2 minutes for each side until browned. Pour apple cider and barbecue sauce into the pot. Turn the ribs to coat.
3. Seal the pressure lid, choose Pressure, set to High, and set the timer to 30 minutes. Press Start. When ready, release the pressure quickly.
4. Place the Cook & Crisp Basket in the pot. Close the crisping lid, choose Air Crisp, set the temperature to 390°F or 199°C, and the time to 5 minutes.
5. Place the ribs with the sauce in the Cook & Crisp Basket. Close the Crisping Lid. Preheat the unit by selecting Air Crisp, setting the temperature to 390°F or 199°C, and setting

the time to 7 minutes. Press Start. When ready, the ribs should be sticky with a brown dark color. Transfer the ribs to a serving plate. Baste with the sauce to serve.

Tender Butter Beef

Servings: 12
Cooking Time: 8 Hours
Ingredients:
- 3 lbs. beef stew meat
- 1/3 cup butter
- 1 ¼ oz. dry onion soup mix
- ¼ cup beef broth, low sodium
- 1 tbsp. cornstarch

Directions:
1. Place beef and butter the cooking pot. Sprinkle onion soup mix over the meat.
2. Add the lid and set to slow cook on low. Cook 7-8 hours, stirring occasionally, untl beef is tender.
3. In a small bowl, whisk together broth and cornstarch until smooth. Stir into beef mixture completely and let cook 10 minutes or until sauce has thickened. Serve over cooked rice or quinoa.

Nutrition Info:
- Calories 197,Total Fat 10g,Total Carbs 3g,Protein 25g,Sodium 388mg.

Herbed Lamb Chops

Servings: 4
Cooking Time: 30 Min
Ingredients:
- 4 lamb chops
- 1 garlic clove, peeled
- ½ tbsp oregano /2.5g
- 1 tbsp plus /5g
- ½ tbsp thyme /2.5g
- 2 tsp olive oil /10ml
- ½ tsp salt /2.5g
- ¼ tsp black pepper /1.25g

Directions:
1. Coat the garlic clove with 1 tsp of olive oil and cook in the Foodi for 10 minutes on Air Crisp mode. Meanwhile, mix the herbs and seasonings with the remaining olive oil.
2. Using a towel, squeeze the hot roasted garlic clove into the herb mixture and stir to combine. Coat the lamb chops with the mixture well, and place in the Foodi.
3. Close the crisping lid and cook for about 8 to 12 minutes on Air Crisp mode at 390 °F or 199°C, until crispy on the outside.

Garlicky Pork Chops

Servings: 2
Cooking Time: 10 Minutes
Ingredients:
- 1 tablespoon coconut butter
- 1 tablespoon coconut oil
- 2 teaspoons cloves garlic, grated
- 2 teaspoons parsley, chopped
- Black pepper and salt to taste
- 4 pork chops, sliced into strips

Directions:
1. Combine all the ingredients except the pork strips. Mix well.
2. Marinate the pork in the mixture for 1 hour. Put the pork on the Ninja Foodi basket.
3. Set it inside the pot. Seal with the crisping lid. Choose air crisp function.
4. Cook at 400 °For 10 minutes.

Nutrition Info:
- Calories: 388; Fat: 23.3g; Carbohydrate: 0.5g; Protein: 18.1g

Beef Bulgogi

Servings: 4
Cooking Time: 10 Minutes
Ingredients:
- 1 lb. lean ground beef
- 10 cloves garlic, chopped
- 1 onion, chopped fine
- 4 tbsp. soy sauce, low sodium
- 2 tbsp. mirin
- 2 tbsp. sugar
- 1 tbsp. apricot jam
- ½ tsp pepper
- 1 tbsp. olive oil
- 5 green onions, chopped
- 1 tsp sesame seeds
- 1 tsp sesame oil

Directions:
1. In a large bowl, combine beef, garlic, onion, soy sauce, mirin, sugar, jam, and pepper, mix well.
2. Add oil to the cooking pot and set to sauté on med-high heat.
3. Add the beef mixture and cook, breaking up the beef with a spatula, 8-10 minutes until meat is fully cooked and all liquid has evaporated.

4. Stir in the green onions. Turn off the heat and add sesame seeds and sesame oil, toss to distribute and serve immediately.

Nutrition Info:
- Calories 419,Total Fat 28g,Total Carbs 19g,Protein 23g,Sodium 602mg.

Beef Congee

Servings: 6
Cooking Time: 1 Hr
Ingredients:
- 2 pounds ground beef /900g
- 1 piece fresh ginger; minced
- 2 cloves garlic; minced
- 6 cups beef stock /1500ml
- 1 cup jasmine rice /130g
- 1 cup kale, roughly chopped /130g
- 1 cups water /250ml
- salt and ground black pepper to taste
- Fresh cilantro; chopped

Directions:
1. Run cold water and rinse rice. Add garlic, rice, and ginger into the Foodi. Pour water and stock into the pot and spread the beef on top of rice.
2. Seal the pressure lid, choose Pressure, set to High, and set the timer to 30 minutes. Press Start. Once ready, release pressure naturally for 10 minutes.
3. Stir in kale to obtain the desired consistency. Add pepper and salt for seasoning. Divide into serving plates and top with cilantro.

Southern Sweet Ham

Servings: 12
Cooking Time: 8 Hours
Ingredients:
- 5 ½ lb. ham, bone-in & cooked
- 1 cup apple cider
- ½ cup dark brown sugar
- 1/3 cup bourbon
- ¼ cup honey
- ¼ cup Dijon mustard
- 4 sprigs fresh thyme

Directions:
1. Place the ham in the cooking pot.
2. In a small bowl, whisk together cider, brown sugar, bourbon, honey, and mustard until smooth. Pour over the ham. Scatter the thyme around the ham.
3. Add the lid and set to slow cook on low. Cook 8 hours or until ham is very tender. Transfer ham to cutting board and let rest 10-15 minutes.
4. Pour the cooking liquid through fine mesh sieve into a bowl. Pour back into the cooking pot. Set to sauté on med-high heat and bring to a simmer, cook 10 minutes or until reduced, stirring occasionally.
5. Slice the ham and serve topped with sauce.

Nutrition Info:
- Calories 372,Total Fat 10g,Total Carbs 20g,Protein 45g,Sodium 2000mg.

Chipotle Beef Brisket

Servings: 4
Cooking Time: 1 Hr 10 Min
Ingredients:
- 2 pounds, beef brisket /900g
- 1 cup beef broth/250ml
- ¼ cup red wine /62.5ml
- 2 tbsp olive oil /30ml
- 1 tbsp Worcestershire sauce /15ml
- ½ tsp ground cumin /2.5g
- ½ tsp garlic powder /2.5g
- 1 tsp chipotle powder /5g
- ¼ tsp cayenne pepper/1.25g
- 2 tsp smoked paprika /10g
- ½ tsp dried oregano /2.5g
- ½ tsp salt /2.5g
- ½ tsp ground black pepper /2.5g
- A handful of parsley; chopped

Directions:
1. In a bowl, combine oregano, cumin, cayenne pepper, garlic powder, salt, paprika, pepper, Worcestershire sauce and chipotle powder; rub the seasoning mixture on the beef to coat. Warm olive oil on Sear/Sauté. Add in beef and cook for 3 to 4 minutes each side until browned completely. Pour in beef broth and red wine.
2. Seal the pressure lid, choose Pressure, set to High, and set the timer to 50 minutes. Press Start. Release the pressure naturally, for about 10 minutes.
3. Place the beef on a cutting board and Allow cooling for 10 minutes before slicing. Arrange the beef slices on a serving platter, pour the cooking sauce over and scatter with parsley to serve.

Adobo Steak

Servings: 4
Cooking Time: 25 Minutes
Ingredients:
- 2 cups of water
- 8 steaks, cubed, 28 ounces pack
- Pepper to taste
- 1 and 3/4 teaspoons adobo seasoning
- 1 can 8 ounces tomato sauce
- 1/3 cup green pitted olives
- 2 tablespoons brine
- 1 small red pepper
- 1/2 a medium onion, sliced

Directions:
1. Chop peppers, onions into ¼ inch strips.
2. Prepare beef by seasoning with adobo and pepper.
3. Add into Ninja Foodi.
4. Stir in remaining ingredients and Lock lid, cook on "HIGH" pressure for 25 minutes.
5. Release pressure naturally.
6. Serve and enjoy.

Nutrition Info:
- Calories: 154; Fat: 5g; Carbohydrates: 3g; Protein: 23g

Lamb Chops And Potato Mash

Servings: 8
Cooking Time: 40 Min
Ingredients:
- 5 potatoes, peeled and chopped
- 4 cilantro leaves, for garnish
- 8 lamb cutlets
- 1 green onion; chopped
- ⅓ cup milk /88ml
- 1 cup beef stock /250ml
- 3 sprigs rosemary leaves; chopped
- 3 tbsp butter, softened /45g
- 1 tbsp olive oil /15ml
- 1 tbsp tomato puree /15ml
- salt to taste

Directions:
1. Rub rosemary leaves and salt to the lamb chops. Warm oil and 2 tbsp or 30g of butter on Sear/Sauté. Add in the lamb chops and cook for 1 minute for each side until browned; set aside on a plate.
2. In the pot, mix tomato puree and green onion; cook for 2-3 minutes. Add beef stock into the pot to deglaze, scrape the bottom to get rid of any browned bits of food.
3. Return lamb cutlets alongside any accumulated juices to the pot. Set a reversible rack on lamb cutlets. Place steamer basket on the reversible rack. Arrange potatoes in the steamer basket.
4. Seal the pressure lid, choose Pressure, set to High, and set the timer to 4 minutes. Press Start.
5. When ready, release the pressure quickly. Remove trivet and steamer basket from pot. In a high speed blender, add potatoes, milk, salt, and remaining tbsp butter. Blend well until you obtain a smooth consistency.
6. Divide the potato mash between serving dishes. Lay lamb chops on the mash. Drizzle with cooking liquid obtained from pressure cooker; apply cilantro sprigs for garnish.

One Pot Ham & Rice

Servings: 4
Cooking Time: 10 Minutes
Ingredients:
- 2 tbsp. water
- ¼ cup celery, chopped
- ¼ cup onion, chopped
- ¼ cup green bell pepper, chopped
- ¼ cup fresh parsley, chopped
- ½ tsp garlic powder
- ¼ tsp pepper
- Nonstick cooking spray
- 5 slices lean deli ham, chopped
- 2 cups brown rice, cooked
- 2 eggs, beaten
- 1 green onion, sliced

Directions:
1. Add water to the cooking pot and set to sauté on medium heat.
2. Add the celery, onion, peppers, parsley, garlic powder, and pepper and cook until water evaporates and vegetables are tender, about 4-5 minutes.
3. Spray the vegetables and pot with cooking spray. Add ham and cook 1-2 minutes until heated through.
4. Stir in rice and mix well. Pour in eggs and cook until they are completely set, stirring occasionally.
5. Sprinkle with green onions and serve immediately.

Nutrition Info:
- Calories 184,Total Fat 4g,Total Carbs 25g,Protein 11g,Sodium 413mg.

Southern-style Lettuce Wraps

Servings: 6
Cooking Time: 30 Minutes
Ingredients:
- 3 pounds boneless pork shoulder, cut into 1- to 2-inch cubes
- 2 cups light beer
- 1 cup brown sugar
- 1 teaspoon chipotle chiles in adobo sauce
- 1 cup barbecue sauce
- 1 head iceberg lettuce, quartered and leaves separated
- 1 cup roasted peanuts, chopped or ground
- Cilantro leaves

Directions:
1. Place the pork, beer, brown sugar, chipotle, and barbecue sauce in the pot. Assemble pressure lid, making sure the pressure release valve is in the SEAL position.
2. Select PRESSURE and set to HI. Set the timer to 30 minutes. Select START/STOP to begin.
3. When pressure cooking is complete, quick release the pressure by turning the pressure release valve to the VENT position. Carefully remove lid when unit has finished releasing pressure.
4. Using a silicone-tipped utensil, shred the pork in the pot. Stir to mix the meat in with the sauce.
5. Place a small amount of pork in a piece of lettuce. Top with peanuts and cilantro to serve.

Nutrition Info:
- Calories: 811, Total Fat: 58g, Sodium: 627mg, Carbohydrates: 22g, Protein: 45g.

Swedish Meatballs With Mashed Cauliflower

Servings: 6
Cooking Time: 1 Hr
Ingredients:
- ¾ pound ground pork /337.5g
- ¾ pound ground beef /337.5g
- 1 head cauliflower; cut into florets
- 1 large egg, beaten
- ½ onion; minced
- 1 ¾ cup heavy cream; divided /438ml
- ¼ cup bread crumbs /32.5g
- ¼ cup sour cream /62.5ml
- 2 cups beef stock /500ml
- ¼ cup fresh chopped parsley /32.5g
- 1 tbsp water /15ml
- 4 tbsp butter; divided /60g
- 3 tbsp flour /45g
- ½ tsp red wine vinegar /2.5ml
- salt and freshly ground black pepper to taste

Directions:
1. In a mixing bowl, mix ground beef, onion, salt, bread crumbs, ground pork, egg, water, and pepper; shape meatballs. Warm 2 tbsp or 30g of butter on Sear/Sauté.
2. Add meatballs and cook until browned, about 5-6 minutes. Set aside to a plate. Pour beef stock in the pot to deglaze, scrape the pan to get rid of browned bits of food.
3. Stir vinegar and flour with the liquid in the pot until smooth; bring to a boil. Stir ¾ cup heavy cream into the liquid. Arrange meatballs into the gravy. Place trivet onto meatballs. Arrange cauliflower florets onto the trivet.
4. Seal the pressure lid, choose Pressure, set to High, and set the timer to 8 minutes. Press Start. When ready, release the pressure quickly.
5. Set the cauliflower in a mixing bowl. Add in the remaining 1 cup or 250ml heavy cream, pepper, sour cream, salt, and 2 or 30g tbsp butter and use a potato masher to mash the mixture until smooth.
6. Spoon the mashed cauliflower onto serving bowls; place a topping of gravy and meatballs. Add parsley for garnishing.

Gingery Beef And Broccoli

Servings: 4
Cooking Time: 70 Min
Ingredients:
- 2 pounds skirt steak; cut into strips /900g
- 1 head broccoli, trimmed into florets
- 3 scallions, thinly sliced
- 4 garlic cloves; minced
- ½ cup coconut aminos /65g
- ½ cup water, plus 3 tbsp. /170ml
- ⅔ cup dark brown sugar /88g
- 1 tbsp olive oil /15ml
- 2 tbsp cornstarch /30g
- ½ tsp ginger puree /2.5ml

Directions:
1. Choose Sear/Sauté on the pot and set to Medium High; hit Start/Stop to preheat the pot. Pour the oil and beef in the preheated pot and brown the beef strips on both sides, about 5 minutes in total. Remove the beef from the pot and set aside.
2. Add the garlic to the oil and Sear/Sauté for 1 minute or until fragrant. Stir in the coconut aminos, ½ cup or 125ml of water, brown sugar, and ginger to the pot. Mix evenly and add the beef. Seal the pressure lid, choose Pressure, set to

High, and set the time to 10 minutes. Choose Start/Stop to begin cooking.

3. Meanwhile, in a small bowl whisk combine the cornstarch and the remaining water.

4. When done cooking, perform a quick pressure release. Choose Sear/Sauté and set to Medium Low. Choose Start/Stop. Pour in the cornstarch mixture and stir continuously until the sauce becomes syrupy. Add the broccoli, stir to coat in the sauce, and cook for another 5 minutes. Once ready, garnish with scallions, and serve.

Beef And Cabbage Stew

Servings: 4
Cooking Time: 30 Min
Ingredients:
- 1 lb. ground beef /450g
- 1 large head cabbage; cut in chunks
- 1 cup diced tomatoes /130g
- 1 ½ cup beef broth /375ml
- ¼ cup Plain vinegar /62.5ml
- 1 cup rice /130g
- ½ cup chopped onion /65g
- 4 cloves garlic; minced
- 1 bay leaf
- 2 tbsp Worcestershire sauce /30ml
- 2 tbsp butter /30g
- 1 tbsp paprika powder/15g
- 1 tbsp dried oregano /15g
- Salt and black pepper to taste
- Chopped parsley to garnish

Directions:
1. Set the Foodi on Sear/Sauté mode. Melt the butter and add the beef. Brown it for about 6 minutes and add in the onions, garlic, and bay leaf. Stir and cook for 2 more minutes.
2. Stir in the oregano, paprika, salt, pepper, rice, cabbage, vinegar, broth, and Worcestershire sauce. Cook for 3 minutes, stirring occassionally.
3. Add the tomatoes but don't stir. Close the lid, secure the pressure valve, and select Pressure Cook mode on High for 5 minutes. Press Start/Stop.
4. Once the timer is done, let the pot sit closed for 5 minutes and then do a quick pressure. Open the lid. Stir the sauce, remove the bay leaf, and adjust the seasoning with salt. Dish the cabbage sauce in serving bowls and serve with bread rolls.

Rosemary Crusted Lamb Chops

Servings: 3
Cooking Time: 10 Minutes
Ingredients:
- 2 tbsp. fresh rosemary, chopped fine
- 2 tsp salt
- 1 tsp pepper
- 1 clove garlic, chopped fine
- 4 tbsp. olive oil, divided
- 1 lb. lamb chops

Directions:
1. In a small bowl, combine rosemary, salt, pepper, garlic, and 2 tablespoon oil, mix well. Coat lamb on both sides. Cover and let sit 30 minutes.
2. Add the remaining oil to the cooking pot and set to seat on medium heat.
3. If you are using double rib chops, sear on all sides, about 2-3 minutes per side for medium rare chops. If you are using single rib chops cook about 1 minute on each side for medium rare. For a medium chop, turn off the heat and cover the pot, let lamb sit for 5 minutes.
4. Transfer chops to a plate and tent with foil, let rest 5 minutes before serving.

Nutrition Info:
- Calories 272,Total Fat 23g,Total Carbs 1g,Protein 16g,Sodium 938mg.

Speedy Pork Stir Fry

Servings: 4
Cooking Time: 5 Minutes
Ingredients:
- 2 tbsp. soy sauce, low sodium
- 1 tsp sugar
- 1 tsp cornstarch
- 1 lb. pork loin, cut in ¼-inch strips
- 4 tbsp. peanut oil
- 5 cloves garlic, sliced thin
- 1 tsp. red pepper flakes
- 10 green onions, sliced
- ½ tsp sesame oil

Directions:
1. In a large bowl, whisk together soy sauce, sugar, and cornstarch until smooth.
2. Add the pork to the bowl and toss to coat. Let sit for 10 minutes.
3. Add the oil to the cooking pot and set to sauté on med-high heat.
4. Add the garlic and pepper flakes and cook, stirring, about 30 seconds or until garlic starts to brown.
5. Add the pork mixture and cook until meat is no longer pink, stirring constantly.

6. Add the green onions and cook 1 minute more. Turn off the heat and stir in the sesame oil. Serve as is or over hot, cooked rice.

Nutrition Info:
- Calories 182,Total Fat 12g,Total Carbs 3g,Protein 15g,Sodium 279mg.

Braised Short Ribs With Creamy Sauce

Servings: 6
Cooking Time: 1 Hr 55 Min
Ingredients:
- 3 pounds beef short ribs /1350g
- 1 can diced tomatoes /435g
- 1 celery stalk; chopped
- 3 garlic cloves; chopped
- 1 onion; chopped
- 1 large carrot; chopped
- 2 cups beef broth /500ml
- ½ cup cheese cream /65g
- ½ cup dry red wine /125ml
- ¼ cup red wine vinegar /62.5ml
- 2 bay leaves
- 2 tbsp olive oil /30ml
- 2 tbsp chopped parsley /30g
- ¼ tsp red pepper flakes /1.25g
- 2 tsp salt; divided /10g
- 1½ tsp freshly ground black pepper; divided /7.5g

Directions:
1. Season your short ribs with 1 tsp black pepper and 1 tsp salt. Warm olive oil on Sear/Sauté. Add in short ribs and sear for 3 minutes each side until browned. Set aside on a bowl.
2. Drain everything only to be left with 1 tbsp of the remaining fat from the pot. Set on Sear/Sauté, and stir-fry garlic, carrot, onion, and celery in the hot fat for 4 to 6 minutes until fragrant.
3. Stir in broth, wine, red pepper flakes, vinegar, tomatoes, bay leaves, and remaining pepper and salt; turn the Foodi to Sear/Sauté on Low and bring the mixture to a boil.
4. With the bone-side up, lay short ribs into the braising liquid. Seal the pressure lid, choose Pressure, set to High, and set the timer to 40 minutes. Press Start.
5. When ready, release the pressure quickly. Set the short ribs on a plate. Get rid of bay leaves. Skim and get rid of the fat from the surface of braising liquid.
6. Using an immersion blender, blend the liquid for 1 minute; add cream cheese, pepper and salt and blitz until smooth Arrange the ribs onto a serving plate, pour the sauce over and top with parsley.

Sausage With Noodles And Braised Cabbage

Servings: 4
Cooking Time: 35 Min
Ingredients:
- 1½ pounds smoked sausage; cut into 4 pieces /675g
- 3 ounces serrano ham; diced /90g
- 5 ounces wide egg noodles /150g
- 4 cups shredded green cabbage /520g
- 1 small onion; sliced
- ⅓ cup dry white wine/88ml
- 1 cup chicken stock /250ml
- 1 tsp salt /5g
- ¼ tsp black pepper /1.25g
- Cooking spray

Directions:
1. On the Foodi, choose Sear/Sauté and adjust to Medium. Press Start to preheat the pot for 5 minutes. Put the ham in the pot and cook for 6 minutes until crisp. Using a slotted spoon, transfer the ham to a paper towel-lined plate to drain, leaving the fat in the pot.
2. Sauté the onion to the pot for about 2 minutes or until the onion starts to soften. Pour in the wine and simmer until the wine reduces slightly while scraping the bottom of the pot with a wooden spoon to let off any browned bits.
3. Pour in the chicken stock, salt, black pepper, and noodles. Stir, while pushing the noodles as much as possible into the sauce. Put the cabbage on top of the noodles and the sausages on the cabbage.
4. Lock the pressure lid into place and seal. Choose Pressure; adjust the pressure to High and the cook time to 3 minutes.
5. When the cooking time is over, do a quick pressure release, and carefully open the lid. Stir the noodles and cabbage and adjust the taste with seasoning.
6. Grease the reversible rack with cooking spray and fix in the upper position of the pot. Transfer the sausages to the rack.
7. Close the crisping lid and Choose Bake/Roast; adjust the temperature to 390°F or 199°C and the cook time to 8 minutes; press Start.
8. After 4 minutes, open the lid and check the sausages. When browned, turn the sausages, close the lid, and cook to brown the other side. Ladle the cabbage and noodles into a bowl and top with the bacon. Serve with the sausages.

Fish & Seafood Recipes

Mediterranean Cod

Servings: 4
Cooking Time: 20 Min
Ingredients:
- 4 fillets cod
- 1 bunch fresh thyme sprigs
- 1 pound cherry tomatoes, halved /450g
- 1 clove garlic, pressed
- 1 cup white rice /130g
- 2 cups water /500ml
- 1 cup Kalamata olives /130g
- 2 tbsp pickled capers /30g
- 1 tbsp olive oil; divided /15ml
- 1 tsp olive oil /15ml
- 1 pinch ground black pepper
- 3 pinches salt

Directions:
1. Line a parchment paper to the steamer basket of your Foodi. Place about half the tomatoes in a single layer on the paper. Sprinkle with thyme, reserving some for garnish. Arrange cod fillets on the top of tomatoes. Sprinkle with a little bit of olive oil.
2. Spread the garlic, pepper, salt, and remaining tomatoes over the fish. In the pot, mix rice and water. Lay a trivet over the rice and water. Lower steamer basket onto the trivet.
3. Seal the pressure lid, choose Pressure, set to High, and set the timer to 7 minutes. Press Start. When ready, release the pressure quickly.
4. Remove the steamer basket and trivet from the pot. Use a fork to fluff rice. Plate the fish fillets and apply a garnish of olives, reserved thyme, pepper, remaining olive oil, and capers. Serve with rice.

Pepper Smothered Cod

Servings: 4
Cooking Time: 20 Minutes
Ingredients:
- ¼ cup olive oil
- ½ cup red onion, chopped
- 2 tsp garlic, chopped
- ½ cup red bell pepper, chopped
- ½ cup green bell pepper, chopped
- Salt and pepper, to taste
- 4 tbsp. flour
- 2 cups chicken broth, low sodium
- ½ cup tomato, seeded & chopped
- 2 tsp fresh thyme, chopped
- 4 cod filets

Directions:
1. Set to sauté on med-high heat and add oil to the cooking pot.
2. Add the onion and garlic and cook, stirring, 1 minute.
3. Add the peppers, salt, and pepper and cook, stirring frequently about 2-3 minutes, or until peppers start to get tender.
4. Stir in the flour and cook until it turns a light brown.
5. Pour in the broth and cook, stirring, until smooth and the sauce starts to thicken. Stir in tomato and thyme.
6. Season the fish with salt and pepper. Place in the pot and add the lid. Cook 3-4 minutes, then turn the fish over and cook another 3-4 minute or until fish flakes easily with a fork. Transfer the fish to serving plates and top with sauce. Serve immediately.

Nutrition Info:
- Calories 249,Total Fat 14g,Total Carbs 11g,Protein 19g,Sodium 1107mg.

Glazed Salmon

Servings: 4
Cooking Time: 25 Minutes
Ingredients:
- 1-2 Coho salmon filets
- 1 cup of water
- 1/4 cup of soy sauce
- 1/4 cup brown erythritol
- 1 tablespoon choc zero maple syrup
- 1 and 1/2 tablespoons ginger roots, minced
- 1/2 teaspoon white pepper
- 2 tablespoons cornstarch
- 1/4 cup of cold water

Directions:
1. Preheat Ninja Foodi by pressing the "GRILL" option and setting it to "HIGH" for 15 minutes.
2. Take a medium saucepan over medium heat, combine sauce ingredients. except for salmon, cornstarch and cold water and bring to a low boil.
3. Then add cornstarch and water in another bowl, whisk cornstarch mixture slowly into sauce until it thickens.
4. Stir in one chunk of pecan wood to the hot coal of your grill.
5. Brush sauce onto the salmon filet.

6. Place on the grill grate, then close the hood.
7. Cook for 15 minutes.
8. Brush the salmon with another coat of sauce.
9. Serve and enjoy.

Nutrition Info:
- Calories: 163; Fat: 0g; Carbohydrates: 15g; Protein: 0g

New England Lobster Rolls

Servings: 4
Cooking Time: 20 Minutes

Ingredients:
- 4 lobster tails
- ¼ cup mayonnaise
- 1 celery stalk, minced
- Zest of 1 lemon
- Juice of 1 lemon
- ¼ teaspoon celery seed
- Kosher salt
- Freshly ground black pepper
- 4 split-top hot dog buns
- 4 tablespoons unsalted butter, at room temperature
- 4 leaves butter lettuce

Directions:
1. Insert Cook & Crisp Basket into the pot and close the crisping lid. Select AIR CRISP, set temperature to 375°F, and set time to 15 minutes. Select START/STOP to begin. Let preheat for 5 minutes.
2. Once unit has preheated, open lid and add the lobster tails to the basket. Close the lid and cook for 10 minutes.
3. In a medium bowl, mix together the mayonnaise, celery, lemon zest and juice, and celery seed, and add salt and pepper.
4. Fill a large bowl with a tray of ice cubes and enough water to cover the ice.
5. When cooking is complete, open lid. Transfer the lobster into the ice bath for 5 minutes. Close lid to keep unit warm.
6. Spread butter on the hot dog buns. Open lid and place the buns in the basket. Close crisping lid.
7. Select AIR CRISP, set temperature to 375°F, and set time to 4 minutes. Select START/STOP to begin.
8. Remove the lobster meat from the shells and roughly chop. Place in the bowl with the mayonnaise mixture and stir.
9. When cooking is complete, open lid and remove the buns. Place lettuce in each bun, then fill with the lobster salad.

Nutrition Info:
- Calories: 408, Total Fat: 24g, Sodium: 798mg, Carbohydrates: 22g, Protein: 26g.

Tangy Catfish & Mushrooms

Servings: 4
Cooking Time: 10 Minutes

Ingredients:
- 2 tbsp. olive oil
- 4 catfish fillets
- 1/8 tsp salt
- ¼ tsp pepper
- 1 tbsp. fresh lemon juice
- ¼ lb. mushrooms, sliced
- 1 onion, chopped
- ¼ cup fresh parsley, chopped

Directions:
1. Add the oil to the cooking pot and set to sauté on medium heat.
2. Sprinkle the fish with salt and pepper and add to the pot. Drizzle lemon juice over the top.
3. Add the remaining ingredients and cook 3-4 minutes. Turn fish over and cook another 3-4 minutes or until it flakes with a fork and mushrooms are tender.
4. Transfer fish to serving plates and top with mushrooms. Serve immediately.

Nutrition Info:
- Calories 187, Total Fat 10g, Total Carbs 4g, Protein 20g, Sodium 131mg.

Spiced Red Snapper

Servings: 6
Cooking Time: 20 Minutes

Ingredients:
- Nonstick cooking spray
- 1 onion, sliced
- 14 ½ oz. stewed tomatoes, undrained, chopped
- 1/3 cup dry white wine
- 3 tbsp. fresh lemon juice
- 1 tsp cumin
- 1/8 tsp cinnamon
- 6 red snapper fillets

Directions:
1. Spray the cooking pot with cooking spray.
2. Set to sauté on med-high heat and add the onion. Cook, stirring, 3-4 minutes or until onions are soft.
3. Add tomatoes, wine, lemon juice, cumin,, and cinnamon and cook about 5 minutes or until sauce has thickened slightly.

4. Add the fish and spoon sauce over the top. Add the lid and reduce heat to medium. Cook 8-10 minutes until fish flakes with a fork.
5. Transfer fish to serving plates and top with sauce. Serve immediately.

Nutrition Info:
- Calories 155,Total Fat 2g,Total Carbs 8g,Protein 25g,Sodium 201mg.

Crab Alfredo

Servings: 4
Cooking Time: 25 Minutes

Ingredients:
- ½ cup butter, unsalted
- ½ red bell pepper, seeded & chopped
- 2 tbsp. cream cheese, low fat
- 2 cups half and half
- ¾ cup parmesan cheese, reduced fat
- 1 tsp garlic powder
- 2 cups penne pasta, cooked & drained
- 6 oz. lump crab meat, cooked

Directions:
1. Add butter to the cooking pot and set to sauté on medium heat.
2. When butter has melted, add bell pepper and cook until it starts to soften, about 3-5 minutes.
3. Add the cream cheese and cook, stirring until it melts.
4. Stir in half and half and parmesan cheese, and garlic powder until smooth. Reduce heat to low and simmer 15 minutes.
5. Stir in cooked penne and crab meat and cook just until heated through. Serve immediately.

Nutrition Info:
- Calories 388,Total Fat 23g,Total Carbs 26g,Protein 19g,Sodium 613mg.

Cajun Shrimp

Servings: 4
Cooking Time: 7 Minutes

Ingredients:
- 1 ¼ pound shrimp
- 1/4 teaspoon cayenne pepper
- 1/2 teaspoon old bay seasoning
- 1/4 teaspoon smoked paprika
- 1 pinch of salt
- 1 tablespoon olive oil

Directions:
1. Preheat Ninja Foodi by pressing the "AIR CRISP" option and setting it to "390 °F" and timer to 10 minutes.
2. Dip the shrimp into a spice mixture and oil.
3. Transfer the prepared shrimp to your Ninja Foodi Grill cooking basket and cook for 5 minutes.
4. Serve and enjoy.

Nutrition Info:
- Calories: 170; Fat: 2g; Carbohydrates: 5g; Protein: 23g

Shrimp And Chorizo Potpie

Servings:6
Cooking Time: 23 Minutes

Ingredients:
- ¼ cup unsalted butter
- ½ large onion, diced
- 1 celery stalk, diced
- 1 carrot, peeled and diced
- 8 ounces chorizo, fully cooked, cut into ½-inch wheels
- ¼ cup all-purpose flour
- 16 ounces frozen tail-off shrimp, cleaned and deveined
- ¾ cup chicken stock
- 1 tablespoon Cajun spice mix
- ½ cup heavy (whipping) cream
- Sea salt
- Freshly ground black pepper
- 1 refrigerated store-bought pie crust, at room temperature

Directions:
1. Select SEAR/SAUTÉ and set to MD:HI. Select START/STOP to begin. Let preheat for 5 minutes.
2. Add the butter. Once melted, add the onion, celery, carrot, and sausage, and cook until softened, about 3 minutes. Stir in the flour and cook 2 minutes, stirring occasionally.
3. Add the shrimp, stock, Cajun spice mix, and cream and season with salt and pepper. Stir until sauce thickens and bubbles, about 3 minutes.
4. Lay the pie crust evenly on top of the filling, folding over the edges if necessary. Make a small cut in center of pie crust so that steam can escape during baking. Close crisping lid.
5. Select BROIL and set time to 10 minutes. Select START/STOP to begin.
6. When cooking is complete, open lid and remove pot from unit. Let rest 10 to 15 minutes before serving.

Nutrition Info:
- Calories: 528,Total Fat: 37g,Sodium: 776mg,Carbohydrates: 19g,Protein: 28g.

Crab Cakes

Servings: 4
Cooking Time: 55 Min
Ingredients:
- ½ cup cooked crab meat /65g
- ¼ cup breadcrumbs /32.5g
- ¼ cup chopped celery /32.5g
- ¼ cup chopped red pepper /32.5g
- ¼ cup chopped red onion /32.5g
- Zest of ½ lemon
- 3 tbsp mayonnaise /45mk
- 1 tbsp chopped basil /15g
- 2 tbsp chopped parsley /30g
- Old Bay seasoning, as desired
- Cooking spray

Directions:
1. Place all Ingredients in a large bowl and mix well until thoroughly incorporated. Make 4 large crab cakes from the mixture and place on a lined sheet. Refrigerate for 30 minutes, to set.
2. Spay the air basket with cooking spray and arrange the crab cakes in it.
3. Close the crisping lid and cook for 7 minutes on each side on Air Crisp at 390 °F or 199°C.

Salmon Florentine

Servings: 4
Cooking Time: 15 Minutes
Ingredients:
- 2 tbsp. olive oil, divided
- 4 salmon filets
- ½ tsp salt
- ¼ tsp pepper
- 4 cloves garlic, chopped fine
- 10 oz. fresh spinach
- ½ tbsp. lemon juice
- ¼ tsp basil

Directions:
1. Add 1 tablespoon oil to the cooking pot and set to sauté on medium heat.
2. Season salmon with salt and pepper and add to the pot. Cook 8-10 minutes or until fish flakes easily with a fork, turning over halfway through cooking time. Transfer to a plate.
3. Add remaining oil and let heat up. Add remaining ingredients and cook 2-3 minutes until spinach is wilted.
4. Place fish on serving plates and top with spinach mixture. Serve immediately.

Nutrition Info:
- Calories 436,Total Fat 30g,Total Carbs 4g,Protein 37g,Sodium 448mg.

Fried Salmon

Servings: 1
Cooking Time: 13 Min
Ingredients:
- 1 salmon fillet.
- ¼ tsp garlic powder /1.25g
- 1 tbsp soy sauce /15ml
- Salt and pepper

Directions:
1. Combine the soy sauce with the garlic powder, salt, and pepper. Brush the mixture over the salmon. Place the salmon onto a sheet of parchment paper and inside the Ninja Foodi.
2. Close the crisping lid and cook for 10 minutes on Air Crisp at 350 °F or 177°C, until crispy on the outside and tender on the inside.

Spicy Grilled Shrimp

Servings: 4
Cooking Time: 6 Minutes
Ingredients:
- 1 teaspoon garlic salt
- 1/2 teaspoon black pepper
- 1 tablespoon paprika
- 1 tablespoon garlic powder
- 2 tablespoons olive oil
- 1-pound jumbo shrimps, peeled and deveined
- 2 tablespoons brown erythritol

Directions:
1. Take a mixing bowl and stir in the listed ingredients to mix well.
2. Let it chill and marinate for 30-60 minutes.
3. Preheat Ninja Foodi by pressing the "GRILL" option and setting it to "MED" and timer to 6 minutes.
4. Let it preheat until you hear a beep.
5. Set prepared shrimps over grill grate, Lock and secure the Ninja Foodi's lid and cook for 3 minutes, flip and cook for 3 minutes more.
6. Serve and enjoy.

Nutrition Info:
- Calories: 370; Fat: 27g; Carbohydrates: 23g; Protein: 6g

Caribbean Catfish With Mango Salsa

Servings: 4
Cooking Time: 10 Minutes
Ingredients:
- 1 red pepper, roasted & chopped
- 1 mango, peeled & chopped
- 1 orange, peeled & chopped
- ¼ cup cilantro, chopped fine
- ¼ cup green onion, chopped fine
- 1 tsp jalapeno, chopped
- 1 tbsp. olive oil
- 1 tsp salt, divided
- ½ tsp pepper, divided
- ½ cup panko bread crumbs
- ½ cup coconut, shredded
- 4 catfish fillets
- Nonstick cooking spray

Directions:
1. In a medium bowl, combine red pepper, mango, orange, cilantro, green onion, jalapeno, olive oil, ¼ tsp salt, and ¼ tsp pepper. Cover and let sit until ready to use.
2. In a shallow dish, stir together bread crumbs and coconut until combined.
3. Season catfish with salt and pepper. Dredge in bread crumbs coating both sides thoroughly.
4. Spray the fryer basket with cooking spray. Lay the catfish in the basket in a single layer. Add the tender-crisp lid and set to air fry on 375°F. Cook fish 8-10 minutes per side until golden brown and fish flakes easily with a fork.
5. Transfer fish to serving plates and top with mango salsa. Serve immediately.

Nutrition Info:
- Calories 357, Total Fat 12g, Total Carbs 34g, Protein 30g, Sodium 534mg.

Italian Flounder

Servings: 4
Cooking Time: 70 Min
Ingredients:
- 4 flounder fillets
- 3 slices prosciutto; chopped
- 2 bags baby kale /180g
- ½ small red onion; chopped
- ½ cup whipping cream /125ml
- 1 cup panko breadcrumbs /130g
- 2 tbsps chopped fresh parsley /30g
- 3 tbsps unsalted butter, melted and divided /45g
- ¼ tsp fresh ground black pepper /1.25g
- ½ tsp salt; divided /2.5g

Directions:
1. On the Foodi, choose Sear/Sauté and adjust to Medium. Press Start to preheat the inner pot. Add the prosciutto and cook until crispy, about 6 minutes. Stir in the red onions and cook for about 2 minutes or until the onions start to soften. Sprinkle with half of the salt.
2. Fetch the kale into the pot and cook, stirring frequently until wilted and most of the liquid has evaporated, about 4-5 minutes. Mix in the whipping cream.
3. Lay the flounder fillets over the kale in a single layer. Brush 1 tbsp or 15ml of the melted butter over the fillets and sprinkle with the remaining salt and black pepper.
4. Close the crisping lid and choose Bake/Roast. Adjust the temperature to 300°F or 149°C and the cook time to 3 minutes. Press Start.
5. Combine the remaining butter, the parsley and breadcrumbs in a bowl.
6. When done cooking, open the crisping lid. Spoon the breadcrumbs mixture on the fillets.
7. Close the crisping lid and Choose Bake/Roast. Adjust the temperature to 400°F or 205°C and the cook time to 6 minutes. Press Start.
8. After about 4 minutes, open the lid and check the fish. The breadcrumbs should be golden brown and crisp. If not, close the lid and continue to cook for an additional two minutes.

Shrimp Fried Rice

Servings: 6
Cooking Time: 15 Minutes
Ingredients:
- 2 tbsp. sesame oil
- 2 tbsp. olive oil
- 1 lb. medium shrimp, peeled & deveined
- 1 cup frozen peas & carrots
- 1/2 cup corn
- 3 cloves garlic, chopped fine
- ½ tsp ginger
- 3 eggs, lightly beaten
- 4 cups brown rice, cooked
- 3 green onions, sliced
- 3 tbsp. tamari
- ½ tsp salt
- ½ tsp pepper

Directions:

1. Add the sesame and olive oils to the cooking pot and set to sauté on med-high heat.
2. Add the shrimp and cook 3 minutes, or until they turn pink, turning shrimp over halfway through. Use a slotted spoon to transfer shrimp to a plate.
3. Add the peas, carrots, and corn to the pot and cook 2 minutes until vegetables start to soften, stirring occasionally. Add the garlic and ginger and cook 1 minute more.
4. Push the vegetables to one side and add the eggs, cook to scramble, stirring frequently. Add the shrimp, rice, and onions and stir to mix all ingredients together.
5. Drizzle with tamari and season with salt and pepper, stir to combine. Cook 2 minutes or until everything is heated through. Serve immediately.

Nutrition Info:
- Calories 361,Total Fat 13g,Total Carbs 38g,Protein 24g,Sodium 1013mg.

Blackened Tilapia With Cilantro-lime Rice And Avocado Salsa

Servings:4
Cooking Time: 12 Minutes
Ingredients:
- 2 cups white rice, rinsed
- 2 cups water
- ¼ cup blackening seasoning
- 4 tilapia fillets
- 2 tablespoons freshly squeezed lime juice, divided
- 1 bunch cilantro, minced
- 1 tablespoon extra-virgin olive oil
- 2 avocados, diced
- 1 large red onion, diced
- 2 Roma tomatoes, diced
- Kosher salt
- Freshly ground black pepper

Directions:
1. Place the rice and water in the pot and stir. Assemble pressure lid, making sure the pressure release valve is in the SEAL position.
2. Select PRESSURE and set to HI. Set time to 2 minutes. Select START/STOP to begin.
3. Place the blackening seasoning on a plate. Dredge the tilapia fillets in the seasoning.
4. When pressure cooking is complete, allow pressure to naturally release for 10 minutes. After 10 minutes, quick release remaining pressure by turning the pressure release valve to the VENT position. Carefully remove lid when unit has finished releasing pressure.
5. Transfer the rice to a large bowl and stir in 1 tablespoon of lime juice and half the cilantro. Cover the bowl with aluminum foil and set aside.
6. Place the Reversible Rack in the pot and arrange tilapia fillets on top. Close crisping lid.
7. Select BROIL and set time to 10 minutes. Select START/STOP to begin.
8. In a medium bowl, stir together the remaining cilantro, remaining 1 tablespoon of lime juice, olive oil, avocado, onion, tomato, and season with salt and pepper.
9. When cooking is complete, open lid and lift the rack out of the pot. Serve the fish over the rice and top with avocado salsa.

Nutrition Info:
- Calories: 637,Total Fat: 19g,Sodium: 108mg,Carbohydrates: 89g,Protein: 30g.

Creamy Crab Soup

Servings: 4
Cooking Time: 45 Min
Ingredients:
- 2 lb. Crabmeat Lumps /900g
- 2 celery stalk; diced
- 1 white onion; chopped
- ¾ cup heavy cream /188ml
- ½ cup Half and Half cream /125ml
- 1 ½ cup chicken broth /375ml
- ¾ cup Muscadet /98g
- 6 tbsp butter /90g
- 6 tbsp flour /90g
- 3 tsp Worcestershire sauce /15ml
- 3 tsp old bay Seasoning /15ml
- 2 tsp Hot sauce /10ml
- 3 tsp minced garlic /15g
- Salt to taste
- Lemon juice to serve
- Chopped dill to serve

Directions:
1. Melt the butter on Sear/Sauté mode, and mix in the all-purpose flour, in a fast motion to make a rue. Add celery, onion, and garlic.
2. Stir and cook until soft and crispy; for 3 minutes. While stirring, gradually add the half and half cream, heavy cream, and broth.
3. Let simmer for 2 minutes. Add Worcestershire sauce, old bay seasoning, Muscadet, and hot sauce. Stir and let simmer for 15 minutes. Add the crabmeat and mix it well into the sauce.

4. Close the crisping lid and cook on Broil mode for 10 minutes to soften the meat.
5. Dish into serving bowls, garnish with dill and drizzle squirts of lemon juice over. Serve with a side of garlic crusted bread.

Salmon With Dill Chutney

Servings: 2
Cooking Time: 15 Min
Ingredients:
- 2 salmon fillets
- Juice from ½ lemon
- 2 cups water /500ml
- ¼ tsp paprika /1.25g
- salt and freshly ground pepper to taste
- For Chutney:
- ¼ cup extra virgin olive oil /62.5ml
- ¼ cup fresh dill /32.5g
- Juice from ½ lemon
- Sea salt to taste

Directions:
1. In a food processor, blend all the chutney Ingredients until creamy. Set aside. To your Foodi, add the water and place a reversible rack.
2. Arrange salmon fillets skin-side down on the steamer basket. Drizzle lemon juice over salmon and apply a seasoning of paprika.
3. Seal the pressure lid, choose Pressure, set to High, and set the timer to 3 minutes; press Start. When ready, release the pressure quickly. Season the fillets with pepper and salt, transfer to a serving plate and top with the dill chutney.

Shrimp & Asparagus Risotto

Servings: 4
Cooking Time: 25 Minutes
Ingredients:
- 1 tbsp. butter
- ½ onion, chopped fine
- 1 clove garlic, chopped fine
- 1 cup Arborio rice
- 5 cups water, divided
- 1 cup clam juice
- 1 tbsp. olive oil
- ½ lb. small shrimp, peeled & deveined
- ½ bunch asparagus, cut in 1-inch pieces
- ¼ cup parmesan cheese

Directions:
1. Add butter to cooking pot and set to sauté on medium heat. Once butter melts, add onion and garlic and cook 5 minutes, stirring frequently.
2. Add the rice and stir to coat with butter mixture. Transfer mixture to a 1-quart baking dish.
3. Pour 1 cup water and clam juice over rice mixture and cover tightly with foil.
4. Pour 2 cups water in the cooking pot and add the rack. Place the rice mixture on the rack, secure the lid and set to pressure cooking on high. Set timer for 10 minutes.
5. When timer goes off release the pressure quickly and remove the baking dish carefully. Drain out any remaining water.
6. Set the cooker back to sauté on med-high and heat the oil. Add the shrimp and asparagus and cook, stirring, just until shrimp start to turn pink.
7. Add the shrimp and asparagus to the rice and stir to mix well. Recover tightly with foil. Pour 2 cups water back in the pot and add the rack.
8. Place the rice mixture back on the rack and secure the lid. Set to pressure cooking on high and set the timer for 4 minutes.
9. When the timer goes off, release the pressure quickly. Remove the foil and stir. Serve immediately sprinkled with parmesan cheese.

Nutrition Info:
- Calories 362,Total Fat 11g,Total Carbs 45g,Protein 20g,Sodium 623mg.

Spicy "grilled" Catfish

Servings: 4
Cooking Time: 10 Minutes
Ingredients:
- Nonstick cooking spray
- 1 tbsp. fresh basil, chopped
- 1 tsp crushed red pepper flakes
- 1 tsp garlic powder
- ½ tsp salt
- ½ tsp pepper
- 4 catfish fillets
- 2 tbsp. olive oil

Directions:
1. Spray the rack with cooking spray and add to the cooking pot.
2. In a small bowl, combine all the spices and mix well.
3. Pat the fish dry with a paper towel. Rub both sides of the fish with the oil and coat with the seasoning mix.
4. Place the fish on the rack and add the tender-crisp lid. Set to roast on 350°F. Cook 7-9 minutes until fish flakes

with a fork, turning over halfway through cooking time. Serve immediately.

Nutrition Info:
- Calories 211,Total Fat 11g,Total Carbs 0g,Protein 26g,Sodium 359mg.

Seafood Chowder

Servings: 4
Cooking Time: 5 Hours

Ingredients:
- 2 cups clam juice
- 3 cups cauliflower, separated into florets
- 1 cup onion, sliced
- ½ cup celery, sliced
- 1/8 tsp saffron, crushed
- 2 cups skim milk, divided
- 8 oz. haddock filet, cut in 1-inch pieces
- 8 oz. cod filet, cut in 1-inch pieces
- ½ cup shrimp, peeled & deveined
- 1 tbsp. cornstarch
- Salt & white pepper, to taste
- 2 slices bacon, cooked crisp & crumbled

Directions:
1. Add the clam juice, vegetables, and saffron to the cooking pot and stir to mix.
2. Add the lid and set to slow cook on high. Cook 4-5 hours, stirring in 1 ½ cups milk in the last 30 minutes. Add the seafood in the last 15 minutes.
3. In a medium bowl, whisk together remaining milk and cornstarch until smooth. Stir into the chowder and continue cooking another 2-3 minutes until it thickens. Season with salt and pepper and serve topped with bacon.

Nutrition Info:
- Calories 245,Total Fat 7g,Total Carbs 15g,Protein 31g,Sodium 761mg.

Orange Glazed Cod & Snap Peas

Servings: 4
Cooking Time: 15 Minutes

Ingredients:
- 2 tsp olive oil
- 1 tsp ginger
- 2 cloves garlic, chopped fine
- 1 bunch green onions, sliced
- 2/3 cup orange juice, unsweetened
- 1/3 cup water
- 2 tsp soy sauce, low sodium
- 1 tbsp. sugar
- 4 cod fillets, 1-inch thick
- 2 cups sugar snap peas

Directions:
1. Add oil to the cooking pot and set to sauté on med-high heat.
2. Once oil is hot, add ginger, garlic, and half the green onions. Cook, stirring occasionally, 3 minutes or until garlic is soft.
3. Add orange juice, water, soy sauce, and sugar and mix well.
4. Add the rack to the pot. Place the fish in the baking pan and place on rack. Set to bake on 325°F. Add the tender-crisp lid and cook 5 minutes.
5. Add the peas on top of the fish. Recover and cook another 3-5 minutes or until fish flakes easily with a fork.
6. Transfer fish and peas to serving plates and top with sauce and the remaining green onions. Serve immediately.

Nutrition Info:
- Calories 157,Total Fat 3g,Total Carbs 13g,Protein 20g,Sodium 439mg.

Stuffed Cod

Servings: 4
Cooking Time: 40 Minutes

Ingredients:
- ½ cup bread crumbs
- 2 ½ tsp garlic powder, divided
- 1 ½ tsp onion powder, divided
- 1 tbsp. parsley
- ¼ cup parmesan cheese
- ½ tsp salt
- ½ lb. scallops, rinsed & dried
- 7 tbsp. butter, divided
- ½ lb. shrimp, peeled & deveined
- 1 tbsp. flour
- ¾ cup chicken broth, low sodium
- ½ tsp dill
- ½ cup sour cream
- ½ tbsp. lemon juice
- 4 cod filets, patted dry

Directions:
1. Set cooker to bake on 400°F. Place the rack in the cooking pot.
2. In a small bowl, combine bread crumbs, 2 teaspoons garlic powder, 1 teaspoon onion powder, parsley, parmesan cheese, and salt, mix well.
3. Place the scallops in a baking pan and pour 3 tablespoons melted butter over top. Add the bread crumb

mixture, and with a spatula mix together so scallops are coated on all sides.

4. Cover with foil and place in the cooking pot. Add the tender-crisp lid and bake 10 minutes.

5. Uncover and add the shrimp and 3 tablespoons butter to the scallops, use the spatula again to coat the shrimp. Recover the dish and bake another 10 minutes. Remove from cooking pot and uncover to cool.

6. In a small saucepan over medium heat, melt the remaining tablespoon of butter. Add the flour and cook, whisking, for 1 minute.

7. Whisk in broth, remaining garlic and onion powder, and dill until combined. Bring mixture just to boil, whisking constantly, and cook until thickened, about 5 minutes. Remove from heat let cool 5 minutes before stirring in sour cream and lemon juice.

8. Pour the scallop mixture onto a cutting board and chop. Add it back to the baking dish.

9. Spoon stuffing mixture onto the wide end of the fish filets and fold in half. Secure with a toothpick. Place on a small baking sheet.

10. Spoon a small amount of the sauce over fish and place on the rack in the cooking pot. Set to bake on 375°F. Add the tender-crisp lid and cook 20 minutes. Transfer to serving plates and top with more sauce. Serve immediately.

Nutrition Info:
- Calories 483, Total Fat 27g, Total Carbs 19g, Protein 41g, Sodium 1459mg.

Salmon, Cashew & Kale Bowl

Servings: 6
Cooking Time: 15 Minutes
Ingredients:
- 12 oz. salmon filets, skin off
- 2 tbsp. olive oil, divided
- ½ tsp salt
- ¼ tsp pepper
- 2 cloves garlic, chopped fine
- 4 cups kale, stems removed & chopped
- ½ cup carrot, grated
- 2 cups quinoa, cooked according to package directions
- ¼ cup cashews, chopped

Directions:
1. Place the rack in the cooking pot and set to bake on 400°F. Place a sheet of parchment paper on the rack.
2. Brush the salmon with 1 tablespoon of oil and season with salt and pepper. Place the fish on the parchment paper.

3. Add the tender-crisp lid and cook 15 minutes or until salmon reaches desired doneness. Transfer the fish to a plate and keep warm.

4. Set the cooker to sauté on medium heat and add the remaining oil. Once the oil is hot, add garlic, kale, and carrot and cook, stirring frequently, until kale is wilted and soft, about 2-3 minutes.

5. Add the quinoa and cashews and cook just until heated through. Spoon mixture evenly into bowl and top with a piece of salmon. Serve immediately.

Nutrition Info:
- Calories 294, Total Fat 17g, Total Carbs 18g, Protein 17g, Sodium 243mg.

Salmon With Almonds, Cranberries, And Rice

Servings: 4
Cooking Time: 10 Minutes
Ingredients:
- 1½ cups long-grain white rice, rinsed
- 1½ cups water
- ⅓ cup dry cranberries
- ⅓ cup slivered almonds
- Kosher salt
- 4 frozen salmon fillets
- ⅓ cup dry roasted sunflower seeds
- ¼ cup Dijon mustard
- ⅓ cup panko bread crumbs
- 1 tablespoon honey
- 1 tablespoon minced parsley

Directions:
1. Place the rice, water, cranberries, and almonds in the pot. Season with salt and stir. Place Reversible Rack in pot in the higher broil position. Place a circle of aluminum foil on top of the rack, then place the salmon fillets on the foil. Assemble pressure lid, making sure the pressure release valve is in the SEAL position.

2. Select PRESSURE and set to HI. Set time to 2 minutes. Select START/STOP to begin.

3. Add the sunflower seeds, mustard, bread crumbs, honey, and parsley to a small bowl and mix well.

4. When pressure cooking is complete, allow pressure to naturally release for 10 minutes. After 10 minutes, quick release remaining pressure by moving the pressure release valve to the VENT position. Carefully remove lid when unit has finished releasing pressure.

5. Using a spoon, spread a thick, even layer of the sunflower mixture across the top of each fillet. Close crisping lid.

6. Select BROIL and set time to 8 minutes. Select START/STOP to begin. When cooking is complete, open lid and remove the rack and salmon. Use a silicone-coated spatula to fluff the rice. Serve the salmon fillets over the rice.

Nutrition Info:
- Calories: 505, Total Fat: 10g, Sodium: 536mg, Carbohydrates: 75g, Protein: 28g.

Tuna & Avocado Patties

Servings: 6
Cooking Time: 20 Minutes

Ingredients:
- Nonstick cooking spray
- 1 avocado, peeled & pitted
- 10 oz. Albacore tuna, drained
- ¼ cup whole wheat bread crumbs
- ¼ cup red onion, chopped fine
- 2 tbsp. cilantro, chopped
- 1 tbsp. fresh lime juice
- 1 tsp hot sauce
- ½ tsp garlic powder
- ½ tsp salt
- 1 egg

Directions:
1. Spray the fryer basket with cooking spray.
2. In a large bowl, mash the avocado. Add the remaining ingredients and mix well. Form into 6 patties.
3. Place the patties in the basket. Add the tender-crisp lid and set to air fry on 400°F. Cook patties 15 minutes or until crisp and cooked through, turning over halfway through cooking time. Serve.

Nutrition Info:
- Calories 102, Total Fat 5g, Total Carbs 6g, Protein 10g, Sodium 269mg.

Awesome Shrimp Roast

Servings: 2
Cooking Time: 7 Minutes

Ingredients:
- 3 tablespoons chipotle in adobo sauce, minced
- ¼ teaspoon salt
- 1/4 cup BBQ sauce
- ½ orange, juiced
- ½ pound large shrimps

Directions:
1. Preheat Ninja Foodi by pressing the "Bake/Roast" mode and setting it to "400 °F" and timer to 7 minutes.
2. Let it preheat until you hear a beep.
3. Set shrimps over Grill Grate and lock lid, cook until the timer runs out.
4. Serve and enjoy.

Nutrition Info:
- Calories: 173; Fat: 2g; Carbohydrates: 21g; Protein: 17g

Oyster Stew

Servings: 4
Cooking Time: 12 Min

Ingredients:
- 3 jars shucked oysters in liqueur /300g
- 3 Shallots, minced
- 3 cloves garlic, minced
- 2 cups chopped celery /260g
- 2 cups bone broth /500ml
- 2 cups heavy cream /500ml
- 3 tbsp olive oil /45ml
- 3 tbsp chopped parsley /45g
- Salt and white pepper to taste

Directions:
1. Add oil, garlic, shallot, and celery. Stir-fry them for 2 minutes on Sear/Sauté mode, and add the heavy cream, broth, and oysters. Stir once or twice.
2. Close the lid, secure the pressure valve, and select Steam mode on High pressure for 3 minutes. Press Start/Stop. Once the timer has stopped, do a quick pressure release, and open the lid.
3. Season with salt and white pepper. Close the crisping lid and cook for 5 minutes on Broil mode. Stir and dish the oyster stew into serving bowls. Garnish with parsley and top with some croutons.

Parmesan Tilapia

Servings: 4
Cooking Time: 15 Min

Ingredients:
- ¾ cup grated Parmesan cheese /98g
- 4 tilapia fillets
- 1 tbsp olive oil /15ml
- 1 tbsp chopped parsley /15g
- ¼ tsp garlic powder /1.25g
- 2 tsp paprika /10g
- ¼ tsp salt /1.25g

Directions:
1. Mix parsley, Parmesan, garlic, salt, and paprika, in a shallow bowl. Brush the olive oil over the fillets, and then coat them with the Parmesan mixture.
2. Place the tilapia onto a lined baking sheet, and then into the Ninja Foodi.

3. Close the crisping lid and cook for about 4 to 5 minutes on all sides on Air Crisp mode at 350 °F or 177°C.

Panko Crusted Cod

Servings: 4
Cooking Time: 15 Minutes
Ingredients:
- 2 uncooked cod fillets
- 3 teaspoons kosher salt
- ¾ cup panko bread crumbs
- 2 tablespoons butter, melted
- 1/4 cup fresh parsley, minced
- 1 lemon. Zested and juiced

Directions:
1. Pre-heat your Ninja Foodi at 390 °F and place the Air Crisper basket inside.
2. Season cod and salt.
3. Take a suitable and stir in bread crumbs, parsley, lemon juice, zest, butter, and mix well.
4. Coat fillets with the bread crumbs mixture and place fillets in your Air Crisping basket.
5. Lock Air Crisping lid and cook on Air Crisp mode for 15 minutes at 360 °F.
6. Serve and enjoy.

Nutrition Info:
- Calories: 554; Fat: 24g; Carbohydrates: 5g; Protein: 37g

Drunken Saffron Mussels

Servings: 4
Cooking Time: 25 Minutes
Ingredients:
- 2 tablespoons vegetable oil
- 2 shallots, sliced
- 3 garlic cloves, minced
- 1 cup cherry tomatoes, halved
- 2 pounds fresh mussels, washed with cold water, strained, scrubbed, and debearded, as needed
- 2 cups white wine (chardonnay or sauvignon blanc)
- 2 cups heavy cream
- 1½ teaspoons cayenne pepper
- 1½ teaspoons freshly ground black pepper
- ½ teaspoon saffron threads
- 1 loaf sourdough bread, cut into slices, for serving

Directions:
1. Select SEAR/SAUTÉ and set the temperature to HI. Select START/STOP to begin and allow to preheat for 5 minutes.
2. Add oil to the pot and allow to heat for 1 minute. Add the shallots, garlic, and cherry tomatoes. Stir to ensure the ingredients are coated and sauté for 5 minutes.
3. Add the mussels, wine, heavy cream, cayenne, black pepper, and saffron threads to the pot.
4. Assemble the pressure lid, making sure the pressure release valve is in the VENT position.
5. Select STEAM and set the temperature to HI. Set the time to 20 minutes. Select START/STOP to begin.
6. When cooking is complete, carefully remove the lid.
7. Transfer the mussels and broth to bowls or eat straight from the pot. Discard any mussels that have not opened.
8. Serve with the bread and enjoy!

Nutrition Info:
- Calories: 882,Total Fat: 54g,Sodium: 769mg,Carbohydrates: 61g,Protein: 20g.

Flounder Veggie Soup

Servings: 10
Cooking Time: 20 Minutes
Ingredients:
- 2 cups water, divided
- 14 oz. chicken broth, low sodium
- 2 lbs. potatoes, peeled & cubed
- 1 onion, chopped
- 2 stalks celery, chopped
- 1 carrot, chopped
- 1 bay leaf
- 2 12 oz. cans evaporated milk, fat free
- 4 tbsp. butter
- 1 lb. flounder filets, cut in 1/2-inch pieces
- ½ tsp thyme
- ¼ tsp salt
- ¼ tsp pepper

Directions:
1. Add 1 ½ cups water, broth, potatoes, onion, celery, carrot, and the bay leaf to the cooking pot. Stir to mix.
2. Add the lid and set to pressure cooker on high. Set the timer for 8 minutes. When the timer goes off, use quick release to remove the lid.
3. Set cooker to sauté on med-low. Stir in milk, butter, fish, thyme, salt and pepper and bring to a boil.
4. In a small bowl, whisk together remaining water and cornstarch until smooth. Add to the soup and cook, stirring, until thickened. Discard the bay leaf and serve.

Nutrition Info:
- Calories 213,Total Fat 6g,Total Carbs 25g,Protein 14g,Sodium 649mg.

Tilapia & Tamari Garlic Mushrooms

Servings: 4
Cooking Time: 10 Minutes
Ingredients:
- 2 tbsp. sesame oil, divided
- 2 cloves garlic, chopped fine
- 2 cups mushrooms, sliced
- 4 tilapia fillets
- ½ tsp salt
- ¼ tsp pepper
- 1 tbsp. fresh lime juice
- 1 tbsp. tamari
- ¼ cup cilantro, chopped

Directions:
1. Add 1 tablespoon oil to the cooking pot and set to sauté on med-high heat.
2. Add the garlic and mushrooms and cook, stirring occasionally, 2-3 minutes.
3. Add the rack to the pot and top with a sheet of foil. Place the fish on the foil and brush with the remaining oil. Season with salt and pepper and drizzle lime juice over the tops.
4. Add the tender-crisp lid and set to roast on 350°F. Cook 5 minutes or until fish flakes with a fork and the liquid from the mushrooms has evaporated.
5. Transfer fish to serving plates. Stir the tamari into the mushrooms and spoon over fish. Garnish with cilantro and serve.

Nutrition Info:
- Calories 298,Total Fat 12g,Total Carbs 2g,Protein 44g,Sodium 610mg.

Clam Fritters

Servings: 4
Cooking Time: 10 Minutes
Ingredients:
- Nonstick cooking spray
- 1 1/3 cups flour
- 2 tsp baking powder
- 1 tsp Old Bay seasoning
- ¼ tsp cayenne pepper
- ¼ tsp salt
- ¼ tsp pepper
- 13 oz. clams, chopped
- 3 tbsp. clam juice
- 1 tbsp. lemon juice
- 2 eggs
- 1 ½ tbsp. chives, chopped
- 2 tbsp. milk

Directions:
1. Spray the fryer basket with cooking spray and add it to the cooking pot.
2. In a large bowl, combine flour, baking powder, Old Bay, cayenne pepper, salt, and pepper, mix well.
3. In a medium bowl, combine clams, clam juice, lemon juice, eggs, chives, and milk, mix well. Add the liquid ingredients to the dry ingredients and mix until combined.
4. Drop by spoonful into the fryer basket, don't over crowd them. Add the tender-crisp lid and set to air fry on 400°F. Cook 8-10 minutes until golden brown, turning over halfway through cooking time.

Nutrition Info:
- Calories 276,Total Fat 4g,Total Carbs 37g,Protein 21g,Sodium 911mg.

Almond Crusted Haddock

Servings: 4
Cooking Time: 30 Minutes
Ingredients:
- 1 tbsp. sugar
- ¾ tsp cinnamon
- ¼ tsp red pepper
- ½ tsp salt
- 1 ½ lbs. haddock filets
- 1 egg white, beaten
- 2 cups almonds, sliced
- 2 tbsp. butter
- ½ cup Amaretto liqueur

Directions:
1. In a small bowl, combine sugar, cinnamon, red pepper, and salt until combined. Use 1 teaspoon of the mixture to season the fish.
2. Spray the fryer basket with cooking spray and place it in the cooking pot.
3. In a shallow dish, beat the egg white.
4. In a separate shallow dish, place the almonds. Dip each filet in the egg white then coat with almonds. Place them in the fryer basket and spray them lightly with cooking spray.
5. Add the tender-crisp lid and set to air fry on 350°F. Cook the fish 5 minutes, then turn over and spray with cooking spray again. Cook another 2-3 minutes until golden brown. Transfer to serving plate and keep warm.
6. In a small saucepan over medium heat, melt the butter. Add the remaining sugar mixture and Amaretto to the pan. Reduce heat to low, and cook, stirring, 1-2 minutes until sauce has thickened. Pour over fish and serve immediately.

Nutrition Info:

- Calories 576,Total Fat 30g,Total Carbs 26g,Protein 38g,Sodium 715mg.

Chili Mint Steamed Snapper

Servings: 4
Cooking Time: 20 Minutes

Ingredients:
- 2 lb. whole snapper
- 2 tbsp. white wine
- 2 tbsp. soy sauce
- ¼ cup peanut oil
- 2 tsp ginger, cut in fine matchsticks
- 2 red chilies, sliced
- 1 cup fresh mint, chopped

Directions:
1. Pour water in the cooking pot and add the rack.
2. Place the fish in a baking pan and add to the cooker. Add the lid and set to steam for 15 minutes.
3. Transfer fish carefully to serving plate. Pour out any remaining water in the pot.
4. Add the wine and soy sauce to the pot and set to sauté on medium heat. Cook until hot but not boiling. Pour over fish.
5. Add the oil and let it get hot. Add the ginger and cook until crisp, about 1 minute. Turn off the heat and the chilies. Pour this mixture over the fish and sprinkle with mint. Serve immediately.

Nutrition Info:
- Calories 370,Total Fat 17g,Total Carbs 4g,Protein 48g,Sodium 405mg.

Kung Pao Shrimp

Servings: 4
Cooking Time: 15 Minutes

Ingredients:
- 1 tbsp. olive oil
- 1 red bell pepper, seeded & chopped
- 1 green bell pepper, seeded & chopped
- 3 cloves garlic, chopped fine
- 1 lb. large shrimp, peeled & deveined
- ¼ cup soy sauce
- 1 tsp sesame oil
- 1 tsp brown sugar
- 1 tsp Sriracha
- 1/8 tsp red pepper flakes
- 1 tsp cornstarch
- 1 tbsp. water
- ¼ cup peanuts
- ¼ cup green onions, sliced thin

Directions:
1. Add oil to the cooking pot and set to sauté on med-high heat.
2. Add the bell peppers and garlic and cook, 3-5 minutes, until pepper is almost tender.
3. Add the shrimp and cook until they turn pink, 2-3 minutes.
4. In a small bowl, whisk together soy sauce, sesame oil, brown sugar, Sriracha, and pepper flakes until combined.
5. In a separate small bowl, whisk together cornstarch and water until smooth. Whisk into sauce and pour over shrimp mixture. Add the peanuts.
6. Cook, stirring, until the sauce has thickened, about 2-3 minutes. Serve garnished with green onions.

Nutrition Info:
- Calories 212,Total Fat 11g,Total Carbs 10g,Protein 20g,Sodium 1729mg.

Pistachio Crusted Mahi Mahi

Servings: 6
Cooking Time: 20 Minutes

Ingredients:
- Nonstick cooking spray
- 6 fresh Mahi Mahi filets
- 2 tbsp. fresh lemon juice
- ½ tsp nutmeg
- ¼ tsp pepper
- ¼ tsp salt
- ½ cup pistachio nuts, chopped
- 2 tbsp. butter, melted

Directions:
1. Place the rack in the cooking pot. Lightly spray a small baking sheet with cooking spray.
2. Place the fish on the prepared pan. Season with lemon juice and spices. Top with pistachios and drizzle melted butter over the tops.
3. Place the pan on the rack and add the tender-crisp lid. Set to bake on 350°F. Cook fish 15-20 minutes or until it flakes easily with a fork. Serve immediately.

Nutrition Info:
- Calories 464,Total Fat 14g,Total Carbs 3g,Protein 77g,Sodium 405mg.

Shrimp & Zoodles

Servings: 6
Cooking Time:x
Ingredients:
- 2 tbsp. olive oil, divided
- 1 lb. shrimp, peel & devein
- 2 cloves garlic, chopped fine
- 3 zucchini, peel & spiralize
- ½ tsp salt
- ¼ tsp pepper
- ½ tsp red pepper flakes
- 1 tbsp. fresh lemon juice
- 1 cup cherry tomatoes, halved

Directions:
1. Add 1 tablespoon oil to the cooking pot and set to sauté on medium heat. Add shrimp and cook until pink 2-3 minutes. Transfer to a plate and cover.
2. Add remaining oil to the pot with the garlic. Cook 1 minute, stirring.
3. Add the zucchini, salt, pepper, red pepper flakes, lemon juice, and tomatoes and toss to combine. Cook until zucchini is tender, about 5-7 minutes, stirring occasionally.
4. Place shrimp on top of the zucchini mixture, cover, and turn off heat. Let sit for 1 minute. Serve immediately.

Nutrition Info:
- Calories 153,Total Fat 7g,Total Carbs 5g,Protein 19g,Sodium 283mg.

Easy Clam Chowder

Servings: 6
Cooking Time: 3 Hours
Ingredients:
- 5 slices bacon, chopped
- 2 cloves garlic, chopped fine
- ½ onion, chopped
- ½ tsp thyme
- 1 cup chicken broth, low sodium
- 4 oz. cream cheese
- 18 oz. clams, chopped & drained
- 1 bay leaf
- 3 cups cauliflower, separated in florets
- 1 cup almond milk, unsweetened
- 1 cup heavy cream
- 2 tbsp. fresh parsley, chopped

Directions:
1. Add the bacon to the cooking pot and set to sauté on med-high heat. Cook until crisp, transfer to a paper-towel lined plate. Pour out all but 3 tablespoons of the fat.
2. Add the onion and garlic and cook 2-3 minutes until onion is translucent. Add the thyme and cook 1 minute more.
3. Add the broth, cream cheese, clams, bay leaf, and cauliflower, mix until combined. Add the lid and set to slow cook on low. Cook 2-3 hours until cauliflower is tender. Stir in the milk and cream and cook until heated through.
4. Ladle into bowls and top with bacon and parsley. Serve warm.

Nutrition Info:
- Calories 377,Total Fat 24g,Total Carbs 13g,Protein 27g,Sodium 468mg.

Arroz Con Cod

Servings: 4
Cooking Time: 30 Minutes
Ingredients:
- ¼ cup olive oil
- 2 tbsp. garlic, chopped
- ½ cup red onion, chopped
- ½ cup red bell pepper, chopped
- ½ cup green bell pepper, chopped
- 2 cups long grain rice
- 3 tbsp. tomato paste
- 2 tsp turmeric
- 2 tbsp. cumin
- ½ tsp salt
- ¼ tsp pepper
- 4 cups chicken broth
- 1 bay leaf
- 1 lb. cod, cut in bite-size pieces
- ½ cup peas, cooked
- 4 tbsp. pimento, chopped
- 4 tsp cilantro, chopped

Directions:
1. Add the oil to the cooking pot and set to sauté on med-high.
2. Add the garlic, onion, and peppers, and cook, stirring frequently for 2 minutes.
3. Stir in rice, tomato paste, and seasonings, and cook another 2 minutes.
4. Add the broth and bay leaf and bring to a boil. Reduce heat, cover, and let simmer 5 minutes.
5. Add the fish, recover the pot and cook 15-20 minutes until all the liquid is absorbed. Turn off the cooker and let sit for 5 minutes.
6. To serve: spoon onto plates and top with cooked peas, pimento and cilantro.

Nutrition Info:

- Calories 282,Total Fat 15g,Total Carbs 35g,Protein 4g,Sodium 1249mg.

Pistachio Crusted Salmon

Servings: 1
Cooking Time: 15 Min
Ingredients:
- 1 salmon fillet
- 3 tbsp pistachios /45g
- 1 tsp grated Parmesan cheese /5g
- 1 tsp lemon juice /5ml
- 1 tsp mustard /5g
- 1 tsp olive oil /5ml
- Pinch of sea salt
- Pinch of garlic powder
- Pinch of black pepper

Directions:
1. Whisk the mustard and lemon juice together. Season the salmon with salt, pepper, and garlic powder. Brush the olive oil on all sides.
2. Brush the mustard-lemon mixture on top of the salmon. Chop the pistachios finely, and combine them with the Parmesan cheese.
3. Sprinkle them on top of the salmon. Place the salmon in the Ninja Foodi basket with the skin side down.
4. Close the crisping lid and cook for 10 minutes on Air Crisp mode at 350 °F or 177°C.

Spicy Shrimp Pasta With Vodka Sauce

Servings:6
Cooking Time: 11 Minutes
Ingredients:
- 2 tablespoons extra-virgin olive oil
- 2 tablespoons minced garlic
- 1 teaspoon crushed red pepper flakes
- 1 small red onion, diced
- Kosher salt
- Freshly ground black pepper
- ¾ cup vodka
- 2¾ cups vegetable stock
- 1 can crushed tomatoes
- 1 box penne pasta
- 1 pound frozen shrimp, peeled and deveined
- 1 package cream cheese, cubed
- 4 cups shredded mozzarella cheese

Directions:
1. Select SEAR/SAUTÉ and set to MD:HI. Select START/STOP to begin. Let preheat for 5 minutes.
2. Add the olive oil, garlic, and crushed red pepper flakes. Cook until garlic is golden brown, about 1 minute. Add the onions and season with salt and pepper and cook until translucent, about 2 minutes.
3. Stir in the vodka, vegetable stock, crushed tomatoes, penne pasta, and frozen shrimp. Assemble pressure lid, making sure the pressure release valve is in the SEAL position.
4. Select PRESSURE and set temperature to HI. Set time to 6 minutes. Select START/STOP to begin.
5. When pressure cooking is complete, quick release the pressure by turning the pressure release valve to the VENT position. Carefully remove lid when unit has finished releasing pressure.
6. Stir in the cream cheese until it has melted. Layer the mozzarella on top of the pasta. Close crisping lid.
7. Select AIR CRISP, set temperature to 400°F, and set time to 5 minutes. Select START/STOP to begin.
8. When cooking is complete, open lid and serve.

Nutrition Info:
- Calories: 789,Total Fat: 35g,Sodium: 1302mg,Carbohydrates: 63g,Protein: 47g.

Crab Cake Casserole

Servings:8
Cooking Time: 17 Minutes
Ingredients:
- 2 tablespoons canola oil
- 1 large onion, chopped
- 2 celery stalks, chopped
- 1 red bell pepper, chopped
- 1½ cups basmati rice, rinsed
- 2 cups chicken stock
- ¼ cup mayonnaise
- ¼ cup Dijon mustard
- 3 cans lump crab meat
- 1 cup shredded Cheddar cheese, divided
- 1 sleeve butter crackers, crumbled

Directions:
1. Select SEAR/SAUTÉ and set to HI. Select START/STOP to begin. Let preheat for 5 minutes.
2. Add the oil. Once hot, add the onion, celery, and bell pepper and stir. Cook for 5 minutes, stirring occasionally.
3. Stir in the rice and chicken stock. Assemble pressure lid, making sure the pressure release valve is in the SEAL position.

4. Select PRESSURE and set to HI. Set time to 2 minutes. Select START/STOP to begin.
5. When pressure cooking is complete, allow pressure to naturally release for 10 minutes. After 10 minutes, quick release any remaining pressure by moving the pressure release valve to the VENT position. Carefully remove lid when unit has finished releasing pressure.
6. Stir in the mayonnaise, mustard, crab, and ½ cup of Cheddar cheese. Top evenly with the crackers, then top with remaining ½ cup of cheese. Close crisping lid.
7. Select BAKE/ROAST, set temperature to 350°F, and set time to 10 minutes. Select START/STOP to begin.
8. When cooking is complete, open lid and serve immediately.

Nutrition Info:
- Calories: 448,Total Fat: 25g,Sodium: 819mg,Carbohydrates: 46g,Protein: 22g.

Stir Fried Scallops & Veggies

Servings: 6
Cooking Time: 15 Minutes
Ingredients:
- 2 tbsp. peanut oil
- 3 cloves garlic, chopped fine
- 1 tsp crushed red pepper flakes
- 1 lb. bay scallops
- 2 tbsp. sesame seeds
- 1 ½ tsp ginger
- 1 head bok choy, trimmed and chopped
- 16 oz. stir-fry vegetables
- 1 tbsp. soy sauce, low sodium

Directions:
1. Add the oil to the cooking pot and set to saute on med-high heat.
2. Add the garlic, red pepper flakes, and scallops and cook until scallops are golden brown and cooked. Transfer scallops to a bowl and keep warm.
3. Add the sesame seeds and ginger and cook, stirring, 1-2 minutes until all the liquid is gone.
4. Add the cabbage and vegetables and cook 4-5 minutes, stirring occasionally.
5. Add the soy sauce and return the scallops to the pot. Cook 1-2 minutes more until heated through. Serve immediately.

Nutrition Info:
- Calories 172,Total Fat 5g,Total Carbs 17g,Protein 15g,Sodium 485mg.

Mackerel En Papillote With Vegetables

Servings: 6
Cooking Time: 25 Min + 2 H For Marinating
Ingredients:
- 3 large whole mackerel, cut into 2 pieces
- 1 pound asparagus, trimmed /450g
- 1 carrot, cut into sticks
- 1 celery stalk, cut into sticks
- 3 cloves garlic, minced
- 2 lemons, cut into wedges
- 6 medium tomatoes, quartered
- 1 large brown onion; sliced thinly
- 1 Orange Bell pepper, seeded and cut into sticks
- ½ cup butter; at room temperature/65g
- 1 ½ cups water /375ml
- 2 ½ tbsp Pernod /37.5g
- Salt and black pepper to taste

Directions:
1. Cut out 6 pieces of parchment paper a little longer and wider than a piece of fish with kitchen scissors. Then, cut out 6 pieces of foil slightly longer than the parchment papers.
2. Lay the foil wraps on a flat surface and place each parchment paper on each aluminium foil.
3. In a bowl, add tomatoes, onions, garlic, bell pepper, pernod, butter, asparagus, carrot, celery, salt, and pepper. Use a spoon to mix them.
4. Place each fish piece on the layer of parchment and foil wraps. Spoon the vegetable mixture on each fish. Then, wrap the fish and place the fish packets in the refrigerator to marinate for 2 hours. Remove the fish to a flat surface.
5. Open the Ninja Foodi, pour the water in, and fit the reversible rack at the bottom of the pot. Put the packets on the trivet.
6. Seal the lid and select Steam mode on High pressure for 3 minutes. Press Start/Stop to start cooking.
7. Once the timer has ended, do a quick pressure release, and open the lid.
8. Remove the trivet with the fish packets onto a flat surface. Carefully open the foil and using a spatula. Return the packets to the pot, on top of the rack.
9. Close the crisping lid and cook on Air Crisp for 3 minutes at 300 °F or 149°C. Then, remove to serving plates. Serve with lemon wedges.

Mustard And Apricot-glazed Salmon With Smashed Potatoes

Servings: 4
Cooking Time: 25 Minutes

Ingredients:

- 20 ounces baby potatoes, whole
- 1½ cups water
- 4 frozen skinless salmon fillets
- ¼ cup apricot preserves
- 2 teaspoons Dijon mustard
- 2 tablespoons extra-virgin olive oil
- ½ teaspoon kosher salt
- ½ teaspoon freshly ground black pepper

Directions:

1. Place the potatoes and water in the pot. Put Reversible Rack in pot, making sure it is in the higher position. Place salmon on the rack. Assemble pressure lid, making sure the pressure release valve is in the SEAL position.
2. Select PRESSURE and set to HI. Set time to 5 minutes. Select START/STOP to begin.
3. Mix together the apricot preserves and mustard in a small bowl.
4. When pressure cooking is complete, quick release the pressure by turning the pressure release valve to the VENT position. Carefully remove lid when unit has finished releasing pressure.
5. Carefully remove rack with salmon. Remove potatoes from pot and drain. Place the potatoes on a cutting board and, using the back of a knife, carefully press down to flatten each. Drizzle the flattened potatoes with the olive oil and season with salt and pepper.
6. Place Cook & Crisp Basket in the pot. Place the potatoes into the basket and close crisping lid.
7. Select AIR CRISP, set temperature to 390°F, and set time to 15 minutes. Select START/STOP to begin.
8. After 8 minutes, open lid, and using silicone-tipped tongs, gently flip the potatoes. Lower basket back into pot and close lid to resume cooking.
9. When cooking is complete, remove basket from pot. Return the rack with the salmon to the pot, making sure the rack is in the higher position. Gently brush the salmon with the apricot and mustard mixture.
10. Close crisping lid. Select BROIL and set time to 5 minutes. Select START/STOP to begin.
11. When cooking is complete, remove salmon and serve immediately with the potatoes.

Nutrition Info:

- Calories: 359, Total Fat: 11g, Sodium: 711mg, Carbohydrates: 36g, Protein: 31g.

Tuscan Cod

Servings: 4
Cooking Time: 32 Minutes

Ingredients:

- 2 tablespoons canola oil, divided
- 1½ pounds baby red potatoes, cut into ½-inch pieces
- 2½ teaspoons kosher salt, divided
- 1 teaspoon freshly ground black pepper, divided
- 1 cup panko bread crumbs
- 6 tablespoons unsalted butter, divided
- 2 teaspoons poultry seasoning
- Juice of 1 lemon
- 1 medium onion, thinly sliced
- 1½ cups cherry tomatoes, halved
- 4 garlic cloves, quartered lengthwise
- ⅓ cup Kalamata olives, roughly chopped
- 4 fresh cod fillets
- 1 teaspoon fresh mint, finely chopped
- 1 lemon, cut into wedges

Directions:

1. Select SEAR/SAUTÉ and set to HI. Select START/STOP to begin. Let preheat for 5 minutes.
2. Add 1 tablespoon of oil and the potatoes. Season with 1½ teaspoons of salt and ½ teaspoon of pepper. Sauté for about 15 minutes, stirring occasionally, until the potatoes are golden brown.
3. While potatoes are cooking, combine the bread crumbs, 4 tablespoons of butter, poultry seasoning, the remaining 1 teaspoon of salt and ½ teaspoon of pepper, and lemon juice in a medium bowl. Stir well.
4. Once the potatoes are browned, carefully remove them from the pot and set aside. Add the remaining 1 tablespoon of oil, then the onion. Sauté for 2 to 3 minutes, until the onions are lightly browned. Add the tomatoes, garlic, and olives and cook for about 2 minutes more, stirring occasionally. Return the potatoes to the pot, stir. Select START/STOP to pause cooking. Close crisping lid to retain heat.
5. Coat the cod on both sides with the remaining 2 tablespoons of butter. Evenly distribute the breadcrumb mixture on top of the cod, pressing the crumbs down firmly.
6. Open lid and place the Reversible Rack in the pot over the potato mixture, making sure it is the higher position. Place the cod fillets on the rack, bread-side up. Close crisping lid.

7. Select BAKE/ROAST, set temperature to 375°F, and set time to 12 minutes. Select START/STOP to begin.

8. When cooking is complete, leave the cod in the pot with the crisping lid closed for 5 minutes to rest before serving. After resting, the internal temperature of the cod should be at least 145°F and the bread crumbs should be golden brown. Serve with potato mixture and garnish with chopped mint and lemon wedges.

Nutrition Info:
- Calories: 583,Total Fat: 28g,Sodium: 815mg,Carbohydrates: 48g,Protein: 37g.

Cod With Ginger And Scallion Sauce

Servings:4
Cooking Time: 10 Minutes
Ingredients:
- 2 tablespoons rice vinegar
- 2 tablespoons soy sauce
- 1 tablespoon chicken stock
- 1 tablespoon grated fresh ginger
- 4 skinless cod fillets
- Sea salt
- Freshly ground black pepper
- Greens of 6 scallions, thinly sliced

Directions:
1. In a small bowl, mix together the rice vinegar, soy sauce, chicken stock, and ginger.
2. Season the cod fillets on both sides with salt and pepper. Place them in the pot and cover with the vinegar mixture.
3. Select SEAR/SAUTÉ and set to MED. Bring the liquid to a low boil.
4. Once boiling, turn the heat to LO and cover with the pressure lid. Cook for 8 minutes.
5. Remove lid and add the scallion greens to the top of the fish. Cover with the pressure lid and cook for 2 minutes more. Serve.

Nutrition Info:
- Calories: 149,Total Fat: 2g,Sodium: 642mg,Carbohydrates: 2g,Protein: 30g.

Farfalle Tuna Casserole With Cheese

Servings: 4
Cooking Time: 60 Min
Ingredients:
- 6 ounces farfalle /180g
- 1 can full cream milk; divided /360ml
- 2 cans tuna, drained /180g
- 1 medium onion; chopped
- 1 large carrot; chopped
- 1 cup vegetable broth /250ml
- 2 cups shredded Monterey Jack cheese /260g
- 1 cup chopped green beans /130g
- 2½ cups panko bread crumbs /325g
- 3 tbsps butter, melted /45ml
- 1 tbsp olive oil/ 15ml
- 1 tsp salt/ 5g
- 2 tsp s corn starch /10g

Directions:
1. On the Foodi, Choose Sear/Sauté and adjust to Medium. Press Start to preheat the pot.
2. Heat the oil until shimmering and sauté the onion and carrots for 3 minutes, stirring, until softened.
3. Add the farfalle, ¾ cup or 188ml of milk, broth, and salt to the pot. Stir to combine and submerge the farfalle in the liquid with a spoon.
4. Seal the pressure lid, choose pressure; adjust the pressure to Low and the cook time to 5 minutes; press Start. After cooking, do a quick pressure release and carefully open the pressure lid.
5. Choose Sear/Sauté and adjust to Less for low heat. Press Start. Pour the remaining milk on the farfalle.
6. In a medium bowl, mix the cheese and cornstarch evenly and add the cheese mixture by large handfuls to the sauce while stirring until the cheese melts and the sauce thickens. Add the tuna and green beans, gently stir. Heat for 2 minutes.
7. In another bowl, mix the crumbs and melted butter well. Spread the crumbs over the casserole. Close the crisping lid and press Broil. Adjust the cook time to 5 minutes; press Start. When ready, the topping should be crisp and brown. If not, broil for 2 more minutes. Serve immediately.

Coconut Cilantro Shrimp

Servings: 4
Cooking Time: 4 ½ Hours
Ingredients:
- 3 ¾ cups coconut milk, unsweetened
- 1 ¾ cups water
- 2 tbsp. red curry paste
- 2 ½ tsp lemon garlic seasoning
- 1 lb. shrimp, peeled & deveined
- ¼ cup cilantro, chopped

Directions:
1. Place all ingredients, except shrimp and cilantro, in the cooking pot and stir to well to mix.
2. Add the lid and set to slow cook on low heat. Cook 4 hours, stirring occasionally.

3. Stir in shrimp and continue cooking another 15-30 minutes until shrimp turn pink and tender.
4. Transfer mixture to a serving plate and garnish with cilantro. Serve immediately.

Nutrition Info:
- Calories 525, Total Fat 46g, Total Carbs 8g, Protein 28g, Sodium 168mg.

Coconut Shrimp

Servings: 2
Cooking Time: 30 Min

Ingredients:
- 8 large shrimp
- ½ cup orange jam /65g
- ½ cup shredded coconut /65g
- ½ cup breadcrumbs /65g
- 8 oz. coconut milk /240ml
- 1 tbsp honey /15ml
- ½ tsp cayenne pepper/2.5g
- ¼ tsp hot sauce /1.25ml
- 1 tsp mustard /5g
- ¼ tsp salt /1.25g
- ¼ tsp pepper /1.25g

Directions:
1. Combine the breadcrumbs, cayenne pepper, shredded coconut, salt, and pepper in a small bowl. Dip the shrimp in the coconut milk, first, and then in the coconut crumbs.
2. Arrange in the lined Ninja Foodi basket, close the crisping lid and cook for 20 minutes on Air Crisp mode at 350 °F or 177°C.
3. Meanwhile whisk the jam, honey, hot sauce, and mustard. Serve the shrimp with the sauce.

Herb Salmon With Barley Haricot Verts

Servings: 4
Cooking Time: 50 Min

Ingredients:
- 4 salmon fillets
- 8 ounces green beans haricot verts, trimmed /240g
- 2 garlic cloves, minced
- 1 cup pearl barley /130g
- 2 cups water /500ml
- ½ tbsp brown sugar /65g
- ½ tbsp freshly squeezed lemon juice /7.5ml
- 1 tbsp olive oil /15ml
- 4 tbsps melted butter/60ml
- ½ tsp dried thyme /2.5g
- ½ tsp dried rosemary /2.5g
- 1 tsp salt; divided /5g
- 1 tsp freshly ground black pepper; divided /5g

Directions:
1. Pour the barley and water in the pot and mix to combine. Place the reversible rack in the pot. Lay the salmon fillets on the rack. Seal the pressure lid, choose Pressure, set to High and set the time to 2 minutes. Press Start.
2. In a bowl, toss the green beans with olive oil, ½ tsp or 5g of black pepper, and ½ tsp or 2.5g of salt.
3. Then, in another bowl, mix the remaining black pepper and salt, the butter, brown sugar, lemon juice, rosemary, garlic, and rosemary.
4. When done cooking the rice and salmon, perform a quick pressure release. Gently pat the salmon dry with a paper towel, then coat with the buttery herb sauce.
5. Position the haricots vert around the salmon. Close the crisping lid; choose Broil and set the time to 7 minutes; press Start/Stop. When ready, remove the salmon from the rack, and serve with the barley and haricots vert.

Flounder Oreganata

Servings: 4
Cooking Time: 15 Minutes

Ingredients:
- 1/3 cup rolled oats
- ¼ cup panko bread crumbs
- 2 cloves garlic, chopped fine
- 2 tbsp. fresh parsley, chopped, divided
- ½ tsp oregano
- 4 tsp fresh lemon juice
- 1 tsp lemon zest
- 1 tbsp. olive oil
- 1 tsp salt, divided
- ½ tsp pepper
- 4 flounder fillets
- Lemon wedges

Directions:
1. Place the rack in the cooking pot and top with a piece of parchment paper.
2. Add the oats to a food processor and pulse until they are finely ground.
3. In a small bowl, combine oats, bread crumbs, garlic, 1 ½ tablespoons parsley, oregano, lemon juice, zest, oil and ½ tsp salt.
4. Lay the fish on the parchment paper and season with salt and pepper. Spoon bread crumb mixture over the fish, pressing lightly.

5. Add the tender-crisp lid and set to bake on 450°F. Bake 10-12 minutes until topping is golden brown and fish flakes easily with a fork. Serve garnished with parsley and lemon wedges.

Nutrition Info:
- Calories 261, Total Fat 9g, Total Carbs 14g, Protein 30g, Sodium 1459mg.

Sweet & Spicy Shrimp Bowls

Servings: 8
Cooking Time: 5 Minutes

Ingredients:
- ½ cup green onions, chopped
- 1 jalapeno pepper, seeded & chopped
- 1 tsp red chili flakes
- 8 oz. crushed pineapple, drained
- 2 tbsp. honey
- 1 lime, zested & juiced
- 1 tbsp. olive oil
- 2 lbs. large shrimp, peeled & deveined
- ¼ tsp salt
- 2 cups brown rice, cooked

Directions:
1. In a small bowl, combine green onions, jalapeno, chili flakes, pineapple, honey, lime juice, and zest and mix well.
2. Add the oil to the cooking pot and set to saute on medium heat.
3. Sprinkle the shrimp with salt and cook, 3-5 minutes or until they turn pink.
4. Add the shrimp to the pineapple mixture and stir to coat.
5. Spoon rice into bowls and top with shrimp mixture. Serve immediately.

Nutrition Info:
- Calories 188, Total Fat 3g, Total Carbs 23g, Protein 17g, Sodium 644mg.

Smoked Salmon Pilaf With Walnuts

Servings: 4
Cooking Time: 60 Min

Ingredients:
- 4 green onions; chopped (white part separated from the green part)
- 1 smoked salmon fillet, flaked
- 1 medium tomato, seeded and diced
- 1 cup basmati rice /130g
- 1 cup frozen corn, thawed /130g
- 2 cups water /500ml
- ½ cup walnut pieces /65g
- 1 tbsp ghee /15g
- 1 tsp salt /5g
- 2 tsps prepared horseradish /10g

Directions:
1. Pour the walnuts into a heatproof bowl. Put the Crisping basket in the inner pot and the bowl in the basket.
2. Close the crisping lid and Choose Air Crisp; adjust the temperature to 375°F or 191°C and the time to 5 minutes. Press Start to begin toasting the walnuts.
3. After the cooking time is over, carefully take the bowl and basket out of the pot and set aside.
4. On the Foodi, choose Sear/Sauté and adjust to Medium to preheat the inner pot. Add the ghee to melt and sauté the white part of the green onions for about a minute, or until starting to soften.
5. Stir in the rice and corn, stirring occasionally for 2 to 3 minutes, or until starting to be fragrant. Add the water and salt.
6. Seal the pressure lid, choose Pressure; adjust the pressure to High and the cook time to 3 minutes; press Start.
7. After cooking, perform a natural pressure release for 5 minutes, then a quick pressure and carefully open the lid.
8. Fluff the rice gently with a fork. Stir in the flaked salmon, green parts of the green onions, and the horseradish.
9. Add the tomato and allow sitting a few minutes to warm through. Spoon the pilaf into serving bowls and top with the walnuts. Serve.

Tuna Zoodle Bake

Servings: 4
Cooking Time: 20 Minutes

Ingredients:
- Nonstick cooking spray
- 2 zucchini, cut in noodles with a spiralizer
- 1tsp olive oil
- ¼ cup onion, chopped fine
- 6 oz. tuna, drained
- ½ tbsp. tomato paste
- ½ cup tomatoes, diced & drained
- ¼ cup skim milk
- ½ tsp thyme
- ¼ tsp salt
- ¼ tsp pepper
- 1/8 cup parmesan cheese, fat free
- 1/4 cup cheddar cheese, reduced fat, grated

Directions:
1. Spray an 8x8-inch baking pan with cooking spray.
2. Place the zucchini in an even layer in the prepared pan.

3. Add the oil to the cooking pot and set to sauté on med-high heat. Once the oil is hot, add the onion and cook 2 minutes, or until soft.

4. Stir in the tuna and tomato paste and cook 1 minute more. Add the tomatoes, milk, thyme, salt, and pepper and bring to a low simmer. Stir in parmesan cheese and cook until it melts.

5. Pour the tuna mixture over the zucchini and sprinkle cheddar cheese over the top. Wipe out the pat and place the baking pan in it.

6. Add the tender-crisp lid and set to bake on 400°F. Bake 15 minutes until cheese is melted and bubbly. Serve.

Nutrition Info:
- Calories 80,Total Fat 3g,Total Carbs 2g,Protein 11g,Sodium 371mg.

Curried Salmon & Sweet Potatoes

Servings: 4
Cooking Time: 20 Minutes
Ingredients:
- Nonstick cooking spray
- 2 sweet potatoes, peeled & cubed
- 1 tbsp. + 1 tsp olive oil, divided
- ½ tsp salt
- 1 tsp thyme
- 1 tsp curry powder
- 1 tsp honey
- ½ tsp lime zest
- 1/8 tsp crushed red pepper flakes
- 4 salmon filets

Directions:
1. Spray the cooking pot with cooking spray.
2. In a large bowl, combine potatoes, 1 tablespoon oil, salt, and thyme and toss to coat the potatoes. Place in the cooking pot.
3. Add the tender-crisp lid and set to roast on 400°F. Cook potatoes 10 minutes.
4. In a small bowl, whisk together remaining oil, curry powder, honey, zest, and pepper flakes. Lay the salmon on a sheet of foil and brush the curry mixture over the top.
5. Open the lid and stir the potatoes. Add the rack to the cooking pot and place the salmon, with the foil, on the rack.

Close the lid and continue to cook another 10-15 minutes until potatoes are tender and fish flakes easily with a fork. Serve.

Nutrition Info:
- Calories 239,Total Fat 8g,Total Carbs 15g,Protein 25g,Sodium 347mg.

Garlic Shrimp And Veggies

Servings:4
Cooking Time: 5 Minutes
Ingredients:
- 2 tablespoons unsalted butter
- 1 shallot, minced
- 3 garlic cloves, minced
- ¼ cup white wine
- ½ cup chicken stock
- Juice of ½ lemon
- ½ teaspoon sea salt
- ½ teaspoon freshly ground black pepper
- 1½ pounds frozen shrimp, thawed
- 1 large head broccoli, cut into florets

Directions:
1. Add the butter. Select SEAR/SAUTÉ and set to MED. Select START/STOP to begin.
2. Once the butter is melted, add the shallots and cook for 3 minutes. Add the garlic and cook for 1 minute.
3. Deglaze the pot by adding the wine and using a wooden spoon to scrape the bits of garlic and shallot off the bottom of the pot. Stir in the chicken stock, lemon juice, salt, pepper, and shrimp.
4. Place the broccoli florets on top of the shrimp mixture. Assemble pressure lid, making sure the pressure release valve is in the SEAL position.
5. Select PRESSURE and set to HI. Set time to 0 minutes. Select START/STOP to begin.
6. When pressure cooking is complete, quick release the pressure by moving the pressure release valve to the VENT position. Carefully remove lid when the unit has finished releasing pressure. Serve immediately.

Nutrition Info:
- Calories: 281,Total Fat: 8g,Sodium: 692mg,Carbohydrates: 9g,Protein: 39g.

Vegan & Vegetable Recipes

Hawaiian Tofu

Servings: 6
Cooking Time: 3 Hours
Ingredients:
- 1 package extra firm tofu, cubed
- ¼ cup fresh pineapple, cubed
- ¼ cup tamari, low sodium
- 1 tbsp. sesame oil
- 1 tbsp. olive oil
- 1 tbsp. brown rice vinegar
- 2 cloves garlic, chopped
- 2 tsp fresh ginger, chopped
- 4 cups zucchini, chopped
- ¼ cup sesame seeds

Directions:
1. Add the tofu to the cooking pot.
2. Add the pineapple, soy sauce, sesame oil, olive oil, vinegar, garlic, and ginger to a food processor or blender. Process until smooth. Pour over tofu.
3. Add the lid and set to slow cook on low. Cook 3 hours, stirring occasionally.
4. During the last 15 minutes of cooking time, add the zucchini and sesame seeds to the pot and stir to combine. Serve over quinoa or rice.

Nutrition Info:
- Calories 164,Total Fat 13g,Total Carbs 5g,Protein 10g,Sodium 680mg.

Roasted Vegetable Salad

Servings: 1
Cooking Time: 25 Min
Ingredients:
- 1 potato, peeled and chopped
- 1 cup cherry tomatoes/130g
- 1 carrot; sliced diagonally
- ½ small beetroot; sliced
- ¼ onion; sliced
- Juice of 1 lemon
- A handful of rocket salad
- A handful of baby spinach
- 2 tbsp olive oil /30ml
- 3 tbsp canned chickpeas /45g
- ½ tsp cumin /2.5g
- ½ tsp turmeric /2.5g
- ¼ tsp sea salt /1.25g
- Parmesan shavings

Directions:
1. Combine the onion, potato, cherry tomatoes, carrot, beetroot, cumin, seas salt, turmeric, and 1 tbsp olive oil, in a bowl. Place in the Ninja Foodi, close the crisping lid and cook for 20 minutes on Air Crisp mode at 370 °F or 188°C; let cool for 2 minutes.
2. Place the rocket, salad, spinach, lemon juice, and 1 tbsp olive oil, into a serving bowl. Mix to combine; stir in the roasted veggies.Top with chickpeas and Parmesan shavings.

Cauliflower And Asparagus Farfalle

Servings: 4
Cooking Time: 60 Min
Ingredients:
- 1 bunch asparagus, trimmed, cut into 1-inch pieces
- 2 cups cauliflower florets /260g
- 10 ounces farfalle /300g
- 3 garlic cloves, minced
- ¼ cup chopped basil /32.5g
- ½ cup grated Parmesan cheese /65g
- 2½ cups vegetable stock /625ml
- ½ cup heavy cream /125ml
- 1 cup cherry tomatoes, halved /130g
- 3 tbsps melted butter; divided /45ml
- 3 tsp s salt; divided /15g

Directions:
1. Put the Crisping Basket in the Foodi. Close the crisping lid, choose Air Crisp; adjust the temperature to 375°F or 191°C and the time to 2 minutes; press Start. Pour the asparagus, and cauliflower, in a large bowl and drizzle with 1 tbsp of melted butter. Season with ½ tsp of salt and toss. Open the cooker and transfer the vegetables to the basket.
2. Close the crisping lid; choose Air Crisp, adjust the temperature to 375°F or 191°C, and set the timer to 10 minutes. Press Start to begin roasting. After 5 minutes, carefully open the lid and mix the vegetables. Close the lid and continue cooking.
3. When done roasting, take out the basket, and cover the top with aluminum foil; set aside.
4. Place the farfalle into the inner pot and add the remaining butter. Using tongs, toss the farfalle to coat, and add the remaining salt, garlic, and water. Stir to combine.
5. Seal the pressure lid, choose Pressure; adjust the pressure to High and the cook time to 5 minutes; press Start.

After cooking, do a quick pressure release and carefully open the lid.

6. Stir the heavy cream and tomatoes into the pasta, tossing well. Choose Sear/Sauté and adjust to Medium. Press Start to simmer the cream until the sauce has your desired consistency.

7. Gently mix in the asparagus, and cauliflower. Allow warming to soften the vegetables, then stir in the basil and Parmesan cheese. Dish the creamy farfalle and serve warm.

Veggie Skewers

Servings: 4
Cooking Time: 20 Min
Ingredients:
- 2 boiled and mashed potatoes
- ¼ cup chopped fresh mint leaves /32.5g
- ⅔ cup canned beans /88g
- ⅓ cup grated carrots /44g
- ½ cup paneer /65g
- 1 green chili
- 1-inch piece of fresh ginger
- 3 garlic cloves
- 2 tbsp corn flour /30g
- ½ tsp garam masala powder /2.5g
- Salt, to taste

Directions:
1. Soak 12 skewers until ready to use. Place the beans, carrots, garlic, ginger, chili, paneer, and mint, in a food processor and process until smooth; transfer to a bowl.
2. Add the mashed potatoes, corn flour, some salt, and garam masala powder to the bowl. Mix until fully incorporated. Divide the mixture into 12 equal pieces.
3. Shape each of the pieces around a skewer. Close the crisping lid and cook the skewers for 10 minutes on Air Crisp mode at 390 °F or 199°C.

Caramelized Sweet Potatoes

Servings: 4
Cooking Time: 20 Minutes
Ingredients:
- 1 cup water
- 2 large sweet potatoes
- 2 tbsp. butter
- ½ tsp salt
- ¼ tsp pepper

Directions:
1. Add the trivet and water to the cooking pot.
2. Prick the potatoes with a fork and place on the trivet. Add the lid and set to pressure cook on high. Set timer for 15 minutes. Once timer goes off, use natural release to remove the pressure.
3. Transfer potatoes to a cutting board and slice ½-inch thick.
4. Remove the trivet and add butter to the pot. Set to sauté on med-high heat.
5. Add the potatoes and cook, turning occasionally, until potatoes are nicely browned on both sides. Season with salt and pepper and serve.

Nutrition Info:
- Calories 107,Total Fat 6g,Total Carbs 14g,Protein 1g,Sodium 227mg.

Spinach, Tomatoes, And Butternut Squash Stew

Servings: 6
Cooking Time: 65 Min
Ingredients:
- 2 lb. butternut squash, peeled and cubed /900g
- 1 can sundried tomatoes, undrained /450g
- 2 cans chickpeas, drained /450g
- 1 white onion; diced
- 4 garlic cloves, minced
- 4 cups baby spinach /520g
- 4 cups vegetable broth /1000ml
- 1 tbsp butter /15g
- ½ tsp smoked paprika /2.5g
- 1 tsp coriander powder /5g
- 1½ tsp s cumin powder /7.5g
- ½ tsp salt /2.5g
- ½ tsp freshly ground black pepper /2.5g

Directions:
1. Choose Sear/Sauté, set to Medium High, and the timer to 5 minutes; press Start/Stop to preheat the pot. Combine the butter, onion, and garlic in the pot. Cook, stirring occasionally; for 5 minutes or until soft and fragrant.
2. Add the butternut squash, vegetable broth, tomatoes, chickpeas, cumin, paprika, coriander, salt, and black pepper to the pot. Put the pressure lid together and lock in the Seal position.
3. Choose Pressure, set to High, and set the time to 8 minutes; press Start/Stop.
4. When the timer is done reading, perform a quick pressure release. Stir in the spinach to wilt, adjust the taste with salt and black pepper, and serve warm.

Creamy Spinach Soup

Servings: 6
Cooking Time: 20 Minutes
Ingredients:
- Nonstick cooking spray
- 1 tsp garlic, chopped fine
- ½ cup green onions, sliced thin
- 3 ½ cups vegetable broth, low sodium
- 20 oz. fresh spinach, chopped
- 3 tbsp. cornstarch
- 3 cups skim milk
- ½ tsp nutmeg
- 1/8 tsp salt
- ½ tsp pepper

Directions:
1. Spray the cooking pot with cooking spray. Set to sauté on med-high heat.
2. Add the garlic and green onions and cook 3-4 minutes, stirring frequently, until soft. Stir in broth and spinach.
3. Add the lid and set to pressure cook on high. Set the timer for 8 minutes. When the timer goes off, use natural release to remove the pressure.
4. Set back to sauté on medium heat.
5. In a small bowl, whisk together cornstarch and milk until smooth. Stir into soup until combined. Add remaining ingredients and cook, stirring constantly, 6-8 minutes until soup has thickened. Serve immediately.

Nutrition Info:
- Calories 95, Total Fat 1g, Total Carbs 16g, Protein 7g, Sodium 559mg.

Cheesy Spicy Pasta

Servings: 6
Cooking Time: 40 Minutes
Ingredients:
- 1 ½ cups cottage cheese, low fat
- ½ cup ricotta cheese
- ½ cup Greek yogurt
- 2 cups mozzarella cheese, grated, divided
- ¼ cup fresh parsley, chopped
- 2 cups baby spinach
- 1 tbsp. butter
- 1 onion, chopped
- 2 tbsp. garlic, chopped fine
- 14 ½ oz. fire-roasted tomatoes
- 8 oz. tomato sauce
- ½ tsp red pepper flakes
- 1 ½ tsp oregano
- 1 tsp rosemary
- ½ tsp salt
- ½ tsp pepper
- ¾ lb. whole grain pasta, cooked & drained
- 6 tbsp. parmesan cheese

Directions:
1. In a medium bowl, combine cottage cheese, ricotta, yogurt, 1 cup mozzarella, parsley, and spinach, mix well.
2. Add the butter to the cooking pot and set to sauté on med-high. Once the butter melts, add the onion and cook until translucent. Add the garlic and cook 1 minute more.
3. Stir in tomatoes, tomato sauce, and seasonings, reduce heat to low and simmer 5 minutes.
4. Stir in the pasta and the ricotta mixture, mix well. Top with remaining mozzarella and the parmesan cheese.
5. Add the tender-crisp lid and set to bake on 400°F. Bake 25-30 minutes until hot and bubbly. Serve.

Nutrition Info:
- Calories 282, Total Fat 7g, Total Carbs 30g, Protein 28g, Sodium 522mg.

Grilled Tofu Sandwich

Servings: 1
Cooking Time: 20 Min
Ingredients:
- 2 slices of bread
- ¼ cup red cabbage, shredded /32.5g
- 1-inch thick Tofu slice
- 2 tsp olive oil divided /10ml
- ¼ tsp vinegar /1.25ml
- Salt and pepper, to taste

Directions:
1. Place the bread slices and toast for 3 minutes on Roast mode at 350 F; set aside. Brush the tofu with 1 tsp of oil, and place in the basket of the Ninja Foodi. Bake for 5 minutes on each side on Roast mode at 350 °F or 177°C.
2. Combine the cabbage, remaining oil, and vinegar, and season with salt and pepper.
3. Place the tofu on top of one bread slice, place the cabbage over, and top with the other bread slice.

Crème De La Broc

Servings: 6
Cooking Time: 25 Min
Ingredients:
- 1 ½ cups grated yellow and white Cheddar cheese + extra for topping /195g
- 1 ½ oz. cream cheese /195g
- 1 medium Red onion; chopped

- 3 cloves garlic, minced
- 4 cups chopped broccoli florets, only the bushy tops/520g
- 3 cups heavy cream /750ml
- 3 cups vegetable broth /750ml
- 4 tbsp butter /60g
- 4 tbsp flour /60g
- 1 tsp Italian Seasoning /5g
- Salt and black pepper to taste

Directions:
1. Select Sear/Sauté mode, adjust to High and melt the butter once the pot is ready. Add the flour and use a spoon to stir until it clumps up. Gradually pour in the heavy cream while stirring until white sauce forms. Fetch out the butter sauce into a bowl and set aside.
2. Press Stop and add the onions, garlic, broth, broccoli, Italian seasoning, and cream cheese. Use a wooden spoon to stir the mixture.
3. Seal the lid, and select Pressure mode on High pressure for 12 minutes. Press Start/Stop. Once the timer has ended, do a quick pressure release.
4. Add in butter sauce and cheddar cheese, salt, and pepper. Close the crisping lid and cook on Broil mode for 3 minutes. Dish the soup into serving bowls, top it with extra cheese, to serve.

Eggplant Lasagna

Servings: 4
Cooking Time: 25 Min
Ingredients:
- 3 large eggplants; sliced in uniform ¼ inches
- ¼ cup Parmesan cheese, grated /32.5g
- 4 ¼ cups Marinara sauce /1062.5ml
- 1 ½ cups shredded Mozzarella cheese /195g
- Cooking spray
- Chopped fresh basil to garnish

Directions:
1. Open the pot and grease it with cooking spray. Arrange the eggplant slices in a single layer on the bottom of the pot and sprinkle some cheese all over it.
2. Arrange another layer of eggplant slices on the cheese, sprinkle this layer with cheese also, and repeat the layering of eggplant and cheese until both Ingredients are exhausted.
3. Lightly spray the eggplant with cooking spray and pour the marinara sauce all over it. Close the lid and pressure valve, and select Pressure mode on High pressure for 8 minutes. Press Start/Stop.
4. Once the timer has stopped, do a quick pressure release, and open the lid. Sprinkle with grated parmesan cheese, close the crisping lid and cook for 10 minutes on Bake/Roast mode on 380 °F or 194°C.
5. With two napkins in hand, gently remove the inner pot. Allow cooling for 10 minutes before serving. Garnish the lasagna with basil and serve warm as a side dish.

Hearty Veggie Soup

Servings: 12
Cooking Time: 15 Minutes
Ingredients:
- 2 cups water
- 3 ½ cups vegetable broth, low sodium
- 15 oz. red kidney beans, drained & rinsed
- 16 oz. cannellini beans, drained & rinsed
- 28 oz. tomatoes, crushed
- 10 oz. spinach, chopped
- 1 onion, chopped
- 10 oz. mixed vegetables, frozen
- 1 tsp garlic powder
- ½ tsp pepper
- 1 cup elbow macaroni

Directions:
1. Set the cooker to sauté on med-high heat.
2. Add all the ingredients, except macaroni, and stir to combine. Bring to a boil.
3. Stir in macaroni. Add the lid and set to pressure cook on high. Set timer for 10 minutes. When timer goes off, use natural release to remove the pressure. Stir well and serve.

Nutrition Info:
- Calories 181,Total Fat 1g,Total Carbs 34g,Protein 10g,Sodium 478mg.

Eggplant With Kale

Servings: 4
Cooking Time: 15 Minutes
Ingredients:
- Juice of 1 lime
- 1-pound eggplant, roughly cubed
- 1 cup kale, torn
- A pinch of black pepper and salt
- ½ teaspoon chilli powder
- ½ cup chicken stock
- 3 tablespoons olive oil

Directions:
1. Set the Foodi on Sauté mode, stir in the oil, heat it up, add the eggplant and sauté for 2 minutes.
2. Stir in the kale and the rest of the ingredients.
3. Put the Ninja Foodi's lid on and cook on and cook on High for 13 minutes.

4. Release the pressure quickly for 5 minutes, divide the mix between plates and serve.

Nutrition Info:
- Calories: 110; Fat: 3g; Carbohydrates: 4.3g; Protein: 1.1g

Mushroom Poutine

Servings: 4
Cooking Time: 46 Minutes

Ingredients:
- 2 tablespoons unsalted butter
- 1 small yellow onion, diced
- 1 garlic clove, minced
- 8 ounces cremini mushrooms, sliced
- ¼ cup red wine
- 3 cups vegetable stock
- ¼ cup all-purpose flour
- Kosher salt
- Freshly ground black pepper
- 1 pound frozen French fries
- 8 ounces Cheddar cheese, cubed

Directions:
1. Select SEAR/SAUTÉ and set to MED. Select START/STOP to begin. Let preheat for 3 minutes.
2. Add the butter, onion, and garlic. Cook, stirring occasionally, for 5 minutes. Add the mushrooms and sauté for 5 minutes. Add the wine and let it simmer and reduce for 3 minutes.
3. In large bowl, slowly whisk together the stock and flour. Whisk this mixture into the vegetables in the pot. Cook the gravy for 10 minutes. Season with salt and pepper. Transfer the gravy to a medium bowl and set aside. Clean out the pot and return to unit.
4. Insert Cook & Crisp Basket and add the French fries. Close crisping lid.
5. Select AIR CRISP, set temperature to 360°F, and set time to 18 minutes. Select START/STOP to begin.
6. Every 5 minutes, open lid and remove and shake basket to ensure even cooking.
7. Once cooking is complete, remove fries from basket and place in the pot. Add the cheese and stir. Cover with the gravy. Close crisping lid.
8. Select AIR CRISP, set temperature to 375°F, and set time 5 minutes. Select START/STOP to begin.
9. When cooking is complete, serve immediately.

Nutrition Info:
- Calories: 550, Total Fat: 32g, Sodium: 941mg, Carbohydrates: 42g, Protein: 20g.

Garganelli With Cheese And Mushrooms

Servings: 4
Cooking Time: 60 Min

Ingredients:
- 1 large egg
- 8 ounces garganelli /240g
- 8 ounces Swiss cheese, shredded /240g
- 1 recipe sautéed mushrooms
- 1 can full fat evaporated milk /360ml
- 1½ cups panko breadcrumbs /195g
- 1¼ cups water /312.5ml
- 2 tbsps chopped fresh cilantro /30g
- 3 tbsps sour cream /45ml
- 3 tbsps melted unsalted butter /45ml
- 3 tbsps grated Cheddar cheese /45g
- 1½ tsp s salt /7.5g
- 1½ tsp s arrowroot starch /7.5g

Directions:
1. Pour the garganelli into the inner pot, add half of the evaporated milk, the water, and salt. Seal the pressure lid, choose Pressure, set to High and the time to 4 minutes. Press Start.
2. In a bowl, whisk the remaining milk with the egg. In another bowl, combine the arrowroot starch with the Swiss cheese.
3. When the pasta has cooked, perform a natural pressure release for 3 minutes, then a quick pressure release and carefully open the lid. Pour in the milk-egg mixture and a large handful of the starch mixture. Stir to melt the cheese and then add the remaining cheese in 3 or 4 batches while stirring to melt. Mix in the mushrooms, cilantro, and sour cream.
4. In a bowl, mix the breadcrumbs, melted butter, and cheddar cheese. Then, sprinkle the mixture evenly over the pasta. Close the crisping lid. Choose Broil and adjust the time to 5 minutes. Press Start to begin crisping.
5. When done, the top should be brown and crispy, otherwise broil further for 3 minutes, and serve immediately.

Spicy Kimchi And Tofu Fried Rice

Servings: 6
Cooking Time: 30 Minutes

Ingredients:
- 1 cup Texmati brown rice
- 1¼ cups water
- 2 tablespoons canola oil
- 2 garlic cloves, minced

- 1 tablespoon minced fresh ginger
- 8 ounces extra-firm tofu, cut into ½-inch squares
- ½ cup frozen peas and carrots
- 1 large egg, beaten
- ½ cup kimchi, chopped
- 2 scallions, sliced thin
- ¼ cup basil, coarsely chopped
- 1 tablespoon soy sauce
- Kosher salt
- Freshly ground black pepper

Directions:

1. Rinse the rice under cold running water in a fine-mesh strainer.

2. Place the rice and water in the pot. Assemble pressure lid, making sure the pressure release valve is in the SEAL position.

3. Select PRESSURE and set to HI. Set time to 2 minutes. Select START/STOP to begin.

4. When pressure cooking is complete, allow pressure to naturally release for 10 minutes. After 10 minutes, quick release remaining pressure by moving the pressure release valve to the VENT position. Carefully remove lid when unit has finished releasing pressure.

5. Evenly layer the rice on a sheet pan and refrigerate until cool, preferably overnight.

6. Select SEAR/SAUTÉ and set to HI. Select START/STOP to begin. Add the canola oil and let heat for 5 minutes.

7. Add the garlic and ginger and cook for 1 minute. Add the tofu, rice, and peas and carrots, and cook for 5 minutes, stirring occasionally.

8. Move the rice to one side and add the egg to empty side of pot. Cook 30 seconds, stirring occasionally to scramble it. Add the kimchi, scallions, basil, and soy sauce, and stir. Cook for 5 minutes, stirring frequently.

9. Season with salt, pepper, and more soy sauce, if needed. Serve.

Nutrition Info:
- Calories: 229,Total Fat: 9g,Sodium: 928mg,Carbohydrates: 30g,Protein: 8g.

Red Beans And Rice

Servings: 4
Cooking Time: 1 Hr
Ingredients:
- 1 cup red beans, rinsed and stones removed /130g
- ½ cup rice, rinsed /65g
- 1 ½ cup vegetable broth /375ml
- 1 onion; diced
- 1 red bell pepper; diced
- 1 stalk celery; diced
- 1 tbsp fresh thyme leaves, or to taste /15g
- 2 tbsps olive oil /30ml
- ½ tsp cayenne pepper /2.5g
- water as needed
- salt and freshly ground black pepper to taste

Directions:

1. Into the pot, add beans and water to cover about 1-inch. Seal the pressure lid, choose Pressure, set to High, and set the timer to 1 minute. Press Start. When ready, release the pressure quickly. Drain the beans and set aside. Rinse and pat dry the inner pot.

2. Return inner pot to pressure cooker, add oil to the pot and press Sear/Sauté. Add onion to the oil and cook for 3 minutes until soft. Add celery and pepper and cook for 1 to 2 minutes until fragrant. Add garlic and cook for 30 seconds until soft; add rice.

3. Transfer the beans back into inner pot and top with broth. Stir black pepper, thyme, cayenne pepper, and salt into mixture. Seal the pressure lid, choose Pressure, set to High, and set the timer to 15 minutes. Press Start.

4. When ready, release pressure quickly. Add more thyme, black pepper and salt as desired.

Mashed Broccoli With Cream Cheese

Servings: 4
Cooking Time: 12 Min
Ingredients:
- 3 heads broccoli; chopped
- 2 cloves garlic, crushed
- 6 oz. cream cheese /180g
- 2 cups water /500ml
- 2 tbsp butter, unsalted /30g
- Salt and black pepper to taste

Directions:

1. Turn on the Ninja Foodi and select Sear/Sauté mode, adjust to High. Drop in the butter, once it melts add the garlic and cook for 30 seconds while stirring frequently to prevent the garlic from burning.

2. Then, add the broccoli, water, salt, and pepper. Close the lid, secure the pressure valve, and select Pressure mode on High pressure for 5 minutes. Press Start/Stop.

3. Once the timer has ended, do a quick pressure release and use a stick blender to mash the Ingredients until smooth to your desired consistency and well combined.

4. Stir in Cream cheese. Adjust the taste with salt and pepper. Close the crisping lid and cook for 2 minutes on Broil mode. Serve warm.

Parsley Mashed Cauliflower

Servings: 4
Cooking Time: 15 Min
Ingredients:
- 1 head cauliflower
- 1/4 cup heavy cream /62.5g
- 2 cups water /500ml
- 1 tbsp fresh parsley, finely chopped /15g
- 1 tbsp butter /15g
- ¼ tsp celery salt /1.25g
- ⅛ tsp freshly ground black pepper /0.625g

Directions:
1. Into the pot, add water and set trivet on top and lay cauliflower head onto the trivet. Seal the pressure lid, choose Pressure, set to High, and set the timer to 8 minutes. Press Start.
2. When ready, release the pressure quickly. Remove the trivet and drain liquid from the pot before returning to the base.
3. Take back the cauliflower to the pot alongside the pepper, heavy cream, salt and butter; use an immersion blender to blend until smooth. Top with parsley and serve.

Cabbage With Bacon

Servings: 4
Cooking Time: 20 Minutes
Ingredients:
- 4 cups red cabbage, shredded
- ¼ cup veggie stock
- A pinch of black pepper and salt
- 1 tablespoon olive oil
- 1 cup canned tomatoes, crushed
- Zest of 1 lime, grated
- 2 ounces bacon, cooked and crumbled

Directions:
1. Put the reversible rack in the Foodi, add the baking pan inside and grease it with the oil.
2. Add the cabbage, the stock and the other ingredients into the pan.
3. Cook on Baking mode at 380 °F for 20 minutes.
4. Divide the mix between plates and serve.

Nutrition Info:
- Calories: 144; Fat: 3g; Carbohydrates: 4.5g; Protein: 4.4g

Pasta Primavera

Servings: 6
Cooking Time: 18 Minutes
Ingredients:
- ½ red onion, sliced
- 1 carrot, thinly sliced
- 1 head broccoli, cut into florets
- 1 red bell pepper, thinly sliced
- 1 yellow squash, halved lengthwise and sliced into half moons
- 1 zucchini, halved lengthwise and sliced into half moons
- ¼ cup extra-virgin olive oil
- ½ teaspoon dried basil
- ½ teaspoon dried oregano
- ½ teaspoon dried parsley
- ¼ teaspoon dried rosemary
- ¼ teaspoon crushed red pepper flakes
- 1 box penne pasta
- 4 cups water
- 2 tablespoons freshly squeezed lemon juice
- ½ cup grated Parmesan cheese, divided

Directions:
1. Place Cook & Crisp Basket in pot. Close crisping lid. Select AIR CRISP, set temperature to 390°F, and set time to 5 minutes. Select START/STOP to begin preheating.
2. In a large bowl, combine the red onion, carrot, broccoli, bell pepper, yellow squash, zucchini, olive oil, basil, oregano, parsley, rosemary, and red pepper flakes, and toss to combine.
3. Once unit has preheated, add the vegetable mixture to the basket. Close lid.
4. Select AIR CRISP, set temperature to 390°F, and set time to 15 minutes. Select START/STOP to begin.
5. When cooking is complete, remove the vegetables and basket, and set aside.
6. Add the pasta and water. Assemble pressure lid, making sure the pressure release valve is in the SEAL position.
7. Select PRESSURE and set to HI. Set time to 3 minutes. Select START/STOP to begin.
8. When pressure cooking is complete, allow pressure to naturally release for 10 minutes. After 10 minutes, quick release remaining pressure by moving the pressure release valve to the VENT position. Carefully remove lid when unit has finished releasing pressure.
9. Add vegetables to pasta. Add the lemon juice and ¼ cup of Parmesan cheese and stir. Serve and top with remaining cheese.

Nutrition Info:

- Calories: 388, Total Fat: 12g, Sodium: 127mg, Carbohydrates: 60g, Protein: 15g.

Roasted Squash And Rice With Crispy Tofu

Servings: 4
Cooking Time: 70 Min
Ingredients:
- 1 small butternut squash, peeled and diced
- 1 block extra-firm tofu, drained and cubed /450g
- 1 cup jasmine rice, cooked /130g
- ¾ cup water /188ml
- 1 tbsp coconut aminos /15g
- 2 tbsps melted butter; divided /30ml
- 2 tsp s arrowroot starch /10g
- 1 tsp salt /5g
- 1 tsp freshly ground black pepper /5g

Directions:
1. Pour the rice and water into the pot and mix with a spoon. Seal the pressure lid, choose Pressure, set to High and set the time to 2 minutes. Choose Start/Stop to boil the rice.
2. in a bowl, toss the butternut squash with 1 tbsp of melted butter and season with the salt and black pepper. Set aside.
3. In another bowl, mix the remaining butter with the coconut aminos, and toss the tofu in the mixture. Pour the arrowroot starch over the tofu and toss again to combine well.
4. When done cooking the rice, perform a quick pressure release, and carefully open the pressure lid. Put the reversible rack in the pot in the higher position and line with aluminum foil. Arrange the tofu and butternut squash on the rack.
5. Close the crisping lid. Choose Air Crisp, set the temperature to 400°F or 205°C, and set the time to 20 minutes. Choose Start/Stop to begin cooking.
6. After 10 minutes, use tongs to turn the butternut squash and tofu. When done cooking, check for your desired crispiness and serve the tofu and squash with the rice.

Bok Choy And Zoddle Soup

Servings: 6
Cooking Time: 35 Min
Ingredients:
- 1 lb. baby bok choy, stems removed /450g
- 2 zucchinis, spiralized
- 6 oz. Shitake mushrooms, stems removed and sliced to a 2-inch thickness /180g
- 2-inch ginger; chopped
- 2 cloves garlic, peeled
- 3 carrots, peeled and sliced diagonally
- 2 sweet onion; chopped
- 6 cups water /1500ml
- 2 tbsp sesame oil /30ml
- 2 tbsp soy sauce /30ml
- 2 tbsp chili paste /30g
- Salt to taste
- Sesame seeds to garnish
- Chopped green onion to garnish

Directions:
1. In a food processor, add the chili paste, ginger, onion, and garlic; and process them until they are pureed. Turn on the Ninja foodi and select Sear/Sauté mode to High.
2. Pour in the sesame oil, once it has heated add the onion puree and cook for 3 minutes while stirring constantly to prevent burning. Add the water, mushrooms, soy sauce, and carrots.
3. Close the lid, secure the pressure valve, and select Pressure mode on High pressure for 5 minutes. Press Start/Stop.
4. Once the timer has ended, do a quick pressure release and open the lid. Add the zucchini noodles and bok choy, and stir to ensure that they are well submerged in the liquid.
5. Adjust the taste with salt, cover the pot with the crisping lid, and let the vegetables cook for 10 minutes on Broil mode.
6. Use a soup spoon to dish the soup with veggies into soup bowls. Sprinkle with green onions and sesame seeds. Serve as a complete meal.

Mushroom Goulash

Servings: 6
Cooking Time: 40 Minutes
Ingredients:
- 2 tbsp. olive oil, divided
- ½ onion, sliced thin
- 1 red bell pepper, chopped
- 2 lbs. mushrooms, chopped
- ½ tsp salt
- ¼ tsp pepper
- 14 oz. tomatoes, diced
- 2 cups vegetable broth, low sodium
- 1 tsp garlic powder
- 1 ½ tbsp. paprika
- 5 -6 sprigs fresh thyme

Directions:

1. Add half the oil to the cooking pot and set to sauté on med-high.
2. Add the onion and cook until they start to get soft, about 4 minutes. Add the red pepper and cook 3-5 minutes or until onions start to caramelize. Transfer to a plate.
3. Add the remaining oil to the pot and let it get hot. Add the mushrooms and cook until liquid is almost evaporated, stirring occasionally. Season with salt and pepper.
4. Add the peppers and onions back to the pot along with tomatoes, broth, garlic powder, paprika, and thyme, stir to mix well. Bring to a boil, cover, reduce heat to med-low and let simmer 20 minutes. Serve.

Nutrition Info:
- Calories 115,Total Fat 5g,Total Carbs 14g,Protein 6g,Sodium 544mg.

Peanut Tofu & Noodles

Servings: 4
Cooking Time: 10 Minutes
Ingredients:
- Nonstick cooking spray
- 16 oz. firm tofu, cubed
- ½ lb. linguine
- 2 cups broccoli, chopped
- ¼ cup peanut butter
- ¼ cup soy sauce, low sodium
- 2 tbsp. rice vinegar
- 2 tbsp. peanuts, chopped

Directions:
1. Spray the fryer basket with cooking spray.
2. Place tofu in the basket and add the tender-crisp lid. Set to air fry on 400°F. Cook tofu 10 minutes, turning over halfway through cooking time.
3. Prepare pasta according to package directions. Add the broccoli during the last 5 minutes of cooking time. Drain.
4. In a small bowl, whisk together peanut butter, soy sauce, and vinegar until smooth.
5. Add the tofu and sauce to the pasta and toss until evenly distributed. Ladle onto serving plates and top with peanuts. Serve immediately.

Nutrition Info:
- Calories 380,Total Fat 19g,Total Carbs 31g,Protein 30g,Sodium 705mg.

Creamy Golden Casserole

Servings: 6
Cooking Time: 40 Minutes
Ingredients:
- Nonstick cooking spray
- 2 lbs. summer squash, cut in 1-inch pieces
- ¾ cup sharp cheddar cheese, reduced fat, grated & divided
- ¼ cup light mayonnaise
- 2 eggs
- ¼ tsp salt
- ¼ tsp pepper

Directions:
1. Spray a 2-qt baking dish with cooking spray.
2. Add the squash to the cooking pot along with just enough water to cover. Set to saute on high heat and bring to a boil.
3. Reduce heat to medium and cook 8-10 minutes or until squash is tender. Drain.
4. Place the squash in a large bowl and add ½ cup cheese, mayonnaise, eggs, salt, and pepper and mix well. Spoon into prepared dish and sprinkle with remaining cheese.
5. Place the rack in the cooking pot and add the dish. Add the tender-crisp lid and set to bake on 375°F. Bake 30 minutes until heated through and top is golden brown. Serve.

Nutrition Info:
- Calories 120,Total Fat 8g,Total Carbs 6g,Protein 7g,Sodium 303mg.

Paneer Cutlet

Servings: 1
Cooking Time: 15 Min
Ingredients:
- 1 small onion, finely chopped
- 2 cup grated paneer /260g
- 1 cup grated cheese /130g
- ½ tsp chai masala /2.5g
- 1 tsp butter /5g
- ½ tsp garlic powder /2.5g
- ½ tsp oregano /2.5g
- ½ tsp salt /2.5g

Directions:
1. Preheat the Ninja Foodi to 350 °F or 177°C. Oil the Ninja Foodi basket. Mix all Ingredients in a bowl, until well incorporated.
2. Make cutlets out of the mixture and place them on the greased baking dish. Place the baking dish in the Ninja Foodi and cook the cutlets for 10 minutes.

Whole Roasted Broccoli And White Beans With Harissa, Tahini, And Lemon

Servings: 4
Cooking Time: 30 Minutes
Ingredients:
- 2 cups water
- 2 small heads broccoli, cut in half
- 2 tablespoons unsalted butter
- ½ white onion, minced
- 2 garlic cloves, minced
- 1 can cannellini beans, rinsed and drained
- 1 can fire-roasted tomatoes and peppers
- 1 tablespoon spicy harissa
- Sea salt
- Freshly ground black pepper
- ¼ cup tahini
- ¼ cup walnuts, toasted and chopped
- Zest of 1 lemon
- Juice of 1 lemon

Directions:
1. Place Reversible Rack in pot, making sure it is in the lowest position. Pour the water into the pot and place the broccoli on the rack. Assemble the pressure lid, making sure the pressure release valve is in the SEAL position.
2. Select STEAM. Set time to 8 minutes. Select START/STOP to begin.
3. When steaming is complete, quick release the pressure by turning the pressure release valve to the VENT position. Carefully remove lid when unit has finished releasing pressure.
4. Remove rack and broccoli and set aside. Drain the remaining water from the pot and reinsert it in base.
5. Select SEAR/SAUTÉ and set to HI. Select START/STOP to begin. Let preheat for 5 minutes.
6. Add the butter to pot. Once melted, add the onions and garlic and cook for 3 minutes. Add the beans, tomatoes, harissa, and season with salt and pepper. Cook for 4 minutes.
7. Reinsert rack and broccoli. Close crisping lid.
8. Select AIR CRISP, set temperature to 390°F, and set time to 15 minutes. Select START/STOP to begin.
9. After 10 minutes, open lid and flip the broccoli. Close lid and continue cooking.
10. When cooking is complete, remove rack with broccoli from pot. Place the beans in serving dishes and top with the broccoli. Drizzle tahini over the broccoli and sprinkle with walnuts. Garnish with the lemon zest and juice and serve.

Nutrition Info:
- Calories: 426, Total Fat: 25g, Sodium: 435mg, Carbohydrates: 39g, Protein: 15g.

Quick Indian-style Curry

Servings: 8
Cooking Time: 35 Minutes
Ingredients:
- 1 tablespoon vegetable oil
- 1 small onion, diced
- 1 small bell pepper, diced
- 1 large potato, cut into 1-inch cubes
- 1 teaspoon ground turmeric
- 1 teaspoon cumin seeds
- 1 teaspoon ground cumin
- 1 teaspoon garam masala (optional)
- 1 teaspoon curry powder
- 1 jar curry sauce, plus 1 jar water
- 1 can diced tomatoes
- 1 cup dried red lentils
- 8 ounces paneer, cubed (optional)
- 1 cup fresh cilantro, roughly chopped (optional)
- Salt
- Freshly ground black pepper

Directions:
1. Select SEAR/SAUTÉ and set temperature to HI. Select START/STOP to begin and allow to preheat for 5 minutes.
2. Add the oil to the pot and allow to heat for 1 minute. Add the onion and bell pepper and sauté for 3 to 4 minutes.
3. Add the potato, turmeric, cumin seeds, cumin, garam masala, and curry powder. Stir and cook for 5 minutes.
4. Stir in the curry sauce, water, tomatoes, and lentils.
5. Assemble the pressure lid, making sure the pressure release valve is in the SEAL position.
6. Select PRESSURE and set to HI. Set the time to 15 minutes. Select START/STOP to begin.
7. When pressure cooking is complete, allow the pressure to naturally release for 10 minutes. After 10 minutes, quick release any remaining pressure by moving the pressure release valve to the VENT position. Carefully remove the lid when the unit has finished releasing pressure.
8. Stir in the paneer (if using) and cilantro. Taste and season with salt and pepper, as needed.

Nutrition Info:
- Calories: 217, Total Fat: 6g, Sodium: 27mg, Carbohydrates: 33g, Protein: 8g.

Veggie Primavera

Servings: 6
Cooking Time: 25 Minutes
Ingredients:
- 2 tbsp. olive oil
- 1 tsp Italian seasoning
- 1 tsp garlic powder
- ½ tsp salt
- ½ tsp pepper
- 12 oz. baby red potatoes, quartered
- 2 ears corn, husked & cut into 1-inch rounds
- 4 oz. baby carrots
- ½ red onion, cut in wedges
- 4 oz. fresh sugar snap peas

Directions:
1. In a large bowl, combine oil, Italian seasoning, garlic powder, salt, and pepper, mix well.
2. Add remaining ingredients, except peas, and toss to coat the vegetables.
3. Spray the cooking pot with cooking spray and add the vegetable mixture.
4. Add the tender-crisp lid and set to roast on 425°F. Roast vegetables 15 minutes, turning halfway through cooking time.
5. Add the peas and stir to mix. Roast another 10-15 minutes until vegetables are lightly browned and tender. Serve immediately.

Nutrition Info:
- Calories 142,Total Fat 5g,Total Carbs 23g,Protein 3g,Sodium 222mg.

Cheesy Baked Spinach

Servings: 8
Cooking Time: 30 Minutes
Ingredients:
- Nonstick cooking spray
- 15 oz. spinach, thawed, chopped & drained well
- 1 cup wild rice, cooked
- 1 ½ cup cheddar cheese, reduced fat, grated
- 10 ½ oz. cream of mushroom soup, low fat
- 1 tbsp. butter, melted
- 1 tsp onion powder
- ¼ tsp nutmeg

Directions:
1. Place the rack in the cooking pot. Spray a casserole dish with cooking spray.
2. In a large bowl, combine all ingredients and mix well. Spoon into prepared dish and place on the rack.
3. Add the tender-crisp lid and set to bake on 350°F. Bake 30 minutes or until heated through. Serve.

Nutrition Info:
- Calories 113,Total Fat 5g,Total Carbs 10g,Protein 8g,Sodium 492mg.

Steamed Artichokes With Lemon Aioli

Servings: 4
Cooking Time: 20 Min
Ingredients:
- 4 artichokes, trimmed
- 1 small handful parsley; chopped
- 1 lemon, halved
- 3 cloves garlic, crushed
- ½ cup mayonnaise /125ml
- 1 cup water /250ml
- 1 tsp lemon zest /5g
- 1 tbsp lemon juice /15ml
- Salt to taste

Directions:
1. On the artichokes cut ends, rub with lemon. Add water into the pot of pressure cooker. Set the reversible rack over the water,
2. Place the artichokes into the steamer basket with the points upwards; sprinkle each with salt. Seal lid and cook on High pressure for 10 minutes. Press Start. When ready, release the pressure quickly.
3. In a mixing bowl, combine mayonnaise, garlic, lemon juice, and lemon zest. Season to taste with salt. Serve with warm steamed artichokes sprinkled with parsley.

Spicy Cabbage Soup

Servings: 6
Cooking Time: 20 Minutes
Ingredients:
- Nonstick cooking spray
- 2 cups onion, chopped fine
- 14 oz. tomatoes with green chilies
- 8 oz. tomato sauce
- 1 tsp garlic powder
- 4 cups water
- 3 cups green cabbage, shredded
- 1 tbsp. brown sugar

Directions:
1. Spray the cooking pot with cooking spray and set to sauté on med-high heat.

2. Add onions and cook until tender, stirring occasionally, about 3-4 minutes.
3. Add tomatoes with chilies to a blender and process about 30 seconds until pureed.
4. Stir the pureed tomatoes, tomato sauce, garlic, and water into the onions until combined.
5. Add the lid and set to pressure cook on high. Set timer for 6 minutes. When timer goes off, use natural release to remove the pressure.
6. Stir in cabbage and brown sugar. Recover and set to pressure cook on high. Set timer for 8 minutes. When timer goes off, use natural release again. Stir well and serve.

Nutrition Info:
- Calories 56,Total Fat 0g,Total Carbs 13g,Protein 2g,Sodium 283mg.

Carrot Gazpacho

Servings: 4
Cooking Time: 2 Hr 30 Min
Ingredients:
- 1 pound trimmed carrots /450g
- 1 pound tomatoes; chopped /450g
- 1 red onion; chopped
- 2 cloves garlic
- 1 cucumber, peeled and chopped
- 1/4 cup extra-virgin olive oil /62.5ml
- 1 pinch salt
- 2 tbsp lemon juice /30ml
- 2 tbsp white wine vinegar /30ml
- salt and freshly ground black pepper to taste

Directions:
1. To the Foodi add carrots, salt and enough water. Seal the pressure lid, choose Pressure, set to High, and set the timer to 20 minutes. Press Start.
2. Once ready, do a quick release. Set the beets to a bowl and place in the refrigerator to cool.
3. In a blender, add carrots, cucumber, red onion, pepper, garlic, olive oil, tomatoes, lemon juice, vinegar, and salt.
4. Blend until very smooth. Place gazpacho to a serving bowl, chill while covered for 2 hours.

Crispy Kale Chips

Servings: 2
Cooking Time: 9 Min
Ingredients:
- 4 cups kale, stemmed and packed /520g
- 1 tbsp of yeast flakes /15g
- 2 tbsp of olive oil /30ml
- 1 tsp of vegan seasoning /5g
- Salt to taste

Directions:
1. In a bowl, add the oil, the kale, the vegan seasoning, and the yeast and mix well. Dump the coated kale in the Ninja Foodi's basket.
2. Set the heat to 370°F or 188°C, close the crisping lid and fry for a total of 6 minutes on Air Crisp mode. Shake it from time to time.

Zucchinis Spinach Fry

Servings: 4
Cooking Time: 17 Minutes
Ingredients:
- 2 zucchinis, sliced
- 1-pound baby spinach
- ½ cup tomato sauce
- Black pepper and salt
- 1 tablespoon avocado oil
- 1 red onion, chopped
- 1 tablespoon sweet paprika
- ½ teaspoon garlic powder
- ½ teaspoon chilli powder

Directions:
1. Set the Foodi on Sauté, stir in the oil, heat it up, add the onion and sauté for 2 minutes.
2. Add the zucchinis, spinach, and the other ingredients Put the Ninja Foodi's lid on and cook on High for 15 minutes.
3. Release the pressure quickly for 5 minutes, divide everything between plates and serve.

Nutrition Info:
- Calories: 130; Fat: 5.5g; Carbohydrates: 3.3g; Protein: 1g

Cauliflower Steaks & Veggies

Servings: 6
Cooking Time: 45 Minutes
Ingredients:
- ¼ cup butter, melted
- 1 tbsp. olive oil
- 3 tbsp. lemon juice
- 2 tsp fresh parsley, chopped
- ¾ tsp onion powder
- ¾ tsp garlic powder
- ½ tsp salt
- ¼ tsp pepper
- 1 head cauliflower, cut in ½-inch thick slices
- 12 baby carrots
- 6 small potatoes, halved

- 1 zucchini, cut in 1-inch pieces

Directions:

1. In a large bowl, whisk together butter, oil, lemon juice, parsley, onion powder, garlic powder, salt, and pepper.
2. Line a baking sheet with foil. Brush both sides of cauliflower steaks with butter mixture and place on baking sheet.
3. Add remaining vegetables to the butter mixture and toss to coat. Place in the cooking pot. Add the rack and place the cauliflower on the rack.
4. Add the tender-crisp lid and set to roast on 400°F. Bake 40-45 minutes until vegetables are tender and starting to brown, turning over halfway through cooking time. Serve.

Nutrition Info:

- Calories 260,Total Fat 11g,Total Carbs 38g,Protein 6g,Sodium 313mg.

Creamy Carrot Soup

Servings: 4
Cooking Time: 15 Minutes

Ingredients:

- 3 ½ cups chicken broth, low sodium
- 5 carrots, peeled & cut in 1-inch pieces
- 1 large parsnip, peeled & cut in 1-inch pieces
- 1 potato, peeled & cut in 1-inch pieces
- 1 onion, chopped
- 2 ½ cups skim milk
- ¼ tsp thyme
- ¼ tsp pepper

Directions:

1. Add the broth, carrots, parsnip, potato, and onion to the cooking pot and toss to mix.
2. Add the lid and set to pressure cook on high. Set the timer for 8 minutes. When timer goes off, use natural release to remove the pressure.
3. Use an immersion blender to process the vegetables until almost smooth.
4. Set to sauté on medium heat. Stir in remaining ingredients and cook 6-8 minutes or until heated through. Ladle into bowls and serve.

Nutrition Info:

- Calories 226,Total Fat 2g,Total Carbs 42g,Protein 13g,Sodium 206mg.

Sweet Potato Noodles With Cashew Sauce

Servings: 4
Cooking Time: 10 Minutes
Ingredients:

- 1 cup cashews
- ¾ cup water
- ½ tsp salt
- 1 clove garlic
- 2 tbsp. olive oil, divided
- 4 large sweet potatoes, spiralized
- 2 cups baby spinach
- ½ cup fresh basil, chopped

Directions:

1. Add cashews to a small bowl and cover with water. Let soak 2 hours.
2. Drain off the water, rinse, and add to a food processor with ¾ cup water, salt, and garlic. Pulse until smooth.
3. Add half the oil to the cooking pot and set to sauté on med-high heat.
4. Add sweet potatoes and cook 6-7 minutes until tender-crisp.
5. Add spinach and toss until it wilts, 1-2 minutes.
6. Turn off the heat and stir in half the herbs and the cashew sauce.
7. Divide evenly among serving plates, drizzle with olive oil and garnish with remaining herbs. Serve.

Nutrition Info:

- Calories 523,Total Fat 35g,Total Carbs 45g,Protein 13g,Sodium 528mg.

Grilled Cheese

Servings: 2
Cooking Time: 40 Minutes

Ingredients:

- 1 small cauliflower, cut in florets
- ½ cup mozzarella cheese, low fat, grated
- 1 egg
- ¼ tsp onion powder
- ¼ tsp pepper
- ½ cup sharp cheddar cheese, low fat, grated
- 1 tbsp. butter, soft, divided

Directions:

1. Place the cauliflower in a food processor and pulsed until finely chopped.
2. Place in a microwave safe bowl and microwave 8-9 minutes or until soft. Place in a strainer and press out any excess water.
3. Add the cauliflower to a large bowl and add mozzarella, egg, onion powder, salt, and pepper and mix well.
4. Add the rack to the cooking pot. Lay out a sheet of parchment paper and spread cauliflower mixture on it. Shape into 4 equal squares.

5. Place the parchment paper on the rack and add the tender-crisp lid. Set to bake on 400°F. Bake 15-20 minutes or until golden brown. Remove from cooking pot.
6. Add 1 teaspoon to the cooking pot and set to sauté on med-low heat.
7. Sprinkle cheese evenly on 2 cauliflower squares and top with remaining squares. Place in the cooking pot and spread remaining butter over top.
8. Cook 2-4 minutes until golden brown, flip and cook another 2-4 minutes until cheese is melted. Serve.

Nutrition Info:
- Calories 394,Total Fat 28g,Total Carbs 9g,Protein 28g,Sodium 696mg.

Rosemary Sweet Potato Medallions

Servings: 4
Cooking Time: 25 Min

Ingredients:
- 4 sweet potatoes, scrubbed clean and dried
- 1 cup water /250ml
- 2 tbsp butter /30g
- 1 tbsp fresh rosemary /15g
- 1 tsp garlic powder /5g
- salt to taste

Directions:
1. Into the pot, add water and place the reversible rack over the water. Use a fork to prick sweet potatoes all over and set onto the reversible rack.
2. Seal the pressure lid, choose Pressure, set to High, and set the timer to 12 minutes. Press Start. When ready, release the pressure quickly. Transfer sweet potatoes to a cutting board and slice into 1/2-inch medallions and ensure they are peeled.
3. Melt butter in the pressure cooker on Sear/Sauté. Add in the medallions and cook each side for 2 to 3 minutes until browned. Apply salt and garlic powder to season. Serve topped with fresh rosemary.

Potato Filled Bread Rolls

Servings: 4
Cooking Time: 25 Min

Ingredients:
- 8 slices of bread
- 2 green chilies, deseeded; chopped
- 5 large potatoes, boiled, mashed
- 2 sprigs curry leaf
- 1 medium onion; chopped
- 1 tbsp olive oil /15ml
- ½ tsp mustard seeds /2.5g
- ½ tsp turmeric /2.5g
- Salt, to taste

Directions:
1. Combine the olive oil, onion, curry leaves, and mustard seed, in the Ninja Foodi basket. Cook for 5 minutes. Mix the onion mixture with the mashed potatoes, chilies, turmeric, and some salt. Divide the dough into 8 equal pieces.
2. Trim the sides of the bread, and wet it with some water. Make sure to get rid of the excess water. Take one wet bread slice in your palm and place one of the potato pieces in the center.
3. Roll the bread over the filling, sealing the edges. Place the rolls onto a prepared baking dish, close the crisping lid and cook for 12 minutes on Air Crisp at 350 °F or 177°C.

Balsamic Cabbage With Endives

Servings: 4
Cooking Time: 15 Minutes

Ingredients:
- 1 green cabbage head, shredded
- 2 endives, trimmed and sliced lengthwise
- Black pepper and salt to the taste
- 1 tablespoon olive oil
- 2 shallots, chopped
- ½ cup chicken stock
- 1 tablespoon sweet paprika
- 1 tablespoon balsamic vinegar

Directions:
1. Set the Foodi on Sauté mode, stir in the oil, heat it up, add the shallots and sauté for 2 minutes.
2. Add the cabbage, the endives and the other ingredients.
3. Put the Ninja Foodi's lid on and cook on High for 13 minutes.
4. Release the pressure quickly for 5 minutes, divide the mix between plates and serve.

Nutrition Info:
- Calories: 120; Fat: 2g; Carbohydrates: 3.3g; Protein: 4

Pasta Veggie Toss

Servings: 8
Cooking Time: 10 Minutes

Ingredients:
- 2 tbsp. olive oil
- ½ red onion, chopped
- ½ lb. asparagus, trimmed & cut in 1-inch pieces
- ½ lb. mushrooms, sliced
- 2 cloves garlic, chopped fine
- ¼ cup dry white win
- 3 oz. sun dried tomatoes, reconstituted & sliced

- ½ tsp salt
- ½ tsp pepper
- ½ cup half and half
- 10 oz. baby spinach, chopped
- 1 tbsp. fresh basil, chopped
- 8 oz. bow tie pasta, cooked & drained

Directions:
1. Add the oil to the cooking pot and set to sauté on med-high heat.
2. Add the onions and asparagus and cook, stirring occasionally, 3 minutes.
3. Add the mushrooms and garlic and cook 2-3 minutes until softened.
4. Stir in the wine, tomatoes, salt, and pepper and cook 2-3 minutes until heated through.
5. Add the half and half and cook until heated through again.
6. Place the pasta in a large bowl and add sauce, spinach, and basil and toss to coat. Serve immediately.

Nutrition Info:
- Calories 192,Total Fat 5g,Total Carbs 34g,Protein 7g,Sodium 218mg.

Broccoli Cauliflower

Servings: 4
Cooking Time: 15 Minutes
Ingredients:
- 2 cups broccoli florets
- 1 cup cauliflower florets
- 2 tablespoons lime juice
- 1 tablespoon avocado oil
- 1/3 cup tomato sauce
- 2 teaspoons ginger, grated
- 2 teaspoons garlic, minced
- 1 tablespoon chives, chopped

Directions:
1. Set the Foodi on Sauté mode, stir in the oil, heat it up, add the garlic and the ginger and sauté for 2 minutes.
2. Stir in the broccoli, cauliflower and the rest of the ingredients.
3. Put the Ninja Foodi's lid on and cook on High for 13 minutes.
4. naturally Release the pressure for 10 minutes, divide everything between plates and serve.

Nutrition Info:
- Calories: 118; Fat: 1.5g; Carbohydrates: 4.3g; Protein: 6g

Baby Porcupine Meatballs

Servings: 4
Cooking Time: 30 Min
Ingredients:
- 1 lb. of ground beef /450g
- 1 onion; chopped
- 1 green bell pepper, finely chopped
- 1 garlic clove, minced
- 1 cup rice /130g
- 2 cups of tomato juice /500ml
- 2 tbsp Worcestershire sauce /30ml
- 1 tsp celery salt /5g
- 1 tsp oregano /5g

Directions:
1. Combine the rice, ground beef, onion, celery, salt, green peppers, and garlic. Shape into balls of 1 inch each. Arrange the balls in the basket of the Ninja Foodi. Close the crisping lid and cook for 15 minutes at 320°F or 160°C.
2. After 8 minutes, shape the balls. Heat the tomato juice, cloves, oregano, and Worcestershire sauce in a saucepan over medium heat.
3. Pour in the meatballs, bring to a boil, reduce the heat and simmer for 10 minutes, stirring often. Serve warm.

Tomato Bisque

Servings: 6
Cooking Time: 3 Hours
Ingredients:
- 2 28 oz. cans tomatoes, crushed
- 1 tbsp. sugar
- 1 tbsp. fresh basil, chopped
- 1 tsp garlic powder
- 1 tsp onion powder
- ½ tsp pepper
- 12 oz. evaporated milk, low fat

Directions:
1. Place the tomatoes, sugar, basil, garlic powder, onion powder, and pepper in the cooking pot, stir to mix.
2. Add the lid and set to slow cook on high. Cook 2 ½ hours.
3. Stir in evaporated milk and let cook another 30 minutes. Serve.

Nutrition Info:
- Calories 141,Total Fat 1g,Total Carbs 29g,Protein 9g,Sodium 558mg.

Cauliflower Chunks With Lemon Sauce

Servings: 4
Cooking Time: 15 Minutes
Ingredients:
- 1-pound cauliflower, cut into chunks
- 1 tablespoon dill, chopped
- 1 tablespoon lemon zest, grated
- Juice of ½ lemon
- 2 tablespoons butter, melted
- Black pepper and salt to the taste

Directions:
1. Set the Foodi on Sauté mode, stir in the butter, melt it, add the cauliflower chunks and brown for 5 minutes.
2. Add the lemon zest and the other ingredients set the machine on Air Crisp and cook at 390 °F for 10 minutes.
3. Divide everything between plates and serve.

Nutrition Info:
- Calories: 122; Fat: 3.3g; Carbohydrates: 3g; Protein: 2g

Italian Sausage With Garlic Mash

Servings: 6
Cooking Time: 30 Min
Ingredients:
- 6 Italian sausages
- 4 large potatoes, peeled and cut into 1½-inch chunks
- 2 garlic cloves, smashed
- ⅓ cup butter, melted /44ml
- ¼ cup milk; at room temperature, or more as needed /62.5ml
- 1 ½ cups water /375ml
- 1 tbsp olive oil /15ml
- 1 tbsp chopped chives/15g
- salt and ground black pepper to taste

Directions:
1. Select Sear/Sauté, set to Medium High, and choose Start/Stop to preheat the pot and heat olive oil. Cook for 8-10 minutes, turning periodically until browned. Set aside. Wipe the pot with paper towels. Add in water and set the reversible rack over water. Place potatoes onto the reversible rack.
2. Seal the pressure lid, choose Pressure, set to High, and set the timer to 12 minutes. Press Start.
3. When ready, release the pressure quickly. Remove reversible rack from the pot. Drain water from the pot. Return potatoes to pot. Add in salt, butter, pepper, garlic, and milk and use a hand masher to mash until no large lumps remain.
4. Using an immersion blender, blend potatoes on Low for 1 minute until fluffy and light. Avoid over-blending to ensure the potatoes do not become gluey!
5. Transfer the mash to a serving plate, top with sausages and scatter chopped chives over to serve.

Veggie Taco Soup

Servings: 6
Cooking Time: 4 Hours
Ingredients:
- Nonstick cooking spray
- 6 corn tortillas, cut in strips
- 3 ½ cups vegetable broth, low sodium
- 14 ½ oz. tomatoes, diced, undrained
- 15 oz. spicy chili beans, undrained
- 4 oz. green chilies, diced & drained
- ¾ cup onions, chopped
- 1 clove garlic, chopped fine
- 2 tsp red wine vinegar
- ¼ tsp crushed red pepper flakes
- ¼ cup cilantro, chopped
- ½ tsp salt

Directions:
1. Spray fryer basket with cooking spray. Add the tortilla strips and spray with cooking spray.
2. Add the tender-crisp lid and set to air fry on 375°F. Cook until crisp, about 5 minutes, turning every couple of minutes. Set aside.
3. Add all ingredients, except cilantro, salt, and tortillas, to the cooking pot, mix well.
4. Add the lid and set to slow cook on high. Cook 3-4 hours, stirring occasionally.
5. Add salt and cilantro and stir well. Ladle into bowls and top with tortilla strips. Serve.

Nutrition Info:
- Calories 172,Total Fat 1g,Total Carbs 33g,Protein 8g,Sodium 617mg.

Burrito Bowls

Servings: 4
Cooking Time: 30 Min
Ingredients:
- 1 can diced tomatoes /435g
- 1 can black beans, drained and rinsed /435g
- 1 ½ cups vegetable stock /375ml
- 1 cup frozen corn kernels /130g
- 1 cup quinoa, rinsed /130g
- 1 avocado; sliced
- 1 onion

- 2 garlic cloves, minced
- 2 tbsp chopped cilantro /30g
- 1 tbsp roughly chopped fresh coriander /15g
- 2 tbsp olive oil /30ml
- 1 tbsp chili powder /15g
- 2 tsp ground cumin /10g
- 2 tsp paprika /10g
- 1 tsp salt /5g
- ½ tsp black pepper /2.5g
- ¼ tsp cayenne pepper /1.25g
- Cheddar cheese, grated for garnish

Directions:
1. Warm oil on Sear/Sauté. Add in onion and cook for 3 to 5 minutes until fragrant. Add garlic and cook for 2 more minutes until soft and golden brown. Add in chili powder, paprika, cayenne pepper, salt, cumin, and black pepper and cook for 1 minute until spices are soft.
2. Pour quinoa into onion and spice mixture and stir to coat quinoa completely in spices. Add diced tomatoes, black beans, vegetable stock, and corn; stir to combine.
3. Seal the pressure lid, choose Pressure, set to High, and set the timer to 7 minutes. Press Start. When ready, release the pressure quickly. Open the lid and let sit for 6 minutes until flavors combine. Use a fork to fluff quinoa and season with pepper and salt if desired.
4. Into quinoa and beans mixture, stir in cilantro and divide among plates. Top with cheese and avocado slices.

Colorful Vegetable Medley

Servings: 4
Cooking Time: 15 Min
Ingredients:
- 16 asparagus, trimmed
- 1 small head broccoli, broken into florets
- 1 small head cauliflower, broken into florets
- 5 ounces green beans /150g
- 2 carrots, peeled and cut on bias into 1/4-inch rounds
- 1 cup water /250ml
- salt to taste

Directions:
1. Into the pot, add water and set trivet on top of water and place steamer basket on top of the trivet. In an even layer, spread green beans, broccoli, cauliflower, asparagus, and carrots in the steamer basket.
2. Seal the pressure lid, choose Pressure, set to High, and set the timer to 3 minutes on High. When ready, release the pressure quickly. Remove steamer basket from cooker and add salt to vegetables for seasoning. Serve immediately.

Pasta With Roasted Veggies

Servings: 6
Cooking Time: 25 Min
Ingredients:
- 1 lb. penne, cooked /450g
- 1 acorn squash; sliced
- 4 oz. mushrooms; sliced /120g
- 1 zucchini; sliced
- 1 pepper; sliced
- 1 cup grape tomatoes, halved /130g
- ½ cup kalamata olives, pitted, halved /65g
- ¼ cup olive oil /62.5ml
- 3 tbsp balsamic vinegar /45ml
- 2 tbsp chopped basil /30g
- 1 tsp Italian seasoning /5g
- Salt and pepper, to taste

Directions:
1. Combine the pepper, zucchini, squash, mushrooms, and olive oil, in a large bowl. Season with salt and pepper. Close the crisping lid and cook the veggies for 15 minutes on Air Crisp mode at 380 °F or 194°C.
2. In a large bowl, combine the penne, roasted vegetables, olives, tomatoes, Italian seasoning, and vinegar. Sprinkle basil and serve.

Mashed Potatoes With Spinach

Servings: 6
Cooking Time: 30 Min
Ingredients:
- 3 pounds potatoes, peeled and quartered /1350g
- 2 cups spinach; chopped /260g
- ½ cup milk /125ml
- ⅓ cup butter /44g
- 1½ cups water /375ml
- 2 tbsp chopped fresh chives /30g
- ½ tsp salt /2.5g
- fresh black pepper to taste

Directions:
1. In the cooker, mix water, salt and potatoes. Seal the pressure lid, choose Pressure, set to High, and set the timer to 8 minutes. Press Start. When ready, release the pressure quickly. Drain the potatoes, and reserve the liquid in a bowl. In a large bowl, mash the potatoes.
2. Mix with butter and milk; season with pepper and salt. With reserved cooking liquid, thin the potatoes to attain the desired consistency.

3. Put the spinach in the remaining potato liquid and stir until wilted; season with salt and pepper. Drain and serve with potato mash. Garnish with black pepper and chives.

Hot & Sour Soup

Servings: 5
Cooking Time: 20 Minutes
Ingredients:
- 3 ½ cups chicken broth, low sodium, divided
- ½ lb. firm tofu, cut in 1-inch cubes
- ¼ lb. mushrooms, sliced
- 3 tbsp. soy sauce, low sodium
- 3 tbsp. vinegar
- 1 tsp ginger
- ½ tsp pepper
- 2 tbsp. cornstarch
- 1 egg, lightly beaten
- ½ cup fresh bean sprouts
- ½ tsp sesame oil

Directions:
1. Add 3 ¼ cups broth, tofu, mushrooms, soy sauce, vinegar, ginger, and pepper to the cooking pot and stir well.
2. Set to sauté on medium heat and bring to a boil.
3. In a small bowl, whisk together remaining broth and cornstarch until smooth. Reduce heat to low and whisk in cornstarch mixture until thickened.
4. Slowly stir in egg to form egg "ribbons". Add bean sprouts and simmer 1-2 minutes or until heated through. Stir in sesame oil and serve immediately.
5. Slowly stir in egg to form egg strands. Add bean sprouts and simmer 1 to 2 minutes, or until heated through, stirring occasionally.

Nutrition Info:
- Calories 123, Total Fat 6g, Total Carbs 8g, Protein 11g, Sodium 978mg.

Cheesy Chilies

Servings: 4
Cooking Time: 25 Minutes
Ingredients:
- Nonstick cooking spray
- 2 poblano chilies, halved, seeded, stems on
- 1 cup cottage cheese, drained
- ¼ cup green onion, chopped
- ½ cup Colby-Jack cheese, grated

Directions:
1. Spray the fryer basket with cooking spray.
2. Place the chilies in the basket and add the tender-crisp lid. Set to broil. Cook chilies until skin is charred on all sides. Transfer to a bag and let cool. When cool, remove the skin.
3. Spray an 8x8-inch baking pan with cooking spray.
4. Place chilies in the prepared pan. Spoon cottage cheese in the chilies and sprinkle with green onion and Colby Jack cheese.
5. Place the rack in the cooking pot and add the baking pan. Add the tender-crisp lid and set to bake on 350°F. Bake 15-20 minutes until hot and cheese is melted. Serve immediately.

Nutrition Info:
- Calories 119, Total Fat 7g, Total Carbs 5g, Protein 10g, Sodium 313mg.

Pomegranate Radish Mix

Servings: 4
Cooking Time: 8 Minutes
Ingredients:
- 1-pound radishes, roughly cubed
- Black pepper and salt to the taste
- 2 garlic cloves, minced
- ½ cup chicken stock
- 2 tablespoons pomegranate juice
- ¼ cup pomegranate seeds

Directions:
1. In your Ninja Foodi, combine the radishes with the stock and the other ingredients.
2. Put the Ninja Foodi's lid on and cook on High for 8 minutes.
3. Release the pressure quickly for 5 minutes, divide everything between plates and serve.

Nutrition Info:
- Calories: 133; Fat: 2.3g; Carbohydrates: 2.4g; Protein: 2g

Steamed Asparagus And Pine Nuts

Servings: 4
Cooking Time: 15 Min
Ingredients:
- 1 ½ lb. asparagus, ends trimmed /675g
- ½ cup chopped Pine Nuts /65g
- 1 cup water /250ml
- 1 tbsp butter /15g
- 1 tbsp olive oil to garnish/15ml
- Salt and pepper, to taste

Directions:
1. Open the Ninja Foodi, pour the water in, and fit the reversible rack at the bottom. Place the asparagus on the

rack, close the crisping lid, select Air Crisp mode, and set the time to 8 minutes on 380 °F or 194°C. Press Start/Stop.

2. At the 4-minute mark, carefully turn the asparagus over. When ready, remove to a plate, sprinkle with salt and pepper, and set aside.

3. Select Sear/Sauté on your Ninja Foodi, set to Medium and melt the butter. Add the pine nuts and cook for 2-3 minutes until golden. Scatter over the asparagus the pine nuts, and drizzle olive oil.

Eggplant Casserole

Servings: 8
Cooking Time: 1 Hour
Ingredients:
- Nonstick cooking spray
- 1 lb. eggplant, peeled, cubed
- ½ cup seasoned bread crumbs, divided
- 2 eggs
- ¼ tsp Italian seasoning
- ½ tsp garlic powder
- 1/8 tsp salt
- 1/8 tsp pepper
- 2 tomatoes, sliced

Directions:

1. Spray an 8x8-inch baking dish with cooking spray.

2. Add enough water to the cooking pot to come 2 inches up the sides. Set to sauté on high heat and bring to a boil.

3. Add the eggplant, reduce heat to medium, cover and cook 20-30 minutes until soft. Drain.

4. Add the eggplant to a large bowl and mash with a fork. Stir in ¼ cup bread crumbs, eggs, Italian seasoning, garlic, salt, and pepper and mix well.

5. Add the rack to the cooking pot. Spread the eggplant mixture in the prepared dish. Top with sliced tomatoes. Sprinkle tomatoes with remaining bread crumbs and spray with cooking spray. Place the dish on the rack.

6. Add the tender-crisp lid and set to bake on 350°F. Bake 25-30 minutes or until tomatoes are tender and starting to brown around the edges. Serve.

Nutrition Info:
- Calories 67, Total Fat 2g, Total Carbs 10g, Protein 3g, Sodium 181mg.

Minestrone With Pancetta

Servings: 6
Cooking Time: 40 Min
Ingredients:
- 2 ounces pancetta; chopped /60g
- 1 can diced tomatoes/450g
- 1 can chickpeas, rinsed and drained /450g
- 1 onion; diced
- 1 parsnip, peeled and chopped
- 2 carrots, peeled and sliced into rounds
- 2 celery stalks,
- 2 garlic cloves, minced
- 6 cups chicken broth /1500ml
- ½ cup grated Parmesan cheese/65g
- 2 cups green beans, trimmed and chopped /260g
- 1½ cups small shaped pasta /195g
- 1 tbsp dried basil/ 15g
- 1 tbsp dried oregano/15g
- 2 tbsp olive oil /30ml
- 1 tbsp dried thyme /15g
- salt and ground black pepper to taste

Directions:

1. Warm oil on Sear/Sauté. Add onion, carrots, garlic, pancetta, celery, and parsnip, and cook for 5 minutes until they become soft.

2. Stir in basil, oregano, green beans, broth, tomatoes, pepper, salt, thyme, vegetable broth, chickpeas, and pasta.

3. Seal the pressure lid, choose Pressure, set to High, and set the timer to 6 minutes. Press Start.

4. Release pressure naturally for 10 minutes then release the remaining pressure quickly. Ladle the soup into bowls and serve garnished with grated parmesan cheese.

Desserts Recipes

Brown Sugar And Butter Bars

Servings: 6
Cooking Time: 55 Min
Ingredients:
- 1 ½ cups Water /375ml
- 1 cup Oats /130g
- ½ cup Brown Sugar /65g
- ½ cup Sugar /65g
- 1 cup Flour /130g
- ½ cup Peanut Butter, softened /65g
- ½ cup Butter, softened /65g
- 1 Egg
- ½ tsp Baking Soda /2.5g
- ½ tsp Salt /2.5g

Directions:
1. Grease a springform pan and line it with parchment paper. Set aside. Beat together the eggs, peanut butter, butter, salt, white sugar, and brown sugar. Fold in the oats, flour, and baking soda.
2. Press the batter into the pan. Cover the pan with a paper towel and with a piece of foil. Pour the water into the Foodi and add a reversible rack. Lower the springform pan onto the rack.
3. Seal the pressure lid, choose Pressure, set to High, and set the time to 35 minutes. Press Start. When ready, do a quick release. Wait for 15 minutes before inverting onto a plate and cutting into bars.

Mini Chocolate Cheesecakes

Servings: 4
Cooking Time: 18 Minutes
Ingredients:
- 1 egg
- 8 ounces cream cheese, softened
- ¼ cup Erythritol
- 1 tablespoon powdered peanut butter
- ¾ tablespoon cacao powder

Directions:
1. Grease the Ninja Foodi's insert.
2. In a blender, stir in the eggs and cream cheese and pulse until smooth.
3. Add the rest of the ingredients and pulse until well combined.
4. Transfer the mixture into 2 8-ounce mason jars evenly.
5. In the Ninja Foodi's insert, place 1 cup of water.
6. Set a "Reversible Rack" in the Ninja Foodi's insert.
7. Place the mason jars over the "Reversible Rack".
8. Close the Ninja Foodi's lid with a pressure lid and place the pressure valve in the "Seal" position.
9. Select "Pressure" mode and set it to "High" for 18 minutes.
10. Press the "Start/Stop" button to initiate cooking.
11. Switch the pressure valve to "Vent" and do a "Natural" release.
12. Open the Ninja Foodi's lid and place the ramekins onto a wire rack to cool.
13. Refrigerate to chill for at least 6-8 hours before serving.

Nutrition Info:
- Calories: 222; Fats: 28.4g; Carbohydrates: 2.9g; Proteins: 6.5g

Flourless Chocolate Cake

Servings: 8
Cooking Time: 40 Minutes
Ingredients:
- Unsalted butter, at room temperature, for greasing the pan
- 9½ tablespoons unsalted butter, melted and cooled
- 4 large eggs, whites and yolks separated
- 1 cup granulated sugar, divided
- ½ cup unsweetened cocoa powder
- ¼ teaspoon vanilla extract
- ¼ teaspoon sea salt
- 1 cup plus 2 tablespoons semisweet chocolate chips, melted
- OPTIONAL TOPPINGS:
- Whipped cream
- Fruit sauce

Directions:
1. Grease a Ninja Multi-Purpose Pan or an 8-inch baking pan with butter and line the pan with a circle of parchment paper. Grease the parchment paper with butter.
2. Close crisping lid. Select BAKE/ROAST, set temperature to 350°F, and set time to 5 minutes. Select START/STOP to begin preheating.
3. In a large bowl, beat the melted butter and egg yolks. Add ½ cup of sugar, cocoa powder, vanilla extract, and salt. Slowly add the melted chocolate and stir.
4. In a medium bowl, beat the egg whites until soft peaks form. Add the remaining ½ cup of sugar and beat until stiff peaks form.

5. Gently fold the egg white mixture into the chocolate mixture. Pour the batter into the prepared pan.
6. When unit has preheated, place pan on Reversible Rack, making sure the rack is in the lower position. Open lid and place rack with pan in pot. Close crisping lid.
7. Select BAKE/ROAST, set temperature to 350°F, and set time to 40 minutes. Select START/STOP to begin.
8. After 30 minutes, check for doneness. If a toothpick inserted into the cake comes out clean, the cake is done. If not, close lid and continue baking until done.
9. When cooking is complete, carefully remove pan from pot and place it on a cooling rack for 5 minutes, then serve.

Nutrition Info:
- Calories: 437, Total Fat: 29g, Sodium: 109mg, Carbohydrates: 49g, Protein: 7g.

Classic Custard

Servings: 4
Cooking Time: 30 Minutes

Ingredients:
- Nonstick cooking spray
- 4 eggs
- ½ cup half and half
- 2 cups almond milk, unsweetened
- 1/3 cup Stevia
- 1 tsp vanilla
- ¼ tsp cinnamon

Directions:
1. Spray four ramekins with cooking spray.
2. In a large bowl, whisk all the ingredients together until combined. Pour into prepared ramekins
3. Place the ramekins in the cooking pot and pour enough water around them it comes ½ inch up the sides of the ramekins.
4. Add the tender-crisp lid and set to bake on 350°F. Bake 30 minutes or until custard is set. Transfer to a wire rack and let cool before serving.

Nutrition Info:
- Calories 135, Total Fat 5g, Total Carbs 23g, Protein 11g, Sodium 164mg.

Chocolate Peanut Butter And Jelly Puffs

Servings: 4
Cooking Time: 15 Minutes

Ingredients:
- 1 tube prepared flaky biscuit dough
- 2 milk chocolate bars
- Cooking spray
- 16 teaspoons (about ⅓ cup) creamy peanut butter
- 1 cup confectioners' sugar
- 1 tablespoon whole milk
- ¼ cup raspberry jam

Directions:
1. Remove biscuits from tube. There is a natural width-wise separation in each biscuit. Gently peel each biscuit in half using this separation.
2. Break the chocolate into 16 small pieces.
3. Spray a baking sheet with cooking spray.
4. Using your hands, stretch a biscuit half until it is about 3-inches in diameter. Place a teaspoon of peanut butter in center of each biscuit half, then place piece of chocolate on top. Pull an edge of dough over the top of the chocolate and pinch together to seal. Continue pulling the dough over the top of the chocolate and pinching until the chocolate is completely covered. The dough is pliable, so gently form it into a ball with your hands. Place on the prepared baking sheet. Repeat this step with the remaining biscuit dough, peanut butter, and chocolate.
5. Place the baking sheet in the refrigerator for 5 minutes.
6. Place Cook & Crisp Basket in pot. Close crisping lid. Select AIR CRISP, set temperature to 360°F, and set time to 20 minutes. Select START/STOP to begin. Let preheat for 5 minutes.
7. Remove the biscuits from the refrigerator and spray the tops with cooking spray. Open lid and spray the basket with cooking spray. Place 5 biscuit balls in the basket. Close lid and cook for 5 minutes.
8. When cooking is complete, remove the biscuit balls from the basket. Repeat step 7 two more times with remaining biscuit balls.
9. Mix together the confectioners' sugar, milk, and jam in a small bowl to make a frosting.
10. When the cooked biscuit balls are cool enough to handle, dunk the top of each into the frosting. As frosting is beginning to set, garnish with any toppings desired, such as sprinkles, crushed toffee or candy, or mini marshmallows.

Nutrition Info:
- Calories: 663, Total Fat: 25g, Sodium: 1094mg, Carbohydrates: 101g, Protein: 14g.

Crispy Coconut Pie

Servings: 8
Cooking Time: 1 Hour

Ingredients:
- 3 eggs
- 1 ½ cup Stevia
- 1 cup coconut, grated

- ½ cup butter, melted
- 1 tbsp. vinegar
- 1 tsp vanilla
- 1/8 tsp salt
- 1 9" pie crust, raw

Directions:
1. In a large bowl, beat the eggs.
2. Add remaining ingredients and mix well. Pour into pie crust.
3. Use a foil sling to carefully place the pie in the cooking pot. Add the tender-crisp lid and set to bake on 350°F. Bake 1 hour or until top is nicely browned and crisp.
4. Transfer to a wire rack to cool before serving.

Nutrition Info:
- Calories 427,Total Fat 22g,Total Carbs 45g,Protein 3g,Sodium 304mg.

Coconut Cream "custard" Bars

Servings:8
Cooking Time: 20 Minutes
Ingredients:
- 1¼ cups all-purpose flour
- 6 tablespoons unsalted butter, melted
- 2 tablespoons granulated sugar
- ½ cup unsweetened shredded coconut, divided
- ½ cup chopped almonds, divided
- Cooking spray
- 1 package instant vanilla pudding
- 1 cup milk
- 1 cup heavy (whipping) cream
- 4 tablespoons finely chopped dark chocolate, divided

Directions:
1. Select BAKE/ROAST, set temperature to 375°F, and set time to 15 minutes. Select START/STOP to begin. Let preheat for 5 minutes.
2. To make the crust, combine the flour, butter, sugar, ¼ cup of coconut, and ¼ cup of almonds in a large bowl and stir until a crumbly dough forms.
3. Grease the Ninja Multi-Purpose Pan or an 8-inch round baking dish with cooking spray. Place the dough in the pan and press it into an even layer covering the bottom.
4. Once unit has preheated, place pan on Reversible Rack, making sure the rack is in the lower position. Open lid and place rack in pot. Close crisping lid. Reduce temperature to 325°F.
5. Place remaining ¼ cup each of almonds and coconut in a Ninja Loaf Pan or any small loaf pan and set aside.
6. When cooking is complete, remove rack with pan and let cool for 10 minutes.
7. Quickly place the loaf pan with coconut and almonds in the bottom of the pot. Close crisping lid.
8. Select AIR CRISP, set temperature to 350°F, and set time to 10 minutes. Select START/STOP to begin.
9. While the nuts and coconut toast, whisk together the instant pudding with the milk, cream, and 3 tablespoons of chocolate.
10. After 5 minutes, open lid and stir the coconut and almonds. Close lid and continue cooking for another 5 minutes.
11. When cooking is complete, open lid and remove pan from pot. Add the almonds and coconut to the pudding. Stir until fully incorporated. Pour this in a smooth, even layer on top of the crust.
12. Refrigerate for about 10 minutes. Garnish with the remaining 1 tablespoon of chocolate, cut into wedges, and serve.

Nutrition Info:
- Calories: 476,Total Fat: 33g,Sodium: 215mg,Carbohydrates: 39g,Protein: 6g.

Pumpkin Custard

Servings: 6
Cooking Time: 2 Hours 30 Minutes
Ingredients:
- Butter flavored cooking spray
- 4 eggs
- ½ cup Stevia
- 1 cup pumpkin puree
- 1 tsp vanilla
- ½ cup almond flour, sifted
- 1 tsp pumpkin pie spice
- 1/8 tsp salt
- 4 tbsp. coconut oil, melted

Directions:
1. Spray the cooking pot with cooking spray.
2. In a medium bowl, beat eggs until smooth and slightly thickened, about 5 minutes.
3. Gradually beat in Stevia.
4. Add pumpkin and vanilla and mix well.
5. Add the flour, pie spice, and salt and beat to mix.
6. Slowly add coconut oil, beating as you do it. Pour mixture into the cooking pot.
7. Place two paper towels over the top of the cooking pot and add the lid. Set to slow cooking on low. Set timer for 2 hours.
8. Cook until custard is done, the center should be set and the sides should begin to pull away from the pot. Serve warm.

Nutrition Info:
- Calories 145, Total Fat 12g, Total Carbs 22g, Protein 5g, Sodium 162mg.

Cherry Clafoutti

Servings: 6
Cooking Time: 20 Minutes
Ingredients:
- 2 cups water
- Butter flavored cooking spray
- 2 cups cherries, pitted
- ¾ cup sour cream, low fat
- 4 egg yolks, at room temperature
- 1/3 cup honey
- ¼ cup milk
- 1 tbsp. vanilla
- ½ cup flour

Directions:
1. Place the rack in the cooking pot. Pour in the water. Spray a 2-quart baking dish with cooking spray.
2. Place the cherries in the prepared dish.
3. In a large bowl, whisk together sour cream, egg yolks, honey, milk, and vanilla, mix well.
4. Stir in flour until combined. Pour over cherries. Place the dish on the rack.
5. Secure the lid and set to pressure cooking on low. Set timer for 25 minutes. When timer goes off, use quick release to remove the lid.
6. Transfer dish to wire rack to cool 10 minutes. Slice and serve warm.

Nutrition Info:
- Calories 184, Total Fat 6g, Total Carbs 27g, Protein 4g, Sodium 35mg.

Chocolate Cake

Servings: 16
Cooking Time: 30 Minutes
Ingredients:
- Butter flavored cooking spray
- 8 Eggs
- 1 lb. semi-sweet chocolate chips
- 1 cup butter

Directions:
1. Place the rack in the cooking pot. Line the bottom of an 8-inch springform pan with parchment paper. Spray with cooking spray and wrap foil around the outside of the pan.
2. In a large bowl, beat eggs until double in size, about 6-8 minutes.
3. Place the chocolate chips and butter in a microwave safe bowl. Microwave at 30 second intervals until melted and smooth.
4. Fold 1/3 of the eggs into chocolate, folding gently just until eggs are incorporated. Repeat two more times.
5. Pour the batter into the prepared pan. Pour 1 ½ cups water into the cooking pot. Place the cake on the rack.
6. Add the tender-crisp lid and set to air fry on 325°F. Bake 25-30 minutes or until center is set.
7. Transfer to wire rack to cool. When cool, invert onto serving plate, top with fresh berries if desired. Slice and serve.

Nutrition Info:
- Calories 302, Total Fat 25g, Total Carbs 15g, Protein 5g, Sodium 130mg.

Créme Brulee

Servings: 4
Cooking Time: 30 Min + 6 Hours Of Cooling
Ingredients:
- 3 cups heavy whipping cream /750ml
- 7 large egg yolks
- 2 cups water /500mll
- 6 tbsp sugar /90g
- 2 tbsp vanilla extract /30ml

Directions:
1. In a mixing bowl, add the yolks, vanilla, whipping cream, and half of the swerve sugar. Use a whisk to mix them until they are well combined. Pour the mixture into the ramekins and cover them with aluminium foil.
2. Open the Foodi, fit the reversible rack into the pot, and pour in the water.
3. Place 3 ramekins on the rack and place the remaining ramekins to sit on the edges of the ramekins below.
4. Close the lid, secure the pressure valve, and select Pressure mode on High for 8 minutes. Press Start/Stop.
5. Once the timer has stopped, do a natural pressure release for 10 minutes, then a quick pressure release to let out the remaining pressure.
6. With a napkin in hand, remove the ramekins onto a flat surface and then into a refrigerator to chill for at least 6 hours. After refrigeration, remove the ramekins and remove the aluminium foil.
7. Equally, sprinkle the remaining sugar on it and return to the pot. Close the crisping lid, select Bake/Roast mode, set the timer to 4 minutes on 380 °F or 194°C. Serve the crème brulee chilled with whipped cream.

Cinnamon Apple Cake

Servings: 10
Cooking Time: 40 Minutes
Ingredients:
- Butter flavored cooking spray
- ½ cup coconut oil, soft
- ½ cup + 1 tbsp. honey, divided
- 1 egg
- 1 tsp vanilla
- 1¼ cups + 2 tbsp. whole wheat flour, divided
- 1 tsp baking powder
- ½ tsp baking soda
- 2 tsp cinnamon, divided
- ½ tsp salt
- 2 cups apple, chopped
- ¼ cup oats
- ½ cup pecans, chopped

Directions:
1. Spray an 8-inch cake pan with cooking spray.
2. In a large bowl, beat together oil, ½ cup honey, egg, and vanilla until smooth.
3. In a medium bowl, stir together 1 ¼ cups flour, baking powder, baking soda, 1 teaspoon cinnamon, and salt.
4. Add apples to dry ingredients and toss to combine. And mixture to wet ingredients and mix well. Pour into prepared pan.
5. In a small bowl, combine remaining flour, cinnamon, oats, pecans, and 1 tablespoon honey and mix well. Sprinkle over the top of the cake batter.
6. Add the cake to the cooking pot along with the tender-crisp lid. Set to bake on 325°F. Bake 35-40 minutes until edges begin to brown.
7. Transfer to a wire rack and let cool in the pan 10 minutes. Then invert onto serving plate and let cool completely before serving.

Nutrition Info:
- Calories 267,Total Fat 16g,Total Carbs 31g,Protein 3g,Sodium 111mg.

Vanilla Pound Cake

Servings: 8
Cooking Time: 45 Minutes
Ingredients:
- Nonstick cooking spray
- 1 cup butter, unsalted, soft
- 1 cup sugar
- 4 eggs
- 2 tsp vanilla
- ½ tsp salt
- 2 cups flour

Directions:
1. Add the rack to the cooking pot. Spray a loaf pan with cooking spray.
2. In a large bowl, on high speed, beat butter and sugar until fluffy.
3. Beat in eggs, one at a time, until combined. Stir in vanilla and salt.
4. Turn mixer to low and add flour a 1/3 at a time. Beat just until combined. Pour into prepared pan.
5. Place the pan on the rack and add the tender-crisp lid. Set to bake on 350°F. Bake 45-50 minutes or until cake passes the toothpick test.
6. Let cool in pan 15 minutes then invert onto a wire rack and let cool completely.

Nutrition Info:
- Calories 389,Total Fat 18g,Total Carbs 49g,Protein 7g,Sodium 192mg.

Pumpkin Latte Cake

Servings: 16
Cooking Time: 3 Hours
Ingredients:
- Butter flavored cooking spray
- 28 oz. pumpkin puree
- 2 cups whole wheat pastry flour
- 3 eggs
- 1 2/3 cups Stevia
- 2/3 cup almond milk, unsweetened
- ¼ cup coconut oil, melted
- 2 tbsp. pumpkin pie spice, divided
- 2 tsp baking powder
- 2 tsp vanilla
- 2 tbsp. espresso powder
- ½ cup honey

Directions:
1. Line the bottom only of the cooking pot with parchment paper. Spray with cooking spray.
2. In a large bowl, beat ½ the pumpkin, flour, 2 eggs, Stevia, milk, oil, 1 ½ tablespoons pie spice, baking powder, vanilla, and espresso together until smooth.
3. In a separate bowl, whisk together remaining pumpkin, egg, pie spice, and honey until smooth.
4. Pour half the cake batter into the cooking pot. Spread the pumpkin mixture on top. Then pour in remaining cake batter.
5. Add the lid and set to slow cooking on low. Cook 2-3 hours until cake passes the toothpick test.

6. Let cool in the pot for 10 minutes, then invert onto serving plate and let cool completely before serving.

Nutrition Info:
- Calories 150, Total Fat 6g, Total Carbs 47g, Protein 4g, Sodium 22mg.

Coconut Lime Snack Cake

Servings: 8
Cooking Time: 20 Minutes

Ingredients:
- Butter flavored cooking spray
- 2 eggs
- ½ cup coconut milk
- 3 tbsp. honey
- 1 tsp vanilla
- ¼ cup + 1 tbsp. fresh lime juice, divided
- 1 tbsp. + 1 tsp lime zest, divided
- 2 ¼ cup almond flour, sifted
- 1 tsp baking soda
- ½ cup coconut, unsweetened & shredded
- ½ cup powdered Stevia

Directions:
1. Place the rack in the cooking pot. Spray an 8-inch baking pan with cooking spray.
2. In a large bowl, beat eggs, milk, honey, vanilla, ¼ cup lime juice and tablespoon zest until thick and frothy, about 6-8 minutes.
3. Fold in flour, baking soda, and coconut just until combined. Pour into prepared pan.
4. Place the cake on the rack and add the tender-crisp lid. Set to bake on 350°F. Bake 15-20 minutes or until cake passes the toothpick test.
5. Let cool in the pan for 10 minutes, then invert onto a serving plate.
6. In a small bowl, whisk together powdered sugar, remaining tablespoon lime juice, and remaining teaspoon lime zest. Drizzle over the top of cooled cake. Serve.

Nutrition Info:
- Calories 183, Total Fat 13g, Total Carbs 28g, Protein 5g, Sodium 35mg.

Sweet And Salty Bars

Servings: 12
Cooking Time: 10 Minutes

Ingredients:
- 1 cup light corn syrup
- 1 cup granulated sugar
- 1 teaspoon vanilla extract
- 1 bag mini marshmallows
- 1 cup crunchy peanut butter
- 1 bag potato chips with ridges, slightly crushed
- 1 cup pretzels, slightly crushed
- 1 bag hard-shelled candy-coated chocolates

Directions:
1. Select SEAR/SAUTÉ and set temperature to MD:HI. Select START/STOP to begin. Let preheat for 5 minutes.
2. Add the corn syrup, sugar, and vanilla and stir until the sugar is melted.
3. Add the marshmallows and peanut butter and stir until the marshmallows are melted.
4. Add the potato chips and pretzels and stir until everything is evenly coated in the marshmallow mixture.
5. Pour the mixture into a 9-by-13-inch pan and place the chocolate candies on top, slightly pressing them in. Let cool, then cut into squares and serve.

Nutrition Info:
- Calories: 585, Total Fat: 21g, Sodium: 403mg, Carbohydrates: 96g, Protein: 9g.

Yogurt Cheesecake

Servings: 8
Cooking Time: 40 Minutes

Ingredients:
- 4 cups plain Greek Yogurt
- 1 cup Erythritol
- ½ teaspoon vanilla extract

Directions:
1. Line a cake pans with Parchment paper.
2. In a suitable, stir in the yogurt and Erythritol and with a hand mixer, mix well.
3. Stir in vanilla extract and mix to combine.
4. Add the mixture into the prepared pan and cover with a paper kitchen towel.
5. Then with a piece of foil, cover the pan tightly.
6. In the Ninja Foodi's insert, place 1 cup of water.
7. Set a "Reversible Rack" in the Ninja Foodi's insert.
8. Place the ramekins over the "Reversible Rack".
9. Close the Ninja Foodi's lid with a pressure lid and place the pressure valve to the "Seal" position.
10. Select "Pressure" mode and set it to "High" for 40 minutes.
11. Press the "Start/Stop" button to initiate cooking.
12. Switch the pressure valve to "Vent" and do a "Quick" release.
13. Place the pan onto a wire rack and remove the foil and paper towel.
14. Again, cover the pan with a new paper towel and refrigerate to cool overnight.

Nutrition Info:
- Calories: 88; Fats: 1.5g; Carbohydrates: 8.7g; Proteins: 7g

Coconut Milk Crème Caramel

Servings: 4
Cooking Time: 20 Min
Ingredients:
- 7 ounces Condensed Coconut Milk /210ml
- 1 ½ cups Water /375ml
- ½ cup Coconut Milk /125ml
- 2 Eggs
- ½ tsp Vanilla /2.5ml
- 4 tbsp Caramel Syrup /60ml

Directions:
1. Divide the caramel syrup between 4 small ramekins. Pour water in the Foodi and add the reversible rack. In a bowl, beat the rest of the ingredients. Divide them between the ramekins. Cover them with aluminum foil and lower onto the reversible rack.
2. Seal the pressure lid, and choose Pressure, set to High, and set the time to 15 minutes. Press Start. Once cooking is completed, do a quick pressure release. Let cool completely. To unmold the flan, insert a spatula along the ramekin' sides and flip onto a dish.

Almond Banana Dessert

Servings: 1
Cooking Time: 8 Min
Ingredients:
- 1 Banana; sliced
- 2 tbsp Almond Butter /30g
- 1 tbsp Coconut oil /15ml
- ½ tsp Cinnamon /2.5g

Directions:
1. Melt oil on Sear/Sauté mode. Add banana slices and fry them for a couple of minutes, or until golden on both sides. Top the fried bananas with almond butter and sprinkle with cinnamon.

Carrot Raisin Cookie Bars

Servings: 16
Cooking Time: 15 Minutes
Ingredients:
- Butter flavored cooking spray
- ½ cup brown sugar
- ½ cup sugar
- ½ cup coconut oil, melted
- ½ cup applesauce, unsweetened
- 2 eggs
- 1 tsp vanilla
- ½ cup almond flour
- 1 tsp baking soda
- 1 tsp baking powder
- ¼ tsp salt
- 1 tsp cinnamon
- ½ tsp nutmeg
- ½ tsp ginger
- 2 cups oats
- 1 ½ cups carrots, finely grated
- 1 cup raisins

Directions:
1. Place the rack in the cooking pot. Spray an 8x8-inch pan with cooking spray.
2. In a large bowl, combine sugars, oil, applesauce, eggs, and vanilla, mix well.
3. Stir in dry ingredients until combined. Fold in carrots and raisins. Press evenly in prepared pan.
4. Place the pan on the rack and add the tender-crisp lid. Set to bake on 350°F. Bake 12-15 minutes or until golden brown and cooked through.
5. Remove to wire rack to cool before cutting and serving.

Nutrition Info:
- Calories 115, Total Fat 7g, Total Carbs 19g, Protein 3g, Sodium 56mg.

Banana Cinnamon Snack Cake

Servings: 16
Cooking Time: 25 Minutes
Ingredients:
- Butter flavored cooking spray
- 1 ½ cup flour
- ½ cup sugar
- 2 tsp baking powder
- 1 tsp baking soda
- 2 tsp cinnamon
- ½ tsp salt
- 1 cup vanilla yogurt, low fat
- 2 bananas, mashed
- 2 tbsp. coconut oil, melted
- 1 egg
- 1 tsp vanilla

Directions:
1. Place the rack in the cooking pot. Spray an 8-inch baking dish with cooking spray.
2. In a large bowl, combine dry ingredients and mix well.

3. Add remaining ingredients and mix until combined. Pour into prepared dish and place on rack.
4. Add the tender-crisp lid and set to bake on 400 °F. Bake 20-25 minutes until golden brown and the cake passes the toothpick test.
5. Cool in pan 10 minutes, then invert onto serving plate and cool completely.

Nutrition Info:
- Calories 111,Total Fat 3g,Total Carbs 20g,Protein 2g,Sodium 164mg.

Chocolate Fondue

Servings: 12
Cooking Time: 5 Min
Ingredients:
- 10 ounces Milk Chocolate; chopped into small pieces /300g
- 1 ½ cups Lukewarm Water /375ml
- 8 ounces Heavy Whipping Cream /240ml
- 2 tsp Coconut Liqueur /60ml
- ¼ tsp Cinnamon Powder /1.25g
- A pinch of Salt

Directions:
1. Melt the chocolate in a heat-proof recipient. Add the remaining ingredients, except for the liqueur. Transfer this recipient to the metal reversible rack. Pour 1 ½ cups or 375ml of water into the cooker, and place a reversible rack inside.
2. Seal the pressure lid, choose Pressure, set to High, and set the time to 5 minutes. Press Start. Once the cooking is complete, do a quick pressure release. Pull out the container with tongs. Mix in the coconut liqueur and serve right now. Enjoy!

Blackberry Crisp

Servings: 6
Cooking Time: 45 Minutes
Ingredients:
- 6 cups blackberries
- 2 tbsp. sugar, divided
- 1 tbsp. cornstarch
- 1 cup oats
- ½ cup almond flour
- ½ cup almonds, chopped
- 1 tsp cinnamon
- ¼ tsp salt
- ¼ cup coconut oil, melted

Directions:

1. Add the rack to the cooking pot. Spray an 8-inch baking dish with cooking spray.
2. In a large bowl, add the blackberries, 1 tablespoon sugar, and cornstarch, toss to coat. Pour into prepared dish.
3. In the same bowl, combine oats, flour, nuts, cinnamon, salt, coconut oil, and remaining sugar, mix well. Pour over berries.
4. Place the dish on the rack. Add the tender-crisp lid and set to bake on 350°F. Bake 30-35 minutes or until top is golden brown. Transfer to wire rack to cool before serving.

Nutrition Info:
- Calories 282,Total Fat 13g,Total Carbs 38g,Protein 6g,Sodium 100mg.

Buttery Cranberry Cake

Servings: 8
Cooking Time: 40 Minutes
Ingredients:
- Butter flavored cooking spray
- 2 eggs
- 1 cup sugar
- 3/8 cup butter, softened
- ½ tsp vanilla
- 1 cup flour
- 6 oz. fresh cranberries

Directions:
1. Set cooker to bake on 350°F. Spray an 8-inch baking pan with cooking spray.
2. In a large bowl, beat eggs and sugar until light in color and slightly thickened, about 5-7 minutes.
3. Add butter and vanilla and continue beating another 2 minutes.
4. Stir in flour just until combined. Gently fold in cranberries.
5. Spread batter in prepared pan and place in the cooking pot. Add the tender-crisp lid and bake 35-40 minutes or until the cake passes the toothpick test.
6. Remove from cooker and let cool in pan 10 minutes before transferring to a wire rack to cool completely.

Nutrition Info:
- Calories 259,Total Fat 10g,Total Carbs 40g,Protein 3g,Sodium 88mg.

Coffee Cake

Servings:8
Cooking Time: 30 Minutes
Ingredients:
- Cooking spray
- 1 box yellow cake mix

- 1 cup water
- ⅓ cup vegetable oil
- 3 large eggs
- 4 cups all-purpose flour
- 1 cup granulated sugar
- 3 tablespoons cinnamon
- 2 cups unsalted butter, melted
- Confectioners' sugar, for garnish

Directions:
1. Grease a Ninja Tube Pan or a 7-inch Bundt pan with cooking spray.
2. Close crisping lid. Select BAKE/ROAST, set temperature to 325°F, and set time to 5 minutes. Select START/STOP to begin preheating.
3. In a large bowl, mix together the cake mix, water, oil, and eggs until combined. Pour the batter into the prepared pan.
4. When unit has preheated, place pan on Reversible Rack, making sure the rack is in the lower position. Open lid and place rack with pan in pot. Close crisping lid.
5. Select BAKE/ROAST, set temperature to 325°F, and set time to 30 minutes. Select START/STOP to begin.
6. In another large bowl, combine the flour, sugar, and cinnamon. Add the butter and mix until well combined and the mixture is a crumble.
7. After 25 minutes, open lid and check for doneness. If a toothpick inserted into the cake comes out clean, the cake is done. If necessary, close lid and continue baking.
8. Open lid and spread the crumble topping on top of the cakes. Close lid and bake for an additional 4 to 5 minutes.
9. When cooking is complete, carefully remove pan from pot and place it on a cooling rack. Let cool. Using a fine mesh sieve, garnish the coffee cake with confectioners' sugar.

Nutrition Info:
- Calories: 1152,Total Fat: 65g,Sodium: 464mg,Carbohydrates: 132g,Protein: 13g.

Pineapple Cake

Servings: 4
Cooking Time: 50 Min
Ingredients:
- 2 oz. dark chocolate, grated /60g
- 4 oz. butter /120g
- 7 oz. pineapple chunks /210g
- 8 oz. self-rising flour /240g
- ½ cup sugar /65g
- 1 egg
- ½ cup pineapple juice /125ml
- 2 tbsp milk /30ml

Directions:
1. Preheat the Foodi to 390 °F or 199°C. Place the butter and flour into a bowl and rub the mixture with your fingers until crumbed. Stir in the pineapple, sugar, chocolate, and juice. Beat the eggs and milk separately, and then add them to the batter.
2. Transfer the batter to a previously prepared (greased or lined) cake pan, and cook for 40 minutes on Roast mode. Let cool for at least 10 minutes before serving.

Double Chocolate Cake

Servings: 12
Cooking Time: 1 Hour
Ingredients:
- ½ cup coconut flour
- 1½ cups Erythritol
- 5 tablespoons cacao powder
- 1 teaspoon baking powder
- ½ teaspoon salt
- 3 eggs
- 3 egg yolks
- ½ cup butter, melted and cooled
- 1 teaspoon vanilla extract
- ½ teaspoon liquid stevia
- 4 ounces 70% dark chocolate chips
- 2 cups hot water

Directions:
1. Grease the Ninja Foodi's insert.
2. In a large bowl, stir in the flour, 1¼ cups of Erythritol, 3 tablespoons of cacao powder, baking powder and salt.
3. In a suitable bowl, add the eggs, egg yolks, butter, vanilla extract and liquid stevia and beat until well combined.
4. Stir in the egg mixture into the flour mixture and mix until just combined.
5. In a small bowl, add hot water, remaining cacao powder and Erythritol and beat until well combined.
6. In the prepared Ninja Foodi's insert, stir in the mixture evenly and top with chocolate chips, followed by the water mixture.
7. Close the Ninja Foodi's lid with a crisping lid and select "Slow Cooker".
8. Set on "Low" for 3 hours.
9. Press the "Start/Stop" button to initiate cooking.
10. Transfer the pan onto a wire rack for about 10 minutes.
11. Flip the baked and cooled cake onto the wire rack to cool completely.
12. Cut into desired-sized slices and serve.

Nutrition Info:

- Calories: 169; Fats: 15.4g; Carbohydrates: 4.4g; Proteins: 3.9g

Vanilla Cheesecake(1)

Servings: 6
Cooking Time: 2 Hours
Ingredients:
- For Crust:
- 1 cup almonds, toasted
- 1 egg
- 2 tablespoons butter
- 4-6 drops liquid stevia
- For Filling:
- 2 8-ounce packages of cream cheese, softened
- 4 tablespoons heavy cream
- 2 eggs
- 1 tablespoon coconut flour
- 1 teaspoon liquid stevia
- 1 teaspoon vanilla extract

Directions:
1. For the crust: in a high-speed food processor, stir in almonds and pulse until a flour-like consistency is achieved.
2. In a suitable, add ground almond, egg, butter and stevia and mix until well combined.
3. In the bottom of a 1½-quart oval pan, place the crust mixture and press to smooth the top surface, leaving a little room on each side.
4. For the filling: in a suitable, stir in all ingredients and with an immersion blender, blend until well combined.
5. Place the prepared filling mixture over the crust evenly.
6. In the Ninja Foodi's insert, place 1 cup of water.
7. Carefully set the pan in the Ninja Foodi's insert.
8. Close the Ninja Foodi's lid with a crisping lid and select "Slow Cooker".
9. Set on "Low" for 2 hours.
10. Press the "Start/Stop" button to initiate cooking.
11. Place the pan onto a wire rack to cool.
12. Refrigerate to chill for at least 6-8 hours before serving.

Nutrition Info:
- Calories: 446; Fats: 42.9g; Carbohydrates: 7.2g; Proteins: 10.6g

Blueberry Peach Crisp

Servings: 8
Cooking Time: 40 Minutes
Ingredients:
- 1 cup blueberries
- 6 peaches, peeled, cored & cut in ½-inch pieces
- ½ cup + 3 tbsp. flour
- ¾ cups Stevia, divided
- ½ tsp cinnamon
- ¼ tsp salt, divided
- Zest & juice of 1 lemon
- 1 cup oats
- 1/3 cup coconut oil, melted

Directions:
1. Place the rack in the cooking pot.
2. In a large bowl, combine blueberries, peaches, 3 tablespoons flour, ¼ cup Stevia, cinnamon, and 1/8 teaspoon salt, toss to coat fruit. Stir in lemon zest and juice just until combined. Pour into an 8-inch baking dish.
3. In a medium bowl, combine oats, ½ cup Stevia, coconut oil, remaining flour and salt and mix with a fork until crumbly. Sprinkle over the top of the fruit.
4. Place the dish on the rack and add the tender-crisp lid. Set to bake on 350 °F. Bake 35-40 minutes until filling is bubbly and top is golden brown. Serve warm.

Nutrition Info:
- Calories 265,Total Fat 11g,Total Carbs 44g,Protein 6g,Sodium 74mg.

Mocha Cake

Servings: 6
Cooking Time: 3 Hours 37 Minutes
Ingredients:
- 2 ounces 70% dark chocolate, chopped
- ¾ cup butter, chopped
- ½ cup heavy cream
- 2 tablespoons instant coffee crystals
- 1 teaspoon vanilla extract
- 1/3 cup almond flour
- ¼ cup unsweetened cacao powder
- 1/8 teaspoon salt
- 5 large eggs
- 2/3 cup Erythritol

Directions:
1. Grease the Ninja Foodi's insert.
2. In a microwave-safe bowl, stir in the chocolate and butter and microwave on High for about 2 minutes or until melted completely, stirring after every 30 seconds.
3. Remove from the microwave and stir well.
4. Set aside to cool.
5. In a small bowl, stir in the heavy cream, coffee crystals, and vanilla extract and beat until well combined.
6. In a suitable bowl, mix the flour, cacao powder and salt.
7. In a large bowl, stir in the eggs and with an electric mixer, beat on high speed until slightly thickened.

8. Slowly, stir in the Erythritol and beat on high speed until thick and pale yellow.
9. Stir in the chocolate mixture and beat on low speed until well combined.
10. Stir in the dry flour mixture and mix until just combined.
11. Slowly stir in the cream mixture and beat on medium speed until well combined.
12. In the prepared Ninja Foodi's insert, add the mixture.
13. Close the Ninja Foodi's lid with a crisping lid and select "Slow Cooker".
14. Set on "Low" for 2½-3½ hours.
15. Press the "Start/Stop" button to initiate cooking.
16. Transfer the pan onto a wire rack for about 10 minutes.
17. Flip the baked and cooled cake onto the wire rack to cool completely.
18. Cut into desired-sized slices and serve.

Nutrition Info:
- Calories: 407; Fats: 39.7g; Carbohydrates: 6.2g; Proteins: 9g

Sweet Potato Pie

Servings: 10
Cooking Time: 45 Minutes
Ingredients:
- Butter flavored cooking spray
- 4 sweet potatoes, baked & cooled
- ½ cup skim milk
- 1 tbsp. maple syrup, sugar free
- ½ cup brown sugar
- 2 eggs
- 1 tbsp. butter, soft
- 1 tsp cinnamon
- 1 tsp vanilla

Directions:
1. Place the rack in the cooking pot. Spray an 8-inch pie plate with cooking spray.
2. Scoop out the flesh of the potatoes and place in a large bowl.
3. Add remaining ingredients and beat until smooth. Pour into pie plate and place on the rack.
4. Add the tender-crisp lid and set to bake on 400°F. Bake 40-45 minutes or until a knife inserted in center comes out clean.
5. Transfer pie to a wire rack to cool. Cover and refrigerate until ready to serve.

Nutrition Info:
- Calories 157,Total Fat 2g,Total Carbs 31g,Protein 3g,Sodium 73mg.

Berry Apple Crisps

Servings: 8
Cooking Time: 30 Minutes
Ingredients:
- Butter flavored cooking spray
- 2 cups apples, peeled & chopped
- 2 cups blueberries
- 1 tbsp. lemon zest
- 1 tbsp. lemon juice
- ¼ cup + 1/3 cup honey, divided
- 1 tsp cinnamon
- ¼ tsp nutmeg
- 2 tbsp. cornstarch
- 2 ½ cups oats, divided
- ¼ cup walnuts, chopped
- 2 tbsp. coconut oil, melted

Directions:
1. Place the rack in the cooking pot. Lightly spray 8 ramekins with cooking spray.
2. In a medium bowl, combine apples, berries, zest, lemon juice and ¼ cup honey.
3. In a small bowl, stir together spices and cornstarch and sprinkle over fruit, toss gently to combine. Spoon into ramekins.
4. Add 1 ½ cups oats to a food processor or blender and pulse until they reach the consistency of flour. Pour into a medium bowl.
5. Stir the remaining oats and nuts into the oat flour. Add oil and 1/3 cup honey and mix until crumbly. Sprinkle over the tops of the ramekins.
6. Place ramekins on the rack and add the tender-crisp lid. Set to bake on 375°F. Bake 25-30 minutes until top is golden brown and filling is bubbly. Let cool slightly before serving.

Nutrition Info:
- Calories 280,Total Fat 8g,Total Carbs 38g,Protein 5g,Sodium 167mg.

Cheat Apple Pie

Servings: 9
Cooking Time: 30 Min
Ingredients:
- 4 apples; diced
- 1 egg, beaten
- 3 large puff pastry sheets
- 2 oz. sugar /60g
- 1 oz. brown sugar /30g
- 2 oz. butter, melted /60ml

- 2 tsp cinnamon /10g
- ¼ tsp salt /1.25g

Directions:
1. Whisk the white sugar, brown sugar, cinnamon, salt, and butter together. Place the apples in a baking dish and coat them with the mixture.
2. Slide the dish into the Foodi and cook for 10 minutes on Roast at 350 °F or 177°C.
3. Meanwhile, roll out the pastry on a floured flat surface, and cut each sheet into 6 equal pieces. Divide the apple filling between the parts.
4. Brush the edges of the pastry squares with the egg. Fold and seal the edges with a fork. Place on a lined baking sheet and cook in the fryer at 350 °F or 177°C for 8 minutes on Roast. Flip over, increase the temperature to 390 °F or 177°C, and cook for 2 more minutes.

Coconut Rice Pudding

Servings:6
Cooking Time: 8 Minutes
Ingredients:
- ¾ cup arborio rice
- 1 can unsweetened full-fat coconut milk
- 1 cup milk
- 1 cup water
- ¾ cup granulated sugar
- ½ teaspoon vanilla extract

Directions:
1. Rinse the rice under cold running water in a fine-mesh strainer.
2. Place the rice, coconut milk, milk, water, sugar, and vanilla in the pot and stir. Assemble pressure lid, making sure the pressure release valve is in the SEAL position.
3. Select PRESSURE and set to HI. Set time to 8 minutes. Select START/STOP to begin.
4. When pressure cooking is complete, allow pressure to naturally release for 10 minutes. After 10 minutes, quick release remaining pressure by moving the pressure release valve to the VENT position. Carefully remove lid when unit has finished releasing pressure.
5. Press a layer of plastic wrap directly on top of the rice (it should be touching) to prevent a skin from forming on top of the pudding. Let pudding cool to room temperature, then refrigerate overnight to set.

Nutrition Info:
- Calories: 363,Total Fat: 18g,Sodium: 31mg,Carbohydrates: 50g,Protein: 5g.

Coconut Pear Delight

Servings: 2
Cooking Time: 15 Min
Ingredients:
- 2 Large Pears, peeled and diced
- ¼ cup Shredded Coconut, unsweetened /32.5g
- ¼ cup Flour /32.5g
- 1 cup Coconut Milk /250ml

Directions:
1. Combine all ingredients in your Foodi. Seal the pressure lid, select Pressureand set the timer to 5 minutes at High pressure. Press Start. When ready, do a quick pressure release. Divide the mixture between two bowls.

Brownie Bites

Servings:10
Cooking Time: 45 Minutes
Ingredients:
- Cooking spray
- 1 box brownie mix, prepared to package instructions
- Confectioners' sugar, for garnish
- Carmel sauce, for garnish

Directions:
1. Coat a silicone egg mold with nonstick cooking spray and set aside.
2. In a large bowl, prepare the brownie mix according to package instructions. Using a cookie scoop, transfer the batter to the prepared mold.
3. Place 1 cup water in the pot. Place the filled molds onto the Reversible Rack in the lower steam position, and lower into the pot.
4. Assemble the pressure lid, making sure the pressure release valve is in the SEAL position.
5. Select PRESSURE and set to HI. Set the time to 45 minutes. Select START/STOP to begin.
6. When pressure cooking is complete, allow the pressure to naturally release for 10 minutes. After 10 minutes, quick release any remaining pressure by moving the pressure release valve to the VENT position. Carefully remove the lid when the unit has finished releasing pressure.
7. Carefully remove the mold from the cooker and let cool for 5 minutes.
8. Flip the brownie onto a plate and garnish with confectioners' sugar and caramel sauce.

Nutrition Info:
- Calories: 288,Total Fat: 5g,Sodium: 168mg,Carbohydrates: 43g,Protein: 2g.

Gingery Chocolate Pudding

Servings: 4
Cooking Time: 20 Min
Ingredients:
- 2 oz. chocolate, coarsely chopped /60g
- 1 ½ cups of Water /375ml
- ¼ cup Cornstarch /32.5g
- 1 cup Almond Milk /250ml
- ¼ cup Sugar /32.5g
- 3 Eggs, separated into whites and yolks
- Zest and Juice from ½ Lime
- 2 tbsp Butter, softened /30g
- ½ tsp Ginger, caramelized /2.5g
- A pinch of Salt

Directions:
1. Combine together the sugar, cornstarch, salt, and softened butter, in a bowl. Mix in lime juice and grated lime zest. Add in the egg yolks, ginger, almond milk, and whisk to mix well.
2. Mix in egg whites. Pour this mixture into custard cups and cover with aluminium foil. Add 1 ½ cups or 375ml of water to the Foodi. Place a reversible rack into the Foodi, and lower the cups onto the rack.
3. Seal the pressure lid, choose Pressure, set to High, and set the time to 25 minutes. Press Start. Once the cooking is complete, do a quick pressure release. Carefully open the pressure lid, and stir in the chocolate. Serve chilled.

White Chocolate Chip Cookies

Servings: 8
Cooking Time: 30 Min
Ingredients:
- 2 oz. white chocolate chips /60g
- 6 oz. self-rising flour /180g
- 3 oz. brown sugar /90g
- 4 oz. butter /120g
- 1 tbsp honey /15ml
- 1 ½ tbsp milk /22.5ml

Directions:
1. Beat the butter and sugar until fluffy. Then, beat in the honey, milk, and flour. Gently fold in the chocolate chips. Drop spoonfuls of the mixture onto a prepared cookie sheet.
2. Close the crisping lid and cook for 18 minutes on Air Crisp mode at 350 °F or 177°C. Once the timer beeps, make sure the cookies are just set.

Hazelnut Cheesecake

Servings:8
Cooking Time: 25 Minutes
Ingredients:
- Unsalted butter, for greasing
- 1 store-bought premade graham cracker crust
- 2 packages cream cheese, at room temperature
- ¼ cup confectioners' sugar, sifted
- 2 eggs
- 1 jar hazelnut spread
- 1 cup water

Directions:
1. Grease the Ninja Multi-Purpose Pan with butter. Place the crust in the pan, crumbling as necessary to fit.
2. In a medium bowl, beat together the cream cheese, sugar, and eggs with a hand mixer until well incorporated. Add the hazelnut spread and beat until well combined. Add the cream cheese mixture over the crust.
3. Pour the water into the pot. Place Reversible Rack in pot, making sure it is in the lower position. Place pan on rack. Assemble pressure lid, making sure the pressure release valve is in the SEAL position.
4. Select PRESSURE and set to HI. Set time to 25 minutes. Select START/STOP to begin.
5. When pressure cooking is complete, allow pressure to naturally release for 10 minutes. After 10 minutes, quick release remaining pressure by moving the pressure release valve to the VENT position. Carefully remove lid when unit has finished releasing pressure.
6. Remove rack and pan from pot. Gently dab the top of the cheesecake with a paper towel to remove excess moisture. Refrigerate for at least 2 hours before serving.

Nutrition Info:
- Calories: 676,Total Fat: 47g,Sodium: 375mg,Carbohydrates: 57g,Protein: 9g.

Pecan Apple Crisp

Servings: 6
Cooking Time: 35 Minutes
Ingredients:
- Butter flavored cooking spray
- 3 apples, peeled & diced
- 1 tbsp. sugar
- 1 3/8 tsp cinnamon, divided
- ¼ cup + ½ tbsp. almond flour, divided
- ½ cup oats
- ¼ cup pecans, chopped
- 1/8 tsp salt
- 1/8 cup coconut oil, melted
- 1/8 cup honey

Directions:

1. Place the rack in the cooking pot. Spray an 8x8-inch baking pan with cooking spray.
2. In a large bowl, combine apples, sugar, 1 teaspoon cinnamon, and ½ tablespoon almond flour, toss to coat the apples. Pour into prepared pan.
3. In a medium bowl, combine oats, remaining flour, pecans, remaining cinnamon, salt, oil, and honey. Use a fork to mix until mixture resembles fine crumbs. Pour over apples.
4. Place on the rack and add the tender-crisp lid. Set to bake on 350°F. Bake 30-35 minutes, or until apples are tender and topping is golden brown.
5. Transfer to a wire rack to cool slightly before serving.

Nutrition Info:
- Calories 293,Total Fat 18g,Total Carbs 30g,Protein 7g,Sodium 62mg.

Irish Cream Flan

Servings: 3
Cooking Time: 10 Minutes
Ingredients:
- ¼ cup + 2 tbsp. sugar, divided
- 1 tbsp. water
- 1 cup half and half
- ¼ cup Irish cream flavored coffee creamer
- ¼ cup Irish cream liqueur
- 2 eggs

Directions:
1. In a small saucepan over medium heat, heat ¼ cup sugar until melted and a deep amber color. Swirl the pan occasionally to distribute the heat.
2. When the sugar reaches the right color remove from heat and carefully stir in the water until combined. Drizzle over the bottoms of 3 ramekins.
3. In a small oven-safe bowl, whisk the eggs.
4. In a small saucepan over medium heat, stir together half and half, creamer, Irish cream, and remaining sugar. Heat to simmering.
5. Gradually whisk the warm liquids into the eggs 2 tablespoons at a time, whisking constantly. After a 1/3 of the cream mixture has been added, slowly pour the remaining mixture into the eggs, whisking constantly until combined.
6. Pour 1 cup water into the cooking pot and add the trivet.
7. Pour the egg mixture into the ramekins and cover tightly with foil. Place them on the trivet.
8. Secure the lid and set to pressure cooking on high. Set the timer for 5 minutes. When the timer goes off, use natural release to remove the lid. Transfer custards to a wire rack and uncover to cool.
9. Cover with plastic wrap and refrigerate at least 4 hours before serving. To serve, use a small knife to loosen the custards from the sides of the ramekin and invert onto serving plate.

Nutrition Info:
- Calories 215,Total Fat 9g,Total Carbs 25g,Protein 7g,Sodium 134mg.

Banana Coconut Pudding

Servings: 8
Cooking Time: 10 Minutes
Ingredients:
- ¼ cup cornstarch
- ¼ tsp salt
- 1/3 cup honey
- 2 egg yolks, lightly beaten
- 1 ½ cups lite coconut milk, canned
- 1 teaspoon vanilla extract
- ½ cup coconut flakes, unsweetened
- 2 bananas, sliced ½-inch thick

Directions:
1. Add the cornstarch and salt to the cooking pot and stir to mix.
2. Whisk in honey and egg yolks until combined.
3. Set to sauté on med-low heat. Slowly whisk in milk until combined.
4. Cook, stirring constantly, 8-10 minutes or until pudding reaches desired thickness.
5. Remove from heat and stir in coconut and vanilla. Layer pudding and banana slices in dessert dishes. Let cool 15 minutes before serving.

Nutrition Info:
- Calories 212,Total Fat 12g,Total Carbs 26g,Protein 2g,Sodium 97mg.

Spiced Poached Pears

Servings: 4
Cooking Time: 4 Hours
Ingredients:
- 4 ripe pears, peeled
- 2 cups fresh orange juice
- ¼ cup maple syrup
- 5 cardamom pods
- 1 cinnamon stick, broke in 2
- 1-inch piece ginger, peeled & sliced

Directions:
1. Slice off the bottom of the pears so they stand upright. Carefully remove the core with a paring knife. Stand in the cooking pot.

2. In a small bowl, whisk together orange juice and syrup. Pour over pears and add the spices.
3. Add the lid and set to slow cooking on low. Cook 3-4 hours or until pears are soft. Baste the pears every hour or so.
4. Serve garnished with whipped cream and chopped walnuts if you like, or just serve them as they are sprinkled with a little cinnamon.

Nutrition Info:
- Calories 219,Total Fat 1g,Total Carbs 53g,Protein 2g,Sodium 6mg.

Cranberry Cheesecake

Servings: 8
Cooking Time: 1 Hr

Ingredients:
- 1/3 cup dried cranberries /44g
- 1 cup water /250ml
- ½ cup sugar /65g
- 1 cup coarsely crumbled cookies/ 130g
- 1 cup mascarpone cheese, room temperature /130g
- 2 eggs, room temperature
- 2 tbsp sour cream /30ml
- 2 tbsp butter, melted /30ml
- ½ tsp vanilla extract /2.5ml

Directions:
1. Fold a 20-inch piece of aluminum foil in half lengthwise twice and set on the pressure cooker. In a bowl, combine melted butter and crushed cookies; press firmly to the bottom and about 1/3 of the way up the sides of a 7-inch springform pan. Freeze the crust while the filling is being prepared.
2. In a separate bowl, beat together mascarpone cheese and sugar to obtain a smooth consistency; stir in vanilla extract and sour cream. Beat one egg and add into the cheese mixture to combine well; do the same with the second egg.
3. Stir cranberries into the filling. Transfer the filling into the crust. Into the pot, add water and set the reversible rack at the bottom. Center the springform pan onto the prepared foil sling. Use the sling to lower the pan onto the reversible rack.
4. Fold foil strips out of the way of the lid. Close the crisping lid and select Bake/Roast; adjust the temperature to 250°F or 122°C and the cook time to 40 minutes. Press Start.
5. When the time is up, open the lid and let to cool the cheesecake. When, transfer the cheesecake to a refrigerator for 2 hours or overnight.
6. Use a paring knife to run along the edges between the pan and cheesecake to remove the cheesecake and set to the plate.

Peach Cobbler

Servings: 6
Cooking Time: 35 Minutes

Ingredients:
- Nonstick cooking spray
- 5 fresh peaches, peeled, pitted & sliced
- 3 tbsp. Stevia
- 1 tsp coconut flour
- ¼ tsp cinnamon
- 1/8 tsp nutmeg
- ½ cup almond flour, sifted
- 1 cup oats, ground fine
- 1 ½ tsp baking powder
- ¼ cup almond milk, unsweetened
- 1 tsp almond extract
- 2 tbsp. honey

Directions:
1. Place the rack in the cooking pot. Spray an 8-inch baking dish with cooking spray.
2. In a large bowl, toss peaches with Stevia, coconut flour, cinnamon, and nutmeg. Place in prepared baking dish.
3. In a medium bowl, combine almond flour, oats, baking powder, milk, almond extract, and honey, mix well. Drop by large spoonful over the top of the peaches. Place in the cooking pot.
4. Add the tender-crisp lid and set to air fry on 350 °F. Bake 35-40 minutes until top is lightly browned. Serve warm.

Nutrition Info:
- Calories 204,Total Fat 7g,Total Carbs 39g,Protein 7g,Sodium 11mg.

Blueberry Lemon Pound Cake

Servings: 12
Cooking Time: 1 Hour 5 Minutes

Ingredients:
- Butter flavored cooking spray
- 1 ¾ cups + 2 tsp flour, divided
- 2 tsp baking powder
- ½ tsp salt
- 1 ½ cups blueberries
- ¾ cup butter, unsalted, soft
- 1 cup ricotta cheese, room temperature
- 1 ½ cups sugar
- 3 eggs, room temperature
- 1 tsp vanilla
- 1 tbsp. lemon zest

Directions:

1. Spray a loaf pan with cooking spray
2. In a medium bowl, combine flour, baking powder, and salt, mix well.
3. Add the blueberries to a bowl and sprinkle 2 tsp flour over them, toss to coat.
4. In a large bowl, beat together butter, ricotta, and sugar on high speed, until pale and fluffy.
5. Reduce speed to medium and beat in eggs, one at a time. Beat in zest and vanilla.
6. Stir in dry ingredients, a fourth at a time, until combined. Fold in blueberries and pour into prepared pan.
7. Add the rack to the cooking pot and place the pan on it. Add the tender-crisp lid and set to bake on 325°F. Bake 1 hour 10 minutes or until cake passes the toothpick test. After 40 minutes, cover the cake with foil.
8. Transfer to wire rack and let cool in pan 15 minutes. Then invert and let cool completely before serving.

Nutrition Info:
- Calories 303,Total Fat 17g,Total Carbs 32g,Protein 6g,Sodium 147mg.

Date Orange Cheesecake

Servings: 8
Cooking Time: 20 Minutes
Ingredients:
- Butter flavored cooking spray
- 2 cups water
- 2 lbs. ricotta cheese
- 4 eggs
- ¼ cup sugar
- ¼ cup honey
- Juice & zest of ½ orange
- ¼ tsp vanilla
- 1 cup dates, soak in warm water 20 minutes, chop fine

Directions:
1. Place the trivet in the cooking pot and add 2 cups water. Spray a deep, 8-inch springform pan with cooking spray.
2. In a large bowl, beat ricotta cheese until smooth.
3. In a medium bowl, beat eggs and sugar 3 minutes. Fold into ricotta cheese.
4. In a small saucepan, heat honey over low heat, do not let it get hot, just warm.
5. Whisk in orange juice, zest, and vanilla until combined. Whisk into cheese mixture until combined.
6. Fold in dates and pour into prepared pan. Cover with foil.
7. Place the cheesecake in the cooking pot and secure the lid. Set to pressure cooking on high. Set the timer for 20 minutes.
8. When timer goes off use natural release to remove the lid. Transfer cheesecake to wire rack to cool completely. Cover and refrigerate at least 4 hours before serving.

Nutrition Info:
- Calories 343,Total Fat 17g,Total Carbs 32g,Protein 16g,Sodium 132mg.

Fried Oreos

Servings:9
Cooking Time: 8 Minutes
Ingredients:
- ½ cup complete pancake mix
- ⅓ cup water
- Cooking spray
- 9 Oreo cookies
- 1 tablespoon confectioners' sugar

Directions:
1. Close crisping lid. Select AIR CRISP, set temperature to 400°F, and set time to 5 minutes. Select START/STOP to begin preheating.
2. In a medium bowl, combine the pancake mix and water until combined.
3. Spray the Cook & Crisp Basket with cooking spray.
4. Dip each cookie into the pancake batter and then arrange them in the basket in a single layer so they are not touching each other. Cook in batches if needed.
5. When unit has preheated, open lid and insert basket into pot. Close crisping lid.
6. Select AIR CRISP, set temperature to 400°F, and set time to 8 minutes. Select START/STOP to begin.
7. After 4 minutes, open lid and flip the cookies. Close lid and continue cooking.
8. When cooking is complete, check for desired crispness. Remove basket and sprinkle the cookies with confectioners' sugar. Serve.

Nutrition Info:
- Calories: 83,Total Fat: 2g,Sodium: 158mg,Carbohydrates: 14g,Protein: 1g.

Mexican Chocolate Walnut Cake

Servings: 8
Cooking Time: 2 ½ Hours
Ingredients:
- Butter flavored cooking spray
- 1½ cups flour
- ½ cup cocoa powder, unsweetened
- 2 tsp baking powder
- 2 tsp ground cinnamon
- ¼ tsp cayenne pepper

- 1/8 tsp salt
- 1 cup sugar
- 3 eggs, beaten
- ¾ cup coconut oil melted
- 2 tsp vanilla
- 2 cups zucchini, grated
- ¾ cup walnuts, chopped, divided

Directions:
1. Spray the cooking pot with cooking spray and line the bottom with parchment paper.
2. In a medium bowl, combine dry ingredients and mix well.
3. In a large bowl, beat sugar and eggs until creamy.
4. Stir in oil, vanilla, zucchini, and ½ cup walnuts until combined. Fold in dry ingredients just until combined.
5. Pour batter into cooking pot and sprinkle remaining nuts over the top. Add the lid and set to slow cooking on high. Cook 2 ½ hours or until cake passes the toothpick test. Transfer cake to a wire rack to cool before serving.

Nutrition Info:
- Calories 452, Total Fat 28g, Total Carbs 48g, Protein 7g, Sodium 189mg.

Strawberry Cheesecake

Servings: 8
Cooking Time: 20 Minutes

Ingredients:
- Butter flavored cooking spray
- 16 oz. cream cheese, soft
- 2/3 cup powdered Stevia
- 1 tsp vanilla
- 2 eggs, room temperature
- 1 cup strawberries, chopped

Directions:
1. Place the trivet in the cooking pot and add enough water to cover bottom by 1 inch. Spray an 8-inch springform pan with cooking spray.
2. In a large bowl, beat cream cheese until smooth.
3. Beat in Stevia and vanilla until combined.
4. Beat in eggs, one at a time and beat until thoroughly combined.
5. Pour into prepared pan. Cover bottom and sides of pan with foil to prevent any water from leaking in. Place the pan on the trivet.
6. Add the lid and select pressure cooking on high. Set timer for 20 minutes.
7. When the timer goes off, use natural release to remove the lid. Transfer cheesecake to wire rack to cool completely.
8. Cover and refrigerate 8 hours or overnight. Top with chopped strawberries before serving.

Nutrition Info:
- Calories 219, Total Fat 21g, Total Carbs 20g, Protein 5g, Sodium 225mg.

Hot Fudge Brownies

Servings: 16
Cooking Time: 25 Minutes

Ingredients:
- Butter flavored cooking spray
- 2/3 cup flour
- 2/3 cup sugar
- ½ cup cocoa powder, unsweetened
- ¼ cup butter, melted
- 2 tbsp. water
- 1 tbsp. vanilla
- ½ tsp baking powder
- 1/3 cup egg substitute
- ¼ cup hot fudge sauce, fat-free, warmed

Directions:
1. Place the rack in the cooking pot. Spray an 8x8-inch baking pan with cooking spray.
2. In a large bowl, combine all ingredients, except hot fudge sauce, and mix well. Spread ½ the batter evenly in prepared pan. Pour hot fudge sauce evenly over batter then spread remaining batter over the top.
3. Place the pan on the rack and add the tender-crisp lid. Set to bake on 350°F. Bake 20-25 minutes or until brownies pass the toothpick test.
4. Transfer to wire rack to cool before serving.

Nutrition Info:
- Calories 102, Total Fat 4g, Total Carbs 17g, Protein 2g, Sodium 35mg.

Sugar Cookie Pizza

Servings: 6
Cooking Time: 35 Minutes

Ingredients:
- 22 ounces premade sugar cookie dough
- 5 tablespoons unsalted butter, at room temperature
- 1 package cream cheese, at room temperature
- 2 cups confectioners' sugar
- 1 teaspoon vanilla extract

Directions:
1. Select BAKE/ROAST, set temperature to 325°F, and set time to 40 minutes. Select START/STOP to begin. Let preheat for 5 minutes.

2. Press the cookie dough into the Ninja Multi-Purpose Pan in an even layer.
3. Once unit is preheated, place the pan on the Reversible Rack and place rack in the pot. Close crisping lid and cook for 35 minutes.
4. Once cooking is complete, remove the pan from the pot. Let cool in the refrigerator for 30 minutes.
5. In a large bowl, whisk together the butter, cream cheese, confectioners' sugar, and vanilla.
6. Once the cookie is chilled, carefully remove it from the pan. Using a spatula, spread the cream cheese mixture over cookie. Chill in the refrigerator for another 30 minutes.
7. Decorate with toppings of choice, such as sliced strawberries, raspberries, blueberries, blackberries, sliced kiwi, sliced mango, or sliced pineapple. Cut and serve.

Nutrition Info:
- Calories: 791,Total Fat: 44g,Sodium: 551mg,Carbohydrates: 92g,Protein: 7g.

Gingerbread

Servings: 12
Cooking Time: 5 Hours
Ingredients:
- Butter flavored cooking spray
- 1½ cups self-rising flour
- ½ cup flour
- 1 tsp cinnamon
- ½ tsp fresh ginger, grated
- ¼ tsp allspice
- ¼ tsp salt
- 8 tbsp. butter, unsalted, soft
- 2/3 cup light molasses
- ¾ cup brown sugar
- 1 egg, beaten
- ½ cup skim milk
- ½ tsp baking soda

Directions:
1. Place the rack in the cooking pot. Spray and flour an 8-inch springform pan.
2. In a large bowl, combine both flours, spices, and salt.
3. Place butter, molasses, and brown sugar in a microwave safe bowl. Microwave on high until butter has melted, mix well.
4. Add butter mixture to dry ingredients and mix well.
5. Whisk in egg until combined.
6. In a measuring cup or small bowl, whisk together milk and baking soda. Add to batter and mix until blended.
7. Pour into prepared pan and place on the rack. Add the lid and set to slow cooking on high. Set timer for 5 hours. Gingerbread is done when it passes the toothpick test.
8. Carefully remove from cooking pot and let cool before cutting and serving.

Nutrition Info:
- Calories 263,Total Fat 9g,Total Carbs 44g,Protein 3g,Sodium 183mg.

Vanilla Chocolate Spread

Servings: 16
Cooking Time: 25 Min
Ingredients:
- 1 ¼ pounds Hazelnuts, halved /562.5g
- ½ cups icing Sugar, sifted /65g
- ½ cup Cocoa Powder /65g
- 10 ounces Water /300ml
- 1 tsp Vanilla Extract /5ml
- ¼ tsp Cardamom, grated /1.25g
- ¼ tsp Cinnamon powder /1.25g
- ½ tsp grated Nutmeg /2.5g

Directions:
1. Place the hazelnut in a blender and blend until you obtain a paste. Place in the cooker along with the remaining ingredients.
2. Seal the pressure lid, choose Pressure, set to High, and set the time to 15 minutes. Press Start. Once the cooking is over, allow for a natural pressure release, for 10 minutes.

Chocolate Chip Cheesecake

Servings: 12
Cooking Time: 50 Minutes
Ingredients:
- Butter flavored cooking spray
- 16 oz. cream cheese, fat free, soft
- ½ cup + 1 tbsp. Stevia, divided
- 3 eggs
- 1 tsp vanilla, divided
- ½ tsp fresh lemon juice, divided
- ½ cup mini chocolate chips
- 1 cup sour cream, fat free

Directions:
1. Spray an 8-inch baking pan with cooking spray.
2. In a large bowl, beat cream cheese and ½ cup Stevia until smooth.
3. Beat in eggs, one at a time, beat well after each addition.
4. Add ½ teaspoon vanilla, and ¼ teaspoon lemon juice and stir until combined. Stir in chocolate chips and spoon into prepared pan.

5. Place the pan in the cooking pot and add the tender-crisp lid. Set to bake on 325°F. Bake 40 minutes, or until top starts to brown.
6. In a small bowl, combine sour cream, remaining Stevia, vanilla, and lemon juice, mix well. Spread over top of cheesecake and bake another 10 minutes.
7. Transfer to a wire rack to cool. Cover with plastic wrap and refrigerate at least 4 hours before serving.

Nutrition Info:
- Calories 127,Total Fat 5g,Total Carbs 22g,Protein 8g,Sodium 312mg.

Fried Snickerdoodle Poppers

Servings: 6
Cooking Time: 30 Min
Ingredients:
- 1 box instant vanilla Jell-O
- 1 ½ cups cinnamon sugar /195g
- 1 can of Pillsbury Grands Flaky Layers Biscuits
- Melted butter, for brushing

Directions:
1. Unroll the flaky biscuits and cut them into fourths. Roll each ¼ into a ball. Arrange the balls on a lined baking sheet, and cook in the Foodi for 7 minutes, or until golden, on Air Crisp mode at 350 °F or 177°C.
2. Prepare the Jell-O following the package's instructions. Using an injector, inject some of the vanilla pudding into each ball. Brush the balls with melted butter and then coat them with cinnamon sugar.

Cinnamon Butternut Squash Pie

Servings: 4
Cooking Time: 30 Min
Ingredients:
- 1-pound Butternut Squash; diced /450g
- ¼ cup Honey /62.5ml
- 1 cup Water /250ml
- ½ cup Milk /125ml
- 1 Egg
- ½ tbsp Cornstarch /7.5g
- ½ tsp Cinnamon /2.5g
- A pinch of Sea Salt

Directions:
1. Pour the water inside your Foodi and add a reversible rack. Lower the butternut squash onto the reversible rack. Seal the pressure lid, and cook on Pressure for 4 minutes at High pressure.
2. Meanwhile, whisk all remaining ingredients in a bowl. Do a quick pressure. Drain the squash and add it to the milk mixture. Pour the batter into a greased baking dish. Place in the cooker, and seal the pressure lid.
3. Choose Pressure, set to High, and set the time to 10 minutes. Press Start. Do a quick pressure release. Transfer pie to wire rack to cool.

Tres Leches Cake

Servings:8
Cooking Time: 38 Minutes
Ingredients:
- 1 box of yellow cake mix
- Cooking spray
- 1 can evaporated milk
- 1 can sweetened condensed milk
- 1 cup heavy (whipping) cream

Directions:
1. Close crisping lid. Select BAKE/ROAST, set temperature to 400°F, and set time to 43 minutes. Select START/STOP to begin. Let preheat for 5 minutes.
2. Prepare the cake batter according to the box instructions.
3. Grease a Ninja Multi-Purpose Pan or a 1½-quart round baking dish with cooking spray. Pour the batter into the pan. Place the pan on Reversible Rack, making sure rack is in the lower position.
4. Once unit has preheated, open lid and place rack with pan in pot. Close lid, and reduce temperature to 315°F. Cook for 38 minutes.
5. In a medium bowl whisk together the evaporated milk, condensed milk, and heavy cream.
6. When cooking is complete, remove rack with pan from pot and let cool for 10 minutes.
7. Remove pan from the rack. Using a long-pronged fork, poke holes every inch or so across the surface of the cake. Slowly pour the milk mixture over the cake. Refrigerate for 1 hour.
8. Once the cake has cooled and absorbed the milk mixture, slice and serve. If desired, top with whipped cream and strawberries.

Nutrition Info:
- Calories: 644,Total Fat: 28g,Sodium: 574mg,Carbohydrates: 89g,Protein: 12g.

Almond Cheesecake

Servings: 8
Cooking Time: 25 Minutes
Ingredients:
- Butter flavored cooking spray
- 16 oz. cream cheese, fat free, soft
- ½ cup + 1 tbsp. sugar

- 3 eggs
- 1 tsp almond extract, divided
- ½ tsp fresh lemon juice, divided
- 1 cup sour cream, low fat
- ¼ cup almonds, sliced

Directions:

1. Spray an 8-inch springform pan with cooking spray.
2. In a large bowl, beat cream cheese and ½ cup sugar until smooth.
3. Beat in eggs, one at a time. Then add ½ teaspoon almond extract and ¼ teaspoon lemon juice and beat until mixed. Pour in prepared pan.
4. Place the pan in the cooking pot and add the tender-crisp lid. Set to bake on 325°F. Bake 15 minutes, center will still be slightly soft.
5. In a small bowl, combine sour cream, remaining sugar, extract, and lemon juice until smooth. Spread over the top of the cheesecake and sprinkle with almonds. Bake another 10 minutes.
6. Let cool completely, cover and refrigerate at least 4 hours before serving.

Nutrition Info:

- Calories 115,Total Fat 2g,Total Carbs 25g,Protein 12g,Sodium 465mg.

Raspberry Crumble

Servings: 6
Cooking Time: 40 Min
Ingredients:

- 1 package frozen raspberries /480g
- ½ cup rolled oats /65g
5.
- ⅓ cup cold unsalted butter; cut into pieces /44g
- ½ cup all-purpose flour /65g
- ⅔ cup brown sugar /88g
- ½ cup water, plus 1 tbsp /265ml
- 2 tbsps arrowroot starch /30g
- 5 tbsps sugar; divided /75g
- 1 tsp freshly squeezed lemon juice /5ml
- 1 tsp cinnamon powder /5g

Directions:

1. Place the raspberries in the baking pan. In a small mixing bowl, combine the arrowroot starch, 1 tbsp or 15ml of water, lemon juice, and 3 tbsps or 45g of sugar. Pour the mixture all over the raspberries.
2. Put the reversible rack in the lower position of the pot. Cover the pan with foil and pour the remaining water into the pot. Put the pan on the rack in the pot. Put the pressure lid together, and lock in the Seal position. Choose Pressure, set to High, and set the time to 10 minutes, then Choose Start/Stop to begin.
3. In a bowl, mix the flour, brown sugar, oats, butter, cinnamon, and remaining sugar until crumble forms. When done pressure-cooking, do a quick release and carefully open the lid.
4. Remove the foil and stir the fruit mixture. After, spread the crumble evenly on the berries. Close the crisping lid; choose Air Crisp, set the temperature to 400°F, and the time to 10 minutes. Choose Start/Stop to begin crisping. Cook until the top has browned and the fruit is bubbling. When done baking, remove the rack with the pan from the pot, and serve.

INDEX

A

Adobo Steak 88

African Pork Stew 78

Almond Banana Dessert 138

Almond Cheesecake 150

Almond Crusted Haddock 103

Almond Lover's Bars 29

Apple Pecan Cookie Bars 24

Apple Pie Oatmeal 49

Apple Walnut Quinoa 49

Applesauce Pumpkin Muffins 50

Apricot Oatmeal 42

Arroz Con Cod 105

Artichoke Bites 28

Asian Chicken Nuggets 21

Awesome Shrimp Roast 101

B

Baby Porcupine Meatballs 127

Bacon & Egg Poppers 41

Bacon And Gruyère Egg Bites 46

Bacon Ranch Chicken Bake 66

Bacon Wrapped Scallops 24

Bacon-wrapped Halloumi Cheese 23

Baked Bacon Macaroni And Cheese 73

Baked Eggs & Kale 39

Baked Eggs In Mushrooms 34

Baked Eggs In Spinach 47

Baked Rigatoni With Beef Tomato Sauce 85

Balsamic Cabbage With Endives 126

Banana Cinnamon Snack Cake 138

Banana Coconut Loaf 41

Banana Coconut Pudding 145

Barbeque Chicken Drumettes 51

Barbeque Sticky Baby Back Ribs With 85

Beef And Cabbage Stew 90

Beef And Garbanzo Bean Chili 79

Beef And Pumpkin Stew 72

Beef Broccoli 84

Beef Bulgogi 86

Beef Chicken Meatloaf 17

Beef Congee 87

Beef Lasagna 77

Beef Pho With Swiss Chard 75

Beef Stew With Beer 80

Beef Stew With Veggies 71

Beef Stroganoff 82

Beef, Barley & Mushroom Stew 72

Bell Pepper Frittata 50

Berry Apple Crisps 142

Blackberry Crisp 139

Blackened Tilapia With Cilantro-lime Rice And Avocado Salsa 97

Blackened Turkey Cutlets 58

Blueberry Lemon Pound Cake 146

Blueberry Peach Crisp 141

Bok Choy And Zoddle Soup 120

Bolognese Pizza 76

Braised Chicken With Mushrooms And Brussel Sprouts 68

Braised Lamb Shanks 71

Braised Short Ribs With Creamy Sauce 91

Breakfast Egg Pizza 38

Breakfast Pies 38

Brie Spread With Cherries & Pistachios 22

Brisket Chili Verde 80

Broccoli Cauliflower 127

Brown Sugar And Butter Bars 132

Brownie Bites 143

Brussels Sprouts Bacon Hash 46

Bunless Burgers 75

Burrito Bowls 128

Butter Pork Chops 79

Buttered Turkey 51

Buttery Chicken Meatballs 31

Buttery Cranberry Cake 139

C

Cabbage With Bacon 119

Cajun Chicken & Pasta 63

Cajun Shrimp 94

Caponata 30

Caramelized Sweet Potatoes 114

Caribbean Catfish With Mango Salsa 96

Caribbean Pork Pot 79

Carne Guisada 83

Carrot Cake Oats 37

Carrot Gazpacho 124

Carrot Raisin Cookie Bars 138

Cauliflower And Asparagus Farfalle 113

Cauliflower Chunks With Lemon Sauce 128

Cauliflower Gratin 15

Cauliflower Nuggets 23

Cauliflower Steaks & Veggies 124

Cheat Apple Pie 142

Cheesy Bacon Brussel Sprouts 16

Cheesy Baked Spinach 123

Cheesy Chicken & Mushrooms 61

Cheesy Chicken & Zucchini Rolls 55

Cheesy Chilies 130

Cheesy Fried Risotto Balls 19

Cheesy Jalapeno Boats 31

Cheesy Onion Dip 18

Cheesy Shakshuka 37

Cheesy Spicy Pasta 115

Cheesy Tomato Bruschetta 31

Cherry Clafoutti 135

Chicken & Black Bean Chowder 57

Chicken And Quinoa Soup 52

Chicken And Sweet Potato Corn Chowder 60

Chicken And Vegetable Egg Rolls 25

Chicken Bites 29

Chicken Bruschetta 55

Chicken Burrito Bowl 52

Chicken Meatballs In Tomato Sauce 59

Chicken Meatballs Primavera 54

Chicken Omelet 47

Chicken Piccata 70

Chicken Pork Nuggets 29

Chicken Pot Pie 63

Chicken Stroganoff With Fetucini 63

Chicken Thighs With Thyme Carrot Roast 65

Chicken With Black Beans 52

Chicken With Crunchy Coconut Dumplings. 53

Chicken With Tomatoes And Capers 59

Chili Cheese Quiche 35

Chili Chicken Dip 28

Chili Mint Steamed Snapper 104

Chinese Bbq Ribs 80

Chipotle Beef Brisket 87

Chocolate Banana Muffins 45

Chocolate Cake 135

Chocolate Chip Cheesecake 149

Chocolate Fondue 139

Chocolate Peanut Butter And Jelly Puffs 133

Cinnamon Apple Cake 136

Cinnamon Butternut Squash Pie 150

Clam Fritters 103

Classic Custard 133

Coconut Cilantro Shrimp 109

Coconut Cream "custard" Bars 134

Coconut Lime Snack Cake 137

Coconut Milk Crème Caramel 138

Coconut Pear Delight 143

Coconut Rice Pudding 143

Coconut Shrimp 110

Cod With Ginger And Scallion Sauce 109

Coffee Cake 139

Colorful Vegetable Medley 129

Crab Alfredo 94

Crab Cake Casserole 106

Crab Cakes 95

Cranberry Cheesecake 146

Cranberry Lemon Quinoa 35

Creamy Carrot Soup 125

Creamy Chicken Carbonara 68

Creamy Crab Soup 97

Creamy Golden Casserole 121

Creamy Spinach Soup 115

Creamy Tuscan Chicken Pasta 64

Crispy Coconut Pie 133

Crispy Delicata Squash 26

Crispy Kale Chips 124

Crispy Roast Pork 83

Crispy Spiced Cauliflower Bites 30

Crunchy Chicken & Almond Casserole 69

Créme Brulee 135

Crème De La Broc 115

Cumin Baby Carrots 17

Curried Chickpea And Roasted Tomato Shakshuka 39

Curried Salmon & Sweet Potatoes 112

D

Date Orange Cheesecake 147

Deviled Eggs(2) 33

Double Berry Dutch Baby 40

Double Chocolate Cake 140

Double Chocolate Quinoa Bowl 48

Drunken Saffron Mussels 102

E

Easy Clam Chowder 105

Egg Spinach Bites 39

Eggplant Casserole 131

Eggplant Lasagna 116

Eggplant With Kale 116

F

Farfalle Tuna Casserole With Cheese 109

Flaxseeds Granola 40

Flounder Oreganata 110

Flounder Veggie Soup 102

Flourless Chocolate Cake 132

French Dip Sandwiches 45

Fried Beef Dumplings 21

Fried Oreos 147

Fried Pin Wheels 13

Fried Salmon 95

Fried Snickerdoodle Poppers 150

G

Garganelli With Cheese And Mushrooms 117

Garlic Chicken And Bacon Pasta 67

Garlic Shrimp And Veggies 112

Garlic Turkey Breasts 56

Garlicky Pork Chops 86

Garlicky Tomato 20

Gingerbread 149

Gingered Butternut Squash 22

Gingery Beef And Broccoli 89

Gingery Chocolate Pudding 144

Glazed Carrots 38

Glazed Salmon 92

Glazed Walnuts 18

Grilled Broccoli 43

Grilled Cheese 125

Grilled Tofu Sandwich 115

Ground Turkey And Potato Chili 64

H

Ham & Broccoli Frittata 44

Ham & Hash Brown Casserole 37

Ham & Spinach Breakfast Bake 36

Ham-stuffed Turkey Rolls 66

Hand-cut French Fries 16

Hawaiian Tofu 113

Hazelnut Cheesecake 144

Healthy Chicken Stew 51

Hearty Breakfast Muffins 48

Hearty Breakfast Skillet 45

Hearty Veggie Soup 116

Herb Roasted Mixed Nuts 13

Herb Salmon With Barley Haricot Verts 110

Herbed Cauliflower Fritters 19

Herbed Lamb Chops 86

Herby Chicken With Asparagus Sauce 57

Herby Fish Skewers 22

Holiday Honey Glazed Ham 74

Honey Bourbon Wings 20

Honey Garlic Chicken 58

Honey Garlic Chicken And Okra 70

Horseradish Roasted Carrots 26

Hot & Sour Soup 130

Hot Crab Dip 18

Hot Dogs With Peppers 77

Hot Fudge Brownies 148

I

Irish Cream Flan 145

Italian Beef Steak 78

Italian Chicken Muffins 64

Italian Flounder 96

Italian Pita Crisps 22

Italian Sausage With Garlic Mash 128

Italian Turkey & Pasta Soup 62

J

Jalapeno Salsa 26

Jamaican Pork 77

Japanese Eggs 23

K

Kale-egg Frittata 44

Kung Pao Shrimp 104

L

Lamb Chops And Potato Mash 88

Lamb Curry 75

Lamb Tagine 84

Lemon Chicken 60

Lettuce Carnitas Wraps 59

M

Mackerel En Papillote With Vegetables 107

Maple Dipped Asparagus 32

Mashed Broccoli With Cream Cheese 118

Mashed Potatoes With Spinach 129

Meatballs With Marinara Sauce 81

Meatballs With Spaghetti Sauce 82

Mediterranean Cod 92

Mexican Chocolate Walnut Cake 147

Minestrone With Pancetta 131

Mini Chocolate Cheesecakes 132

Mini Crab Cakes 15

Mini Shrimp Tacos 13

Mocha Cake 141

Moo Shu Chicken 54

Mushroom Goulash 120

Mushroom Poutine 117

Mushrooms Stuffed With Veggies 14

Mustard And Apricot-glazed Salmon With Smashed Potatoes 108

N

New England Lobster Rolls 93

O

Omelets In The Jar 40

One Pot Ham & Rice 88

Orange Glazed Cod & Snap Peas 99

Oyster Stew 101

P

Pancetta Hash With Baked Eggs 49

Paneer Cutlet 121

Panko Crusted Cod 102

Paprika Buttered Chicken 60

Paprika Hard-boiled Eggs 47

Paprika Shirred Eggs 50

Parmesan Butternut Crisps 27

Parmesan Tilapia 101

Parsley Mashed Cauliflower 119

Pasta Primavera 119

Pasta Veggie Toss 126

Pasta With Roasted Veggies 129

Peach Cobbler 146

Peanut Tofu & Noodles 121

Pecan Apple Crisp 144

Pepper Smothered Cod 92

Peppercorn Meatloaf 74

Pineapple Cake 140

Pineapple Chicken Tenders 59

Pistachio Crusted Mahi Mahi 104

Pistachio Crusted Salmon 106

Pistachio Stuffed Mushrooms 17

Pizza Stuffed Chicken 69

Polish Sausage & Sauerkraut 81

Pomegranate Radish Mix 130

Pork Carnitas Wraps 76

Pork Chops With Gravy 81

Pork Chops With Seasoned Butter 78

Pork Pie 74

Pork Tenderloin With Warm Balsamic And Apple Chutney 71

Potato Filled Bread Rolls 126

Prosciutto, Mozzarella Egg In A Cup 49

Pulled Chicken And Peach Salsa 56

Pumpkin Coconut Breakfast Bake 33

Pumpkin Custard 134

Pumpkin Latte Cake 136

Pumpkin Pecan Oatmeal 33

Pumpkin Steel Cut Oatmeal 35

Q

Quesadilla Casserole 58

Quick Indian-style Curry 122

R

Raspberry And Vanilla Pancake 48

Raspberry Crumble 151

Red Beans And Rice 118

Ricotta Raspberry Breakfast Cake 44

Riviera Chicken 56

Roasted Chicken With Potato Mash 53

Roasted Squash And Rice With Crispy Tofu 120

Roasted Vegetable Salad 113

Rosemary Crusted Lamb Chops 90

Rosemary Lemon Chicken 67

Rosemary Sweet Potato Medallions 126

S

Salmon Florentine 95

Salmon With Almonds, Cranberries, And Rice 100

Salmon With Dill Chutney 98

Salmon, Cashew & Kale Bowl 100

Salsa Chicken With Feta 53

Sausage & Broccoli Frittata 41

Sausage With Celeriac And Potato Mash 83

Sausage With Noodles And Braised Cabbage 91

Sausage Wrapped Scotch Eggs 46

Savory Custards With Ham And Cheese 43

Scalloped Potatoes 27

Seafood Chowder 99

Shallot Pepper Pancakes 16

Shallots With Mushrooms 13

Shredded Chicken Salsa 51

Shredded Chicken With Lentils And Rice 66

Shrimp & Asparagus Risotto 98

Shrimp & Zoodles 105

Shrimp And Chorizo Potpie 94

Shrimp Fried Rice 96

Smoked Salmon Pilaf With Walnuts 111

Soft-boiled Eggs 34

Sour Cream & Cheese Chicken 57

South Of The Border Corn Dip 24

Southern Grits Casserole 34

Southern Sweet Ham 87

Southern-style Lettuce Wraps 89

Southwest Chicken Bake 61

Southwest Tofu Scramble 36

Spanish Lamb & Beans 73

Spanish Potato And Chorizo Frittata 36

Speedy Pork Stir Fry 90

Spiced Poached Pears 145

Spiced Red Snapper 93

Spicy "grilled" Catfish 98

Spicy Cabbage Soup 123

Spicy Chicken Wings. 65

Spicy Glazed Pecans 23

Spicy Grilled Shrimp 95

Spicy Honey Wings 18

Spicy Kimchi And Tofu Fried Rice 117

Spicy Shrimp Pasta With Vodka Sauce 106

Spinach & Sausage Casserole 42

Spinach Casserole 35

Spinach Hummus 14

Spinach Turkey Cups 42

Spinach, Tomatoes, And Butternut Squash Stew 114

Steak And Chips 82

Steak And Minty Cheese 28

Steamed Artichokes With Lemon Aioli 123

Steamed Asparagus And Pine Nuts 130

Sticky Orange Chicken 62

Stir Fried Scallops & Veggies 107

Strawberry Cheesecake 148

Strawberry Muffins 34

Strawberry Oat Breakfast Bars 32

Stuffed Baked Potatoes 33

Stuffed Cod 99

Stuffed Whole Chicken 65

Sugar Cookie Pizza 148

Swedish Meatballs With Mashed Cauliflower 89

Sweet & Spicy Shrimp Bowls 111

Sweet And Salty Bars 137

Sweet Garlicky Chicken Wings 65

Sweet Pickled Cucumbers 14

Sweet Potato Fries 25

Sweet Potato Noodles With Cashew Sauce 125

Sweet Potato Pie 142

T

Tangy Catfish & Mushrooms 93

Tangy Jicama Chips 27

Tender Beef & Onion Rings 85

Tender Butter Beef 86

Tilapia & Tamari Garlic Mushrooms 103

Tiny Tostadas 30

Tomato Bisque 127

Traditional Beef Stroganoff 76

Tres Leches Cake 150

Tuna & Avocado Patties 101

Tuna Zoodle Bake 111

Turkey & Wild Rice Casserole 67

Turkey Croquettes 69

Turkey Enchilada Casserole 61

Turkey Rellenos 56

Turkey Scotch Eggs 17

Tuscan Cod 108

Tuscany Turkey Soup 55

V

Vanilla Cheesecake(1) 141

Vanilla Chocolate Spread 149

Vanilla Pound Cake 136

Veggie Primavera 123

Veggie Skewers 114

Veggie Taco Soup 128

W

Walnut Orange Coffee Cake 47

White Bean Hummus 26

White Chocolate Chip Cookies 144

Whole Roasted Broccoli And White Beans With Harissa, Tahini, And Lemon 122

Wrapped Asparagus In Bacon 32

Y

Yogurt Cheesecake 137

Z

Zucchini Chips 21

Zucchinis Spinach Fry 124

Printed in Great Britain
by Amazon